PORN

Polly Barton is a Japanese literary translator. Her translations include *Where the Wild Ladies Are* by Aoko Matsuda, *There's No Such Thing as an Easy Job* by Kikuko Tsumura and *Spring Garden* by Tomoka Shibasaki. She won the 2019 Fitzcarraldo Editions Essay Prize for *Fifty Sounds*. *Porn: An Oral History* is her second book. She lives in Bristol.

PORN
AN ORAL HISTORY

POLLY BARTON

CONTENTS

'And I dreamed your dream for you, and now
   your dream is real
How can you look at me as if I was just another
   one of your deals?'
—— Dire Straits, 'Romeo and Juliet'

'That brought a flush of shame. Which is what
you will get, of course, if you behave as if things
are other than they are.'
—— Gwendoline Riley, *My Phantoms*

ZERO

Back when I was living in rural Japan, one of my favourite pastimes was hanging out beside the porn section in the local video shop. The video shop was a sizeable place, its numerous racks labelled with all the different categories of film I would have expected to find there, and some more besides, which I wouldn't. There was the 'Sekushii' [Sexy] section, for instance, sandwiched between the very standardly labelled 'Romantic Comedies' and 'Suspense' racks. This label afforded me great delight when I first managed to read it, and I immediately assumed that this must be the porn, but on further inspection, the rack turned out to contain the kinds of films that to my mind would be best described as 'eighties erotic drama'. They might have been sexy by name, but they clearly weren't sexy enough by nature to merit shielding from the eyes of the toddlers who would go thundering down the aisles in search of the newest animation DVD – that was a fate reserved for the porn proper, which had its own separate room, partitioned off from the main shop floor by a pink curtain. This section wasn't labelled in any way, as far as I could see. I only became aware of its existence one day when I was perusing the box sets on the far wall, and witnessed someone else who was also perusing the box sets with me ostensibly disappear into thin air. Was I losing my mind? Like someone who has witnessed a miracle or a tragedy, I stood rooted to the spot, feigning fascination with the videos in front of me, and a couple of minutes later the disappearing man emerged, now with two see-through plastic cases in hand. As he trotted in the direction of the cashiers, I stood back from the shelves and examined the opening into which he had vanished and from which he had reappeared: sure enough there was a hole in the wall veiled by two pieces of thin pink satin fabric. I must have subconsciously registered it before, and assumed it was some kind of employee-only zone.

From that point on, I became fascinated by the pink curtain dance that the porn-renting men would perform. Now and then I would encounter someone who went swanning in directly, but these intrepid types were the anomaly; the protocol was that you had to stand and pretend to be looking at the box sets, and then, after a surreptitious head-turn or two, slip in sideways between the silky pink folds of the curtain. Almost unfailingly there was a graceful, nigh on ethereal quality to this movement that, held up alongside the array of sights they were no doubt going to see on the shelves of that room, brought me an obscure pleasure. I say 'no doubt', because I never myself entered the pink-curtain room. Perhaps subconsciously I wasn't brave enough, and I feared the interaction if and when I encountered someone else in there. It seemed to me, though, that I just wasn't interested. I didn't want to see the rows of DVDs with pictures that would probably make me feel strange and uncomfortable. I just wanted to watch the men as they performed their clandestine ritual, and this I started doing as a matter of course whenever I visited the video shop. I'm fairly sure that my lingering presence by the box-set wall or the neighbouring shelves was perceived as an obstacle, something that made the curtain-slip harder and more embarrassing to execute, and that for me was a point of joy, even pride. I felt no animosity towards the porn-renting men, but neither did I understand why I should cooperate in making their quest any easier. Standing there brought me a faint sense of jubilation, that I think was something to do with feeling the tables had been turned: until that point in my life, I'd felt that porn was a mechanism used to make

me feel embarrassed or somehow hemmed in both exis-
tentially and physically, or at least, which did make me
embarrassed and hemmed in, for a host of reasons that
I found it difficult to unravel. Now, I was in a position of
inviolability. It was almost thrilling to feel that I was tied
to these men's crusade in some way, a witness to their act
of transgression – which was not really a transgression at
all. As I watched them heading towards the counter, their
footsteps no longer remotely ethereal, I would feel a fris-
son of nerves as I pictured and vicariously experienced
that mortifying interaction. Even I had felt embarrassed
in the past when the cashiers had read out the names of
the videos I was renting, as they were obliged to do, for
no reason other than that they contained a lot of foreign
words that I was making them pronounce. How, then, was
a person to cope when the words they were enunciating
were 'Edward Penishands' or 'Super Hornio Brothers'?
Who felt the more embarrassed: the renter or the
cashier? Or did neither of them? Was this transaction so
humdrum by now that there was no mortification left in
it? What percentage of videos taken out here were porn?
Did the pink-curtain cupboard actually account for eighty
per cent of all rentals? Was it a cupboard, or was it de-
ceptively huge? Was it actually as large as the video shop
again? These were the kinds of questions I would ask
myself as I stood smirking by the box sets.

I tell this story not because I think it reflects well on
me but rather because, in a way, it feels inextricable from
my reasons for writing this book. I suppose you could
articulate my pink-curtain fixation as a species of child-
ishness, a fascination for the clandestine, an inability to
leave alone the things that one is not supposed to probe.
Probably, into my thirties, I wouldn't do the same thing.
Yet if I'm a very different person in many ways to that

twenty-one-year-old, I think that my feelings when it comes to porn aren't that altered – or at least they weren't when I began this project.

When I first conceived of this book, and started feeling some urgent need to work on it, the prospect of writing something with the word 'porn' in the title – or as the whole title – felt to me very worrying indeed. Certainly some of the worry came as a generalized knee-jerk reaction to the thought of being associated, professionally, with porn. I fretted that, in a similar way to how people who've worked as porn actors might struggle to find work in different industries, the affiliation might damage my ability to work ever again, especially as a translator. My concern took a more specific form, as well: I was worried, and pre-emptively ashamed, that writing a book about porn would mean people would assume that I was a porn connoisseur. If I was writing a book about porn, I must watch loads of it, and like it, and know a lot about it. That, I thought, was deeply embarrassing.

It was only as I started to delve further into the topic that I began to feel differently. If only I *was* a porn connoisseur, I thought – perhaps a little bashful but mostly forthright in my passion, my desire. If only I was strong in what felt like my right, all of our rights, to indulge in fantasy. Those sorts of positions started to seem to me very attractive by view of their firmness – and, indeed, less embarrassing than the reality. For in truth, my predominant feeling towards porn was not one of love, and nor was it the opposite, one of hate or virulent disapproval. What I had was rather a kind of nebulous, all-pervasive worry and discomfort. I worried about what porn stood for, I worried about what it has done to us, is doing to us and will do to us, and I worried that this worry made me a bad feminist. A stolid love of or belief in porn and a wish to defend it seemed to me, in comparison, an enviable place to write from – as did, in a way, a vehement anti-porn stance. Faced with such a polarizing topic with so many different strands and aspects to it, the worst possible position seemed to be the one I held: ambivalence. Or, to qualify that, a kind of tortured ambivalence. A calm, nuanced on-the-fence position I would have taken, but a mass of tortured, conflicting and mostly unexplored reactions was less than welcome.

Not only did I feel threatened by my own destabilizing, unresolved feelings on the topic, but I also felt uncomfortable about the way it seemed to be so impossible to talk about it in a way that might have helped me sort through those feelings. Thinking about it, I realized I could count the number of conversations I'd had about it on one hand; not a single one had felt exploratory or liberating, and instead the tone had ranged from fraught and perilous to downright confrontational. Outside of these discussions, the silence around the topic didn't feel neutral or chosen, but oppressive, forced upon me, something I wanted to rip away – an urge not dissimilar, I guess, to the wish to stand beside the pink curtain and disrupt, in some minute sense, the tacit pact we all made to turn our heads from acknowledging it.

In a way, it feels bizarre to speak of silence around porn when porn is now so ubiquitous. I'm not exactly clear on when I began to become conscious of the topic coming up more in the things I listened to and read – it was a gradual shift, it seemed, and then before I knew it, it was everywhere. Certainly, around the time that I began brewing the idea for writing some kind of book on porn and my antennae were pricked, I noted I had a run of six months where every single book I read, fiction and non-fiction, included the word at least once. Because it was on the news, in podcasts, it began to wend its way into interactions too. People I barely knew would drop it into conversation, mostly as an example of some aspect of human experience that the internet had altered dramatically. Not knowing of my project, my dad told me on the phone that he had been invited to his son's school to a parents' talk about 'pornography' (I wish I could reproduce in writing his tone of voice when speaking this word, but there was a lot of separating of syllables). I opened up the *Guardian* webpage and there was Billie Eilish, declaring that 'porn destroyed my brain', detailing how she had begun watching at age eleven and as a result had felt unable to say no to many 'not good' things in her sexual encounters. Another day, the front page was filled with the news that a Tory MP had been reported watching porn on his phone in the House of Commons; another Tory MP came out to defend him, stating that finding your way onto a porn site after searching for tractors felt like an understandable mistake to have made. On the back of this, other MPs discussed and questioned the prevalence of a culture of misogyny in Parliament. More and more there was the sense that porn was becoming a part of The Conversation.

Yet, instead of sating my desire to talk about things honestly, to sort through the multiple strands of beliefs we seemed called upon to hold true simultaneously – everyone does it, it's part of a wider culture of misogyny, it's anti-social and offensive, it's a fact of contemporary life, it's something deeply private, it normalizes sexual degradation, it's destroying our brains, it's splashed all over the internet, it's a corollary to masturbation, it's an expression of the untrammelled sexual creativity of the contemporary psyche, it's become more than simply an aid to masturbation, it's an artform, it's addictive, it's a blight on people's ability to create a satisfying sex life – the sudden explosion of porn within public discourse seemed to me to highlight the absence of what I thought of as genuine discussion. We could all, now, lip service it without blushing, yet I still hadn't had a real conversation about it with someone I wasn't going out with. I felt like I could predict most of my friends' practices and opinions about myriad aspects of life – not with total accuracy, maybe, but with some degree of conviction – yet when it came to porn, I had no idea what they might think, or feel, or do, or watch. It didn't fail to cross my mind that this absence of dialogue wasn't universal, and that I had just somehow missed out. In a sense that's true; I now think that there are people for whom porn is a topic of real discussion with others, in what seems to me a genuinely healthy way. Yet, not infrequently, I would spot flashes of discomfort in people's eyes when the subject came up which made me think, *Aha*.

I should say here that, increasingly, I believe that what I'm referring to here as 'discomfort' is complex – that porn is the intersection point for a number of different kinds of discomfort, and that different people experience varying admixtures of these. Porn, and masturbation in general, are subjects about which people are taught to carry a lot of shame, and fear of others' judgement. Even if we happen to have got away without feeling such shame, the question of what it is we desire is uncomfortable to talk about publicly, because it can feel so deeply personal and exposing. Then there is also, I think, a more outward-facing awareness at play: that the topic is a polarizing and controversial one, which elicits strong emotions, and discussion is therefore potentially incendiary. I think about a comment one of my friends made about porn being a 'deeply uncool' topic, which triggered a burst of recognition in me. I wonder if there's some kind of society-wide mechanism whereby, having recognized that delving into our real thoughts on porn brings up too much inflammatory emotional content, we have conveniently deemed it unnecessary and therefore gauche to hash over it – particularly if the hashing over involves discussions of ethics. It's more comfortable for everyone involved to act as though we have reached an acceptance of the reality, that we are at peace with all of the complexities of it, even if the truth is that many of us have not, really, gone through that peacemaking process in any substantive way.

In hindsight, I would say there was a specific trigger for turning to my burbling feelings about porn and re-solving, at last, to give them my full attention. Objectively speaking, it was an extremely minor occurrence. Late one night I got a text message from a man, who shouldn't, at least from my perspective, have been attempting to initi-ate sexual contact with me, in which he mentioned that he was watching porn. That was it, that was all it was, and yet quite unexpectedly it sent me into a tailspin. What shocked me was not the fact of the text – I'm not sure if this experience is unusual or not, but over the years I've received numerous emails, text messages and letters from men casually detailing their masturbatory habits – but rather that I felt, in that moment, that I had no idea how to read it. It was an alien-just-landed-from-outer-space-after-lots-of-preparatory-language-study kind of a feel-ing: I could, of course, understand the literal words of the message, but I was at a loss as to how to interpret its in-tended meaning. Was this a come-on, or at least a species of flirting? Was it intended to make me uncomfortable? Was it signalling his adherence to a moral code of radical honesty? Was it a move to make his viewing feel more

20

transgressive and therefore more stimulating? Or did we now live in a world where I was supposed to parse this as I would 'I'm watching the football'? I genuinely didn't know the answer, and I didn't know if he knew, either. It even struck me as possible that his intention was precisely to bring on this kind of alien feeling.

Adding to this reeling I felt was an unshakeable sense that it was somehow mind-boggling for this particular person to admit to watching porn. Pre-text, if someone had asked me to make a bet on whether he regularly watched porn, I suppose I would have put my money on yes, as I would for almost every man – and yet holding up that image alongside his life, its ethical commitments, and above all the position he held as an arbiter of superior taste somehow produced in me a sense of deep disjunct that I couldn't categorize. I didn't know if I was a prude, I didn't know if this was just me being unstreetsmart, if I was just old and backward. The more I thought about it, the more I realized that this same sense applied to the greater part of my friendship circle, when I floated the idea of them watching porn. The people I most trusted didn't send me messages about watching porn – we knew it was safe not to talk about it, and so we didn't – and yet I had no idea of what they were doing in that regard.

Clearly, a text message that seems impossible to decipher is hardly a rarity, and nor is that indecipherability exclusive to porn-related content. What felt instructive to me, though, was the sudden surge of turmoil this occurrence brought up. The turmoil felt old, and known, and also it felt static – as ever, I had no idea what to do to dispel it. My knowledge of what porn really meant wasn't developing as I let it lie fallow, reading the odd article here and there, and my feelings around it weren't maturing either. On the surface my attitude seemed calm enough, but all it took was a little bit of tumult to stir the whole thing up and make it bubble over again. It was time to do something about it. Rather than just letting this slip from awareness, I needed a scheme or a structure to keep me probing the issue until something in me shifted. I was coming to the end of my previous writing project, and the idea naturally suggested itself to me: how about writing something on porn?

Formulating this plan to myself felt peculiar, in part because I was painfully aware that whichever way I thought about it, I was not the best person to write about porn in any conventional manner. Not only was it not my academic specialism, or even close to that, but even within an amateurish, non-professional context, I knew very little about porn. If I was going to write about it, it would have to be in a way that at the very least didn't preclude my being an ignoramus. Preferably, I would be able to harness that ignorance in some way that would be beneficial to the project. It occurred to me that I could attempt some permutation of the classic 'journey of discovery' where I narrated my journeys to various archives and libraries and San Fernando Valley studios, detailing my reactions and recording the revelations I had along the way, yet the prospect didn't seem particularly appealing. My motivation for writing the book was, above all, a sense that the conversations I viewed as important around porn were not being had, at least not around me – this in connection with a realization that the things in my life that had really altered or deepened my positions on things were almost always conversations with friends or acquaintances. Thinking about what I myself would be interested in reading about porn, I acknowledged that, much as I wanted to patch up the horrendous gaps in my knowledge about it, I didn't want to read a traditional history. I was far more interested in reading something that focused on people outside of the industry – with laypeople, and their experiences with and thoughts about porn. In this way I stumbled towards an idea – less a proposal for a finished book than a plan to lay the groundwork for whatever would come after it. I would talk to people about porn, and somehow find some way to write about that.

The next question was, what people? It seemed obvious to me from the start that this particular project was one I needed to do with acquaintances – that the conversations had to be with people I already had at least some kind of connection or relationship with (although, in the end, I came to speak with a couple of people who I was introduced to by friends, but whom I hadn't met until our interviews). I understood that this would immediately deprive the book of any claim to being comprehensive, yet that had never seemed to me like a possibility anyway. A truly comprehensive survey would have to interview people of all sexualities, ethnicities, ages, genders, abilities, nationalities, social classes, political affiliations, family set-ups, home arrangements – not simply to have a claim to being truly diverse, but because these are all parameters that arguably influence consumption in significant ways. Such a study would also have to encompass people in all aspects of an industry that is sprawling in its size and scope. In other words, it would necessarily be a full-blown research project. That wasn't something that I, as a single author, was equipped to do.

More than that, it wasn't something I desperately wanted to do, either. Rather than provide something with a claim to objectivity, a representation of the full range of thoughts and opinions or, heaven forbid, which attempted to locate some kind of 'standard' or majority position, I wanted with this book to set my sights on what it looked like to talk about these things, amongst friends, almost regardless of the kind of views being expressed and where they lay on the complex map of different stances.

There was also a sense in which this methodology itself became my difficult learning curve – a training, if you will, in putting myself (and the people around me) through the experience of conversing about things that were awkward, difficult, potentially even excruciating. I wanted to see what happened when I waded right in there. I felt that if the book was going to reflect upon or record my own development in some way, the embarrassment couldn't be circumvented. What I needed was not the magical fix of interviewing strangers, where I suddenly felt powerful and impervious to shame, but rather to struggle to have the conversations through that embarrassment. It needed to work itself through the system.

That said, I was still terrified. It was one thing to decide that I'd speak to people I already knew, but which ones, exactly? How well did I have to know somebody to invite them to talk to me about porn? I might have summoned up the determination to confront my embarrassment, but that didn't make it shrink. I found I felt enthusiastic about the idea during the day, but would wake up in the middle of the night with stabs of fear and panic. I drafted an email to people inviting them to join me, but let my uncertainty about the precise list of people to send it to serve as an excuse for stalling; the late-night-terror part of me was pleased, as I dragged my feet and allowed myself to think that maybe it was a bad idea after all. The more I stalled, the more I coulld feel the late-night part digging in its heels, beginning to win out. So one night, falsely brave after a glass of wine, I sat down and filled in a list of email addresses into the bcc field of my draft titled 'A Request'.

The email, which I won't quote in full here for it was

quite lengthy, started with the kind of tentative greeting that was very common in the early stages of the pandemic – 'I hope you are well, or okay, or somehow moving towards something in the future that feels better' – then went in for the kill: 'This is going to be a strange email.' In the strangeness that followed, I asked recipients to consider having 'a conversation with me about your/ our relationship to and feelings around porn, and how it impacts directly and indirectly on your life.' I had initially conceived of renting an Airbnb, I wrote, and asking at least UK participants round for a bottle of wine or a meal, but in light of the COVID-19 situation I wasn't sure whether or not that would come to pass; I was still prioritizing doing the talks in person, if at all possible. For the moment I was looking for some kind of show of hands: would they be, in theory, willing to do this with me?

The adrenaline rush of pressing send left me a little dizzy, and I was ready to think about something else, pretend it had never happened, but almost immediately, the replies began to come in. A few were just: 'I'm in', 'yes'. Others were more hesitant: their senders were reluctant, or not sure, but they'd give it a go. Some people, not that evening, but later, wrote me longer emails, talking about some particular aspect of the topic they'd been musing on of late or, sometimes, mentioning a total lack of conversations in their life about it. Included in my group were some people I didn't know all that well, a couple of whom I had encountered professionally, and I worried that they might find my sudden request strange, and crossing a boundary somehow. Yet nobody's response suggested to me that they felt that way.

So, gradually, I shifted into the execution phase of these pornchats, as I was now calling them to myself. In the end I recorded nineteen, all of which have been included here. There were other people who kindly agreed and whom I planned to include, but at some point I realized that I had more than enough material, and needed to stop if I were to have any hope of assembling it. Some part of me still harbours the hope of continuing the project – looking back, I'd say I went from feeling terrified to starting to positively enjoy pornchatting as an activity. It wasn't just that it was the pandemic, that I was living alone and often feeling bored and lonely, and it provided me with a reason to meet people, sometimes to take trains to go and see them. The main reason I liked it was that it increasingly struck me as a very generative thing to do: to push through the embarrassment, to change your feelings about doing something by exposure, to wilfully enter into conversational territory where both parties felt vulnerable and to allow yourselves to be in a space of experimentation. I felt for myself how freeing it was to talk about this stuff, and I liked watching my conversational partners having the same realization.

And genuinely, I started to observe changes taking place. At the outset of the project, I'd had to whisper the word 'porn', or squeal it. For a period of time around the beginning of recording the chats, I began seeing someone, and the idea of telling him about what I was working on felt difficult; a similar thing applied with my parents. It was amazing to me how quickly this started to shift: how I began to tell people what I was working on without blushing, and eventually drop into conversation with my mum that I'd done a pornchat today, with total casualness. Naturally, all of that could be chalked up to sheer desensitization to the word, and hardly anything to celebrate. Yet there were other, more profound effects too: I started to feel less as though I had a hysterical rat trapped inside my chest. I could entertain positions on the topic calmly, without feeling the kettle begin to steam inside. Of course that was always going to be easier with these people who, however much I knew and liked them, I was not in a sexual or romantic relationship with. It still seemed proof, though, that this hare-brained scheme of mine was having some kind of effect.

I wrote that when I first began this project, I didn't really know what form it would take, but I suppose my default idea, what seemed the most likely outcome, was that I would write a book of thematic essays. I made lists of the kinds of things I might write these essays on: Aesthetics, Age, Being a 'Pervert', Bodies, Ethics, Ethnicity, First Encounters, Gender, Incest, Kink, Masturbation, Money, Misogyny, Objectification, Passivity, Racism, Sex Toys, Shame, Taboo. I collected up quotations from novels, non-fiction, critical theory by Roland Barthes, Eimear McBride, Andrea Long Chu, Virginie Despentes, Maggie Nelson.

Then I started to actually speak to people, and began, very quickly, to see that one of the things that makes porn such a rich topic is the way that all these things are impossible to separate out. I observed how, even when I began the discussions often with one of a few very standard questions – first experiences with porn, or the frequency of conversations on the subject, or else picking up on something the person mentioned in response to my first email – the direction that the conversations went in were unique, and though the same issues came up, they did so from varied angles. It started to feel like the way that these issues swirled around kaleidoscopically was somehow integral to the project.

And something more fundamental revealed itself to me. I began to feel that the voices in which these stories were being told were integral to the accounts themselves.

I could attempt to condense the interviews down, to extract the pure essence of their content, but in doing so, I would lose a sense of the people behind them, and the more I went on, the more grievous I felt this loss to be. I also grew increasingly conscious that would mean putting my own slant on things – and that doing so, after being entrusted with all of this testimony, would be at best a missed opportunity, and at worst, an ethical violation. What's interesting to note now is that having that line of thought before I began the project would have seemed to me overly precious, a sign that I was taking my own project too seriously. It's only porn, the voice from inside me would have said. Never mind that it was a topic that had caused me a lot of anguish in the past, triggered major arguments, felt endlessly fraught – there was something that prevented me externally from acknowledging its weight. Ten minutes into the first chat, though, and I had already realized how wrong I was. Porn was as serious to other people as it was to me, because other people's lives are serious, and porn rubs up against some of the most important aspects of them.

In a similar vein, there was something about the shape of the individual chats that I felt was instructive, and important to represent. What felt valuable within the conversations was not solely the points raised and the conclusions reached, but the chaotic and often contradictory process of reaching them in tandem with another person – perhaps this is true of any conversation, but it felt particularly so of these ones, which were often the first time for people to vocalize their thoughts on certain ideas or try out arguments outside of their own heads. The trajectories of the conversations varied – some had a definite arc, others seemed to go back and forth between two conflicting modes of thought, while still others

28

bounced around energetically from here to there – but whatever the shape was, it seemed to bring something to my understanding of the wider resonance of the conversation, which I felt I wanted the reader to share in. Above all, I felt it was important to preserve a record of what it was like to speak for the first time about something awkward with someone – there was value in preserving the sloppiness of the process, not only in reproducing the mood of the chat, but also in offering a route of insight into the nature of conversation itself.

In what follows, then, I have decided to present the interviews more or less as I had them, but anonymized, and in mildly edited form. Now, I pass my eyes over my list of potential chapter topics and note with some astonishment that most are covered in the conversations. That is not to say that there aren't aspects of the sprawling constellation of issues that fall under the header of porn left untouched, and there are certainly aspects that need more attention and thorough investigation than they are given here. Inevitably, actually speaking with people about porn threw up topics that I'd not thought about much before, and about which I now feel I would love to have further conversations on, after the chance to reflect on them – some of these seem to me areas of great fertility.

In fact, as I was coming towards the end of the project, I found myself thinking of *My Unwritten Books* by George Steiner, a book written towards the end of his life in which he outlines seven books that he had always been minded to write but didn't manage to, for assorted reasons. I feel that there are seven books this book could have been and wasn't, that there are seven or more offshoot books that it could have been. Porn and ethnicity deserves a far, far better exploration than I have been able to give it within this book, as does porn and socio-economic class, and body image. I would like to consider, as critical theorists have, the relationship between porn and eroticism within the contemporary landscape. I would like to write about porn and mimetic desire: training ourselves, wittingly or more often unwittingly, to want what it is that we see, or, as one article wonderfully put it, the question of 'Do we fuck this way because of porn, or does porn look like this because it's how we fuck?' But ultimately, I suspect, we are back to the expertise issue again: these seven books would be better written by somebody else.

As I am sure the reader will have gathered by now, the agenda of this book is not to expound my beliefs about porn. I don't think I entered this project with any such beliefs, certainly not well-formed or fixed ones, and, as my understanding of the topic has grown over the course of the project, I am increasingly unsure what a position or even an opinion on porn could look like for me. If anything, the agenda I'm pushing is rather the inherent value in conversations where one is allowed to try on ideas, say things that one may later regret, and contradict oneself. More particularly, that this is something that is desperately needed in the field of porn, where the opportunity to have these kinds of conversations is less than something lost along the wayside and more something that, for many people and for a complex web of reasons, has never been had in the first place. What follows is an attempt to build a first place.

Bristol, May 2022

ONE

One is a straight woman in her late thirties.
She is in a long-term relationship, and has children.

ONE — I've been so looking forward to this conversation, and only as I walked in the door did I suddenly feel exposed and vulnerable. My worry is not to come across as prudish but the opposite, which is probably saying a lot, because I'm probably so vanilla on the scale of consumption.

POLLY BARTON — *It's interesting you say consumption. I'm interested by the way that when some people hear the word porn – specifically women, actually – they immediately jump to talking about it from the perspective of their partner's consumption, or the consumption of the world at large, or the sex they've had with men who watched a lot of porn. And then there's other people who primarily talk about themselves as consumers. Do you feel like you fall definitively on either side?*

I'm definitely the watcher of porn. I've tried to find out if my partner watches it, but I don't think he does now. I think he'd probably be stunned to know how much I watch – although actually I'm currently watching less, because we're back to sharing a bed. I watched it even right after the babies were born – which is why we were sleeping separately – and I'm conscious that's not exactly a 'new mother' thing. There have been a couple of moments when I'm masturbating and the baby monitor goes off and it's like: Oh for god's sake, I just needed four minutes!

When I think about my ex-boyfriends, they're all such good, upstanding men... My brain knows they couldn't *not* watch porn, because doesn't everybody? Especially guys. I'm sure they have seen it and enjoyed it, from the perspective of sheer probability, right? But I can't picture it, and I never got the impression from them that they were trying things that they learned from porn. I feel really conscious, though, that my daughter is going to grow up in a world where that's more of what's happening. I was maybe lucky in that sense and she won't be. But here I am still watching it, so I'm still contributing to that system.

Do you watch porn exclusively to masturbate or can you imagine just putting it on to —

Unwind or something? No, I can't imagine that. It's exclusively for masturbation. As soon as I've orgasmed, I'm done with porn. I feel like: Get it out of my sight.

I don't watch that much porn, but whenever I do the contrast between before and after is so stark. Much more than with anything else that's a turn-on. What seems just-about-bearably grimy suddenly seems intolerably grimy. Funnily enough, I associate that with a masculine way of being, somehow.

Now I've gotten off I'm not interested?

Yes. As if it's tied into that trope you see portrayed in films of being led by your dick down some avenue you don't really want to go down, and then as soon as the orgasm happens, it's like, What the fuck was that? That's how I feel about porn when I do watch it.

34

I hadn't thought about it until I just said it out loud to you, but I do have this feeling of doing something icky... It's funny, I'm not ashamed that I watch porn – though I don't tell a lot of people about it, so does that mean I *am* ashamed? Or just that it doesn't come up in conversation? Maybe there is shame in that slight feeling of: oh, that was repulsive. But I don't truly believe that it was repulsive. I'm just done with it, I guess. It was a private itch I had to scratch. But now I'm trying to think about the experience of watching a movie that's not porn but which I find erotic and how that's different. I suppose I get titillated sitting in my seat, and then I just keep watching, because there's an actual narrative.

Have you always watched porn?

Yes. I've been sexual from early on. I was telling someone about this the other day, actually, which is weird because it's a really embarrassing story: when I was six, I would go round to a friend's house after school to hang out, so that the parents could share the childcare. Anyway, one day I was masturbating while I was there, without realizing that was what I was doing. I was kneeling on myself in that way. So obviously the woman told my mom what was happening, and my mom was really great about it. She said to me, it's normal to do that, but it's private. It's stuck in my head clearly, but she did it in a way I wouldn't have felt shame about it. Especially considering I grew up in an evangelical don't-have-sex-before-marriage church with books on the shelf by James Dobson saying masturbation was evil. But I think that was an extreme version of what my parents practised, if that makes sense.

Do you think you came to feel shame about it later?

I think I'm embarrassed about it only because I realize I was doing something that's not publicly acceptable. I was only a kid, though. With religion stuff more generally, there were a lot of hangovers. I didn't want to have sex before I was married, for example, long after I stopped believing in God or the Bible. That lingered for a long time. But anyway, about the porn, I did watch it growing up. I remember really clearly how, back on AOL dial-up, I used to use this website called Sublime Directory. I don't know how I stumbled upon it. There was a list of different categories: 'Erotic Fiction', 'Sex Toons', 'Lesbians', and so on. It was just all hyperlinks you clicked on to open up. I don't think it would have been videos, I think it was probably just pictures. I remember reading a lot of erotic stories, too, just about regular people having sex.

What kind of age were you?

Fifteen is probably a good guess. I felt younger than fifteen, but in hindsight... But then, no, actually, because at one point my parents found out somehow that porn was being watched on the computer, and they assumed it was my younger brother and I let them think that. And he's six years younger, so I must've been older for that to be conceivable. So it was high school. I think I was really sexual from a relatively early age. At six I didn't know it was sexual. I just knew it felt good.

These categories feel so fraught, anyway. What does it mean to be sexual when you're a child? I was probably quite similar, quite early. It occupied quite a lot of my consciousness, but I

36

felt I couldn't speak about it with anybody. It was the biggest taboo. How was that for you?

Once I knew it wasn't a shameful thing I was okay with it within myself. Obviously when I was watching porn online, I was masturbating. I would have been downstairs in the den touching myself. And yet when I picture masturbating, it's always upstairs in bed, kneeling over a wad of my blankets. That's how I did it. I wonder if I was just replaying things I had seen, because although I had had kisses with boys from about middle school, I was such a nerd, so it's not as though I had a lot of experiences to draw from in real life. But I don't remember telling any girlfriends that I was doing it or anything like that. I hung out with Christian girls until later in high school, too, so I'm sure we didn't talk about it.

Was there a point at which you started talking to people about it?

I'm not ashamed to talk about masturbating. Although still not to my partner, because it feels like, when you're in a long-term committed relationship, there's a taboo there. It's as if you're cheating on them or something. I'm not ashamed, but I don't want to hurt his feelings. Masturbating is more convenient, or less fraught, than sex sometimes.

But talking about porn... Now I hang out with progressive feminist women, in a culture where it feels like the gender politics of porn are so atrocious. That's the taboo, more than anything else.

So much around this is built on assumptions, and because we don't talk about this stuff, we can't really test those assumptions. The question of whether or not you masturbate when you're in a relationship, for example. I feel like people who think it's normal approach the question with an 'of course you do!', and the others approach it with an 'of course you don't.' But maybe that certainty is a cover for the fear of actually exploring that topic through conversation, rubbing up against someone who feels differently and having to fight your corner.

Do you know Esther Perel?

Yes, I used to listen to her couples therapy podcasts religiously when I was in Japan.

There's one where she talks about the way some people define cheating as watching porn and others define it as actual intercourse, and there's a whole spectrum in between. I should have known all this from the beginning, I suppose – that this is how it would turn out. But you know how sex lives are exciting at first for any relationship, and at the beginning with my partner it felt adventurous enough to me that I just assumed... we were more on the same page? We were so young that I don't think I had fully explored what I wanted anyway. But we haven't really talked about it, not for a long time, and we have our own complications.

Sometimes I wonder if I've just been having this whole journey in my head with what I like and my interests. Not that I haven't had sexual relationships I've enjoyed – and another part of porn, actually, is that it tends to mimic sex I've had that I've enjoyed with people other than my partner. Anyway, that's my embarrassing confession, and it's embarrassing because in an ideal relationship, we would discuss this freely. Set our own

38

parameters and preferences. That should be part of it. And yet it's just not something I'm interested in venturing into. It's not that I'm shy about it. I think my partner knows I've watched porn, I've joke-mentioned it, but I get the impression from his reaction that I'm probably embarrassing him more than engaging with him.

It sounds like you've lost faith that he could excite you?

A little bit, yeah.

That's really tough.

Yeah. But interestingly, I listened to another episode of Esther Perel's podcast, featuring a guy who was watching a lot of porn and a woman who was really upset that he was watching a lot of porn. He would want to try things with her and she would feel, 'But that's not who I am.' That didn't make me think of my partner at all, at the time, but I see now that it should have. I realize now that that's an alternate reality for us.

Can you imagine being in a long-term relationship and not watching porn? I mean, does it feel as though you're doing it because you're not sexually fulfilled? Or do you think that, even if you were, you would still watch porn because it's a different thing altogether?

That's a really good question and I don't know the answer. My inkling is probably that if someone was meeting all of your sexual needs, you wouldn't watch porn. Partly because, who has the time?

What kind of porn do you watch?

As I go to answer that question I realize that I don't know all the terms for this stuff, and any knowledge I have obtained is just by dipping my toe in. There was this article in *New York* magazine about porn that you should read, if you haven't, and it mentioned a few categories of porn where I was like: what is *that*? But for instance, Deeper is a channel on Pornhub that I tend to like, because it tends to be very 'classy', I suppose: people having sex that is dominating, but feels consensual, which is what I like.

The thing is, when my partner set up the internet, he somehow configured it to this security setting and because of everything I've just said, I don't want to ask him to change it. Not that he would mind, I'm sure – but it feels very awkward to say to your spouse: 'I'd like to watch porn, please can you turn the child safety lock off?'

Do you think he did that coincidentally?

Totally. He wouldn't have thought about it: I'm sure it was a default and he left it. Maybe thinking of when our kids are eventually old enough for it to matter. That's how he is. Anyway, I discovered that on Tumblr, you can follow porn blogs. I find it really interesting. Another website I used to like was just called sex.com and it's GIFs, and Tumblr is kind of that, too. Though I will say it's a really strange space to be watching porn in. I haven't used Tumblr for anything else, so I don't have any followers, and I feel safe and anonymous there. But you are watching actual people's accounts of the porn they like. Some guy in Kansas or Istanbul, or a couple of swingers in Texas. And because I like dominating sex, there's a real slippery line between consensual stuff and people just abusing a woman, and the woman looking like she's not enjoying it, which I consider two very different things. So that's scary, because it almost feels like someone's guiding me through their porn. I'm scrolling down and then I get to something that will suddenly be a turn-off. Women with their mascara running, or they start being tied up, or they're being abused and humiliated, there's a lot of calling them 'stupid bitch'. It's awful. I'm aware there's a thin line between that and my thing that I'm saying is okay. Mostly it's fine and I have a very enjoyable evening, it's a quick hit for me, but sometimes it's wrapped up with other things. You're watching the porn from an account of a guy who you later discover has said something vaguely racist and it's like, Fuck! It makes you feel dirty.

I've had that feeling before of being turned on by the dominatey-type sex you're describing, but realizing that it belongs on the continuum with something that I'm really uncomfortable with society-wise. And even with real sex that I've had in the past, there have been things that have turned me on but which I don't feel comfortable endorsing... Consent has to be the dividing line, ultimately, but it is also overwhelmingly difficult to pin down.

Yes. In a way I want to say, Each to their own, where that doesn't infringe on other people's rights. There was this line quoted in a Rebecca Solnit essay about Covid and mask-wearing, something along the lines of: 'My right to swing my arm ends where your nose begins.' It's a thin line, though.

In a past relationship where I had very sensual and really good sex, there was one time he started to choke me. He hadn't done it before and afterwards he said, Actually, I'm never going to do that again. He was more

41

freaked out than I was, thinking about what could have happened. I don't think I want to be choked, but that's part of whatever this is. It's adjacent to it. I'm okay with you slapping me... sometimes. And sometimes I might not be. And not in the face.

Is it always the man who is dominating and the woman who's submissive in the porn you watch?

Yeah. The other way around doesn't appeal because I'm so tall and have historically felt bigger. I'm bigger than my partner, for instance, and part of why I wouldn't even try to make that happen with him is that the physicality of it would make it impossible for me to be in that sexy position. I want someone who's taller. Let's not pretend that he could pin me down or something. Does that make sense? I don't like to feel like the bigger, stronger person.

Have you read The Right to Sex *by Amia Srinivasan? It grew out of an essay she wrote for the* LRB *with the same title, using incels as an inroad into exploring consent and sex and other stuff. She has a chapter in there about porn, and one of the questions she asks is: When heterosexual women watch straight porn, who are they identifying with? Do you have a clear sense of that? If you're watching – I don't know what the correct word is here – dominatey, dominatory...*

It's hard to find a word, isn't it? It's not S and M. And it's not about the costumes either.

Is it about the power dynamic?

Yes, the submissiveness.

So do you feel you are identifying with the submissive woman?

Yes. And I should say, when I do watch porn, it can be anywhere from every other day to once a week or once a couple of weeks, depending, but it's usually a pretty quick experience – it doesn't take me long to get off. I don't think I could ever stand – funnily enough this makes me feel very male and guilty too – but I don't want to watch all the narrative build-up, or rather, attempts at narrative. I'm quick to feel: I don't believe this scenario, you're obviously going to have sex at the end and I just want to see it... Basically I really enjoy very graphic close-ups of genitals having intercourse.

You know how in porn, you don't really get a lot of certain positions, it's always the woman, and you get a lot of her body, and it's really something when you get the back of a man, the back of his testicles. And when I see that, I layer this great-sex ex on top of that. My partner has really lovely testicles, he actually has a very excellent penis, but because our sex life isn't what I had with this other person, he's just not who I visualize when I see this. For me that's what feels rare when I'm scrolling through porn, that kind of close-up.

Have you ever been concerned by the idea your partner might be watching loads of porn, or that you don't know how much he's watching?

Really not, but only because I would feel hypocritical to think that. I can completely picture the other scenario, and of course that's what I hear of more – that it's the guy who's watching a lot of porn. I almost want him to have that and enjoy it, for his sake, but I don't think he is. Partly because he set the parental controls, and he doesn't know about Tumblr. I'm sure he used to. I do have the sense that he was a horny little twenty-something, but I think that's just not who he is right now. And maybe I have that all wrong, but anyway, I really do think – porn aside, because it's fraught – that everyone should have a healthy fantasy and sexual life of their own. It would be nice if he had that, but I'm not sure it's a priority for him.

When I first found out about porn, I linked it up with something very fundamental about the way girls and women are treated in society, and which I'd grown up with – it all seemed of a piece. There's a part of me, even now, that finds it really troubling that someone I am in a relationship with might be watching and getting off on something that I find really misogynist and degrading, and then coming back to me and playing the good feminist, you know?

That's a really good point. It's easy to say I would be fine if my partner was watching porn but actually I think I might find it difficult if it happened. Or depending on what kind it was. Which is partly, again, my own body insecurities, because all the women in porn are beautiful. I'm aware that's a generalization, but that's how they look to me. I had a really frank conversation about porn with a good male friend of mine, and I realized that I just assumed that every woman squirts and I was weird for not squirting. But he was like, Oh no, it's unusual. And that he's had that with someone once and it actually wasn't that nice – I mean, it's just kind of messy. That made me feel so much better.

From porn I just thought there was a disproportionate amount of people who do that. Of course, now that I'm not looking out for it or feeling ashamed about not being that way, I don't see it all the time, but I think it did cause anxiety for a while. That ever-present 'Oh, I'm different' anxiety.

I'm hypocritical in a sense, too, in that I am really okay with a fantasy world where I'm with two men, but I would never want to be a second woman. It really ties in with body insecurity: I can really just see I'd assume the other one is more beautiful and more attractive. And I would feel really... not competitive, exactly, but just unloved in that situation.

Even if the other woman was someone I was a hundred per cent sure I was more attractive than – I can't really imagine how that situation would ever come about, but let's say hypothetically I was – I think I would still feel worried.

I think you're right, that if the person I was with was really sexual too, and had his own separate sexual life, I wouldn't like it. It's interesting to be in a relationship with someone like my partner where that's less of a priority. The great-sex ex didn't really watch porn, but I know that he had seen enough, or I know that he had his own interests and fetishes in a way that was sexy to me. It's a fine line. I wouldn't have wanted him to be like: Could you just be more like this? And when I hear people talk about watching porn together to get turned on, that sounds so foreign to me. I just cannot imagine that turning me on at all.

Or leaving it on while they have sex. I find that idea mind-blowing.

That really blows my mind, too. It sounds terrible.

45

Have you got to a stage where masturbating equals porn? Are there times when you masturbate and don't watch porn?

There are times when I masturbate and don't watch porn. Porn just makes it quicker for me. I started saying this before and went off on a tangent, but I think that approach I have to it makes me feel a bit male, as if I'm just in it to get off. Wasn't there an episode in *Fleabag* where she basically said, I'm tired, I just want to have an orgasm and go to bed? Men probably do that and it's not a big deal, but it does feel sleazy. Then I wonder if it would still feel this way if the porn itself were different. It's so obviously male-centric – you have the beautiful female body, and a man who's either headless, or all but invisible. I know that there's porn that's made for women, but it doesn't do it for me. Anyway, mainstream porn is shot very much from the guy's perspective, the female body is objectified and very beautiful, and I wonder if that element makes it feel more like a transaction, when I'm just trying to get off.

When I was young, a lot of the body anxiety I felt came from women's magazines. It wasn't necessarily generated by them, but it felt as though they sustained it. These days I don't have any contact with them at all, and I feel a lot less body anxiety – for multiple reasons, definitely not just that one. Occasionally I'll come into contact with them in the newsagent or whatever, though, and I'll feel this weird twinge, a kind of flare-up. Like, Wow, that is an old and deep and horrible feeling and I don't want anything to do with that. Hearing what you said made me wonder whether porn does the same thing?

Totally. Because so many of the women are beautiful or

46

anorexic. I think what bothers me is that I've realized I am more attracted when it's beautiful people making porn. It's problematic! With the body image stuff: I've had a baby, you know, and I understand the time it takes. Sure, I would like these jeans to feel more comfortable on me, but I can forgive myself that I can't run every day now, do you know what I mean? And that's okay.

Did you use to run every day?

Yeah. That's probably wrapped up in the body image issues, past eating disorders, etc. With body image stuff, I'm able to exist these days thinking I would rather have dessert than not look like this, but as you say, it does flare up. I've also found that even as I'm living in this body, I wouldn't want to watch someone who looks like me having sex. I wouldn't want to watch someone who has a little roll of stomach having sex. And yet I want to have sex, stomach and all. So I find that really disappointing of myself. Everyone deserves to have sex, you know? To have really good sex. Also, it's worth saying there's not a lot of stomach-roll porn out there either. It's not like I switch away from it. There's just not much to see. Is that true, what I'm saying? I think maybe the issue is that porn is really extreme: it's either really skinny people or it's a fat fetish, which has its own category, and that seems different. Maybe I don't fit in between. I saw Jon Ronson when he did his *The Last Days of August* tour, and I'd heard his podcast before that. I was really struck by this idea that, with porn stars, they do well for a very short period when they're very young, and there's this period where they're out of work...

Yes! Before they become a MILF.

And MILFs are basically... still barely of child-bearing age. I found that really fascinating.

The Right To Sex *touches on profiles on Grindr and other gay male dating apps, and how it's very common for men to specify 'no Asians, no fats', in this very balls-out way. Of course, essentially the same thing happens in straight dating sites...*

It's a lot more coded, isn't it?

Yeah. In the straight world you see that same thing in its unshrouded form in porn categories, where there's suddenly no need to try and dress up what your sexual proclivities are as you define them.

Anyhow, on this question of how much our desires are malleable, I've heard a lot of people talk about actively adding body-positive accounts on Instagram so as to familiarize themselves with fat bodies, bodies other than skinny bodies. And that's more about self-acceptance and social worth than sexual desire, but I don't think they're unrelated. So much of it comes back to the fact that when something isn't treated as normal and/or desirable by society or the communities of which you're a part, it's far harder to feel accepting or desiring of it.

That's the case with everything: you don't know you can do something unless you have an example of it. And you don't think to want it either. I am turned off by super skinny girls, in part because I could never be that, but also because porn is so extreme that the super skinny girls often overlap with the young dominated girls, which is really different from being an adult woman and choosing to be dominated. Sometimes they have bunny ears on, or are dressed as schoolgirls. That's not what I want to see. It's a really specific, consensual but very sexy and dirty thing that I like.

When I was in my twenties, I was friends with this girl. Actually we were friends from school, and when I started hanging around her she was a goth, and throughout university she gradually got more and more into the BDSM community.

Do those two tend to be related?

I thought that they weren't, I thought it was a cliché to think that they were, but I think there is a certain degree of overlap. Anyway, at some point in my twenties, I went with her to this S and M club in Vauxhall, which opened at eleven p.m. and stayed open all night. It was called Hades. The building was really cavernous, with so many different sections and stages and kinds of people. I found it a very disturbing experience, much more than I imagined. I went there feeling quite open to it but there was a lot of stuff I found either utterly uninspiring, or really difficult to deal with. A lot of medical stuff? Anyway, I spent most of the evening wandering around by myself, because my friend was off getting whipped by this whipping expert with all her cooler friends.

Then I stumbled into this room, it was small and dimly lit, and there was a central platform on which there was a couple having vaguely dominatey sex, and the people sitting around the edge were watching them. Neither of them had physiques to die for at all, but the connection between them was so palpable. I assume they were doing it because they got off on people watching them, but it felt nonetheless really soupy and intimate and intense. I suppose I'm thinking about it now because I feel if there was a still from a video of that on a porn site I would probably scroll right past it, you know. But being there – that was a hundred times sexier than anything bloodless between very hot skinny people.

That makes sense. How can you replicate that? That's something porn flattens entirely. You know that these are people who are being paid to have sex and you can't really get around that. Saying that, I guess there's a whole other home-video thing but that makes me feel weird too. The problem is partly that I really like the produced look. And, also, I can't help but feel that here's this young couple in their twenties, they're trying to make a buck and don't know the repercussions of putting themselves on the internet. I end up feeling a bit mumsy about it. Your father would be very disappointed! That said, I haven't watched much of it, probably because by the time that was a thing, I had my own porn.

50

TWO

Two is a gay Australian man in his forties who lives in Japan. He is currently single.

POLLY BARTON — *Can you remember your first encounter with porn?*

TWO — Yes. It's strange in retrospect because the first time I ever saw porn was with my brother and his friends, when we were living in North Queensland. Lots of things happened in that place and one day – I don't think it was a summer holiday? – no, it was a school swimming carnival. We didn't go to the carnival, and one of my brother's friends brought a porno to our house, called *Rachel Ryan RR*. Rachel Ryan was the main porn star and she looked a bit like Debbie Harry, she was this blonde, really sexy, slightly older woman – or at least at that age she seemed older. The movie was a montage of clips of her from different movies, and it had a female presenter, whose name – I still remember all the names – was Trinity Loren. Trinity Loren was in this studio and would introduce the clips. She'd say, 'Rachel doesn't only like the guys, she likes the girls as well...' and then it would cut to a lesbian scene. I remember being shocked by it because in Australia you couldn't get X-rated movies, so that was the first fully explicit porn I'd ever seen. You could only get R-rated movies.

What does that mean?

You don't see erections, you don't see cum. Basically you can't see full genitalia – you see naked people having

51

sex, but you can't see any actual penetration or anything. Most Australian porno was edited versions of X-rated American movies, so it would be more or less exactly the same as the original, but you wouldn't get cum shots or anything like that. Hilariously, the only place in Australia that you could get X-rated movies was in Canberra, which is where all the politicians lived, so people would sometimes go there just to buy them.

So the Rachel Ryan video was R-rated?

No, it was X-rated. I think my brother's friend's uncle had been to America or something, and got it there. Anyway, my brother bought the video off this guy, and I gave him money towards it. Let's say the video was $20, I gave him $5 and he paid $15 or something.

Also, it's so strange to say this, but I used to collect *Playboy* magazines. I had tons of these *Playboy* magazines, and they became a kind of social collateral in school. People knew I had no qualms about walking into a news agency and buying *Playboy*, whereas they were all too scared to do it, because we were so young. So it became a thing where people would give me money, and I would go and buy magazines for them. In fact, one of the things I remember from around the time of Rachel Ryan was that I had a friend called Will, who gave me money to buy this super hardcore European magazine. It was the same with magazines in Australia, you couldn't buy hardcore magazines, but he gave me money to buy this imported magazine with biker women on it. I've no idea why the news agency stocked it, but it was full-on frightening. Really extreme stuff I'd never seen before. I went into the news agency and took it to the counter, and that was the first time the woman at the news agency ever challenged me. She was like: 'Who are you buying this for? Why are you buying this?' I remember really panicking, and saying, 'Oh my dad's in hospital!' Saying something about my dad. Just because I thought she was going to call the police. In the end I succeeded in buying that magazine for him, though – Will got it. The thing was, though, Will's mum was really lovely, I used to go round to his house and talk to her. I got along with his mum really well because she loved books and reading. Then one day, she found the magazine and I guess she asked him about it. We knew because she went to visit my mum at work and said, 'Two's bought this hardcore magazine for Will. I'm not angry, I'm just really surprised because Two's really sensitive and we always talk about books and stuff, so I wonder, you know...' I remember my mum coming home and telling me. I wasn't embarrassed or anything, I just remember thinking, Oh no, now Will's mum doesn't like me.

But yes, Rachel Ryan was the first proper video I remember.

You said you were shocked, but talk me through your other feelings about it. You've told me before that you knew you were gay from very early on, basically from the dawning of consciousness?

Yes, basically.

And you collected Playboy and had this love of women in a kind of aesthetic way. What was it like to see that porn, and to see your brother's reaction to it?

Watching that porno was the first time I'd ever really seen erections and stuff, so I felt, Oh my God, this is really exciting, but also sort of scary and a bit forbidden. It felt aggressive, in a strange way. Frighteningly so. But I was really excited about it because I finally understood what people actually did when they had sex. Up until that point I'd seen tons of sex comedies and stuff, but the sex scenes were always just someone lying on top of someone else in the nude. I'd never seen it in explicit terms. It was completely different from *Playboy*. *Playboy* to me was purely about the aesthetics, I used to buy vintage ones so the models would be on pinball machines in fur jackets and stupid stuff. I thought it was really cool. Porn was different. It was exciting, but it also felt really dark.

Exciting, like arousing?

Yes, definitely arousing. I remember feeling a bit sad too. As if there was nothing left to discover, almost. I remember thinking, This is the limit of what you can see in a movie, there's nothing beyond this. But yeah, totally arousing.

How old were you?

I would have been thirteen. For some perspective on what I was watching and what my knowledge was, I had already read *The Secret Diary of Laura Palmer*, which is fully explicit and very dark, maybe two full years before that, and I'd seen *Blue Velvet* and other heavy movies that other kids probably weren't watching and shouldn't be watching. Even when I was younger, I remember specifically in primary school – I was probably nine or ten – and there were two dogs on the school oval having sex, and this kid goes, 'Look, they're sexing!' I remember

saying, 'Aww, you don't call it sexing, they're *fucking*!' I
said it really loud, and I remember my teacher, who was
standing really far away, turning and looking at me, in
shock. I felt like: How stupid are you?! How would you
not know that you don't say sexing? Ultimately, though,
he was just a kid, and he'd never heard it before, whereas
I'd been reading books that were adult books and watching things that were beyond my years. But that porn was
shocking. I was shocked by it, for sure.

You're a little bit older than me, and with people of my age,
in order to get internet porn as a teenager you needed to be
really on it, into forums and stuff. But you didn't have porn on
the internet...

There was no internet until I was in high school. Was
that where you first saw it, on the internet?

The first time for me was maybe watching Boogie Nights?
And like you with Rachel Ryan RR, *the standout memory*
from that was seeing someone with an erection. Full-frontal
images of women were incredibly common, and I'd seen people
fucking in TV series, but seeing a man with an erection I
thought: Oh wow, this is the real shit. I think I found it –
again, like you – really arousing, but also a dangerous feeling
and somehow unpleasant at the same time. I remember I
had this tiny little TV with an integral VHS player, and for
some reason I had the Boogie Nights *video, and I remember*
watching it on that, and feeling this real sense of darkness
and seediness. Being turned on by it and not really wanting
to be turned on by it, the way that complemented the whole
experience of watching that film.

I just remembered something from when I was much

younger than when I watched *Rachel Ryan*. There's a channel in Australia called SBS, which is basically the foreign channel, it's what people who've immigrated to Australia tend to watch, so it will have a block of French TV shows or whatever. It was free. But it was on this weird channel where you had to twist the aerial around to get reception. Every weekend, they'd show two or three foreign movies, and one of those movies was a French film called *The Wounded Man*[1]. I must have seen that when I was maybe eleven or twelve. It's about this French hustler who's cruising men in a train station, and goes into this toilet, and a guy holds a knife to his throat and gropes him. But then they end up in a relationship. It's not super explicit, but it's full frontal nudity. That was the first time I'd ever seen gay sex or anything close. I had that on tape and I used to watch just the sex scenes over and over again, and that felt really forbidden. If anyone knew that I recorded it, I would have been really scared. So that was actually probably the first porn for me, but it wasn't porn. It was an art movie, basically.

And you'd watch that to be turned on, to masturbate to?

Yes, yes, yes. I used to read about all the movies that were showing in the TV book every Sunday morning, and circle which ones to watch. I must have read the synopsis of it and it must have said gay or something. I watched it again maybe two or three years ago, actually, because I just wanted to see what it was like, and it still feels quite full-on. At the end, he strangles the guy to death as they're having sex.

1   A 1983 film portraying a relationship between a young man and
     an elder hustler, directed by Patrice Chéreau and co-written by
     Chérau and Hervé Guibert.

*That was what I used to do as well: record films and then just
watch the sex scenes. I don't watch much porn, and part of
that is about the aesthetics. It's much more common for me to
watch a film and find the sex scenes a turn-on. I feel like such
a clichéd bore saying this: the sex scenes in arty films are some
of the most arousing stuff that exists, for me.*

Totally. I think the whole focus is wrong, especially with
gay porn. Even the people in it are usually so repulsive
to me. It's the same feeling as going out and listening
to awful music all night at gay clubs. I just think, Why
would I want to do that?

*What has your porn consumption been like throughout your
life? Have you been through stages with it?*

Yeah, I think so. Whenever I've been in relationships
with people, I almost never watch porn, and then there
are other times... I don't know, it's weird. When I first
came to Japan, I didn't watch any porn for years. Before
I had my first boyfriend in Japan, I had no access to gay
life or the gay world here, and I didn't know anything
about it. I didn't know it even existed. I was so interested
in what was out there, I guess.

One night, after I'd been here a couple of years and I
was living in a semi-rural town, I got really drunk and
went into an adult video shop. At that time, my Japanese
was bad, and I remember buying a couple of videos
without really even looking at them because I just wanted to get out of there, just grabbing them and paying
without much thought.

Anyway, one of them turned out to be a regular gay
porno, and the other one was a 'new half' porno. What
would be the proper way to say that in English? A trans

woman with a penis, basically. But the new halves were the dominant ones in the situation.

A new half with another man?

It was a group of new halves with one man.

A new half gang-bang?

Yes. The guy was a really standard-looking chubby forty-something man. I remember thinking: of *all* the videos I could have picked up, how did I end up buying this? Just because one of the guys on the spine had bleached hair. I remember being fascinated by it.

Did you feel turned on by it?

Maybe I felt turned on by his reaction rather than the situation. The situation was just —

It sounds nuts.

Yeah, it was nuts, it was really nuts. Up until that point, I'd really felt that in Japan in general, and in my circle of friends specifically, everyone seemed almost asexual. It felt as if there was no open sexuality around me at that time. Everyone in my friendship circle came across as so innocent, and when I think about it, none of my friends talked about sex at all. I remember thinking, Wow, there's this whole other thing here that I have no idea about. And this is in a semi-rural area, and people are buying this video here. There's something going on here. I found it really interesting. So strange when I think about it.

That makes me think about porn as information source. You know, one of the main focuses of discussions around porn in the media is the way that more and more children now are watching porn not to be turned on, although maybe that too, but to learn how to have sex. I remember worrying about that kind of stuff when I was young: how do I give a hand-job? How do I give a blow-job? These worries, which stemmed from the idea that I didn't know how to do it, and if it ever came around that I would have to do those things then I'd be expected to know, and so I'd get found out as a fraud or a saddo. If there'd been porn readily available then, I'm sure I'd have watched it to try to get that knowledge. And now, I guess, all the kids are doing that – or at least, that's one piece of the puzzle. It's interesting to me that in your case, maybe it wasn't exactly serving as a how-to guide, but it was a precious source of information about what was out there in this country you had just moved to.

Totally. Looking back, I learned so much Japanese from watching those videos. Not only sexual stuff, but basic phrases, things that people said in life that I'd never picked up on before. I remember speaking to someone, I think they were talking about playing tennis, and I asked, '*Hatsutaiken?*' [Is it your first time?] And they looked at me, like, What the fuck? I just thought it meant your first time for anything. I didn't realize it only meant 'lose your virginity'. I remember going beet red, and thinking, Oh my God, they're going to think I'm really dirty.

It's interesting what you were saying about kids, because there's one kid I've taught for a long time, he's in the first year of junior high school now, and he told me last year that his dream was to be a porno director. He specifically said he wanted to work for Pornhub.

There's this game called Nanja Moja, do you know it? It's a kids' card game and there are tons of different monster-creature things. You have to make up names for them the first time a specific kind appears, and if it pops up again, you have to remember the name that someone else has given it. You'd probably really like it, it's really fun. This kids' class is all boys and we started playing it one lesson, and I don't remember why now, but I had to leave the classroom for some reason. And when I came back, I remember opening the door and this kid was shouting out 'Fellatio, fellatio!' I gasped, but I also understood that that was the name that someone had given to that creature, and I knew immediately it was this one kid, the Pornhub director.

In fact, there were lots of really sexual monster names they had given them: anal sex, homo, I think there was double penetration, something penetration, in full katakana[2] pronunciation: *pe-ne-to-rē-shon*. It was so crazy. And so of course I had to tell them that they can't use words like that, but it was so hard not to laugh. It shocked me just how extreme it was. It made me realize, sure, they might not really understand this stuff, but they still know everything, because so many of them have phones now. All those words were search-terms for porn.

Just a few weeks ago, a few of my students were looking at this thing on TikTok in the classroom. It started out as an innocuous video of someone shaking something in the kitchen or something – and they were all crowded around watching this video on one of their phones – and then it cut straight to what I guess was a porn star dancing, with a hard-on bouncing up and

2   One of the two Japanese phonetic scripts, which is commonly used for representing imported words, such as those taken from English.

down. They weren't remotely worried that I might see it, or embarrassed. It was just normal.

Have you talked to this kid about his ambitions to be a porn director?

Yes, I asked him about it. I said, 'Are you serious about that? Why do you want to do that?' As far as he's concerned, it's a really good way of making money and it would be fun. On some level, it still shocks me that he even knows what Pornhub is, but then it doesn't, at the same time. *Of course* they know what it is.

Do you think at that age he watches porn because he's turned on by it, or is it the social capital that it has?

I would guess that at first he was watching it so he could talk about it with people, but I think later on it shifts. I've noticed that happens with kids a lot – they'll talk all the time about *oppai* [boobs] and all this sort of stuff, and then all of a sudden they just stop mentioning it. They become ashamed of it at a certain point, because it becomes real. They realize why people watch porn, and then they're ashamed of it.

Right, as soon as they're using it for masturbation it becomes different. My sense is that lots of men, particularly, find it hard to wank without porn – or maybe it wasn't initially, but it's got to be more that way since the rise of internet. Does that feel true to you?

Maybe. I don't think it's impossible without it, but it's easier. It just becomes natural after a while.

It's the association.

This is what you do, basically. I think so. I think it would be very rare to find people who aren't like that. I don't really talk about it with other people, but that's the impression I get.

Do you have ways of finding porn that you find non-objectionable or do you tolerate the bad stuff?

No, I don't tolerate it. It has to be really specific. It's hard to explain, actually. Number one, if it looks ugly, I won't even look at it. But even that is specific. A pristine studio is ugly to me. Usually, if it's someone with an interesting face or something different in some way, I might look. If it's something that makes me think, Wow, what is this person doing here? If it's an 'Oh sorry, pizzaboy, I have no wallet'-type scenario, I won't watch it. If it's an interview with someone first and then sex happens or something, I find that really fascinating. I'm specific in the things I will not look at, basically. I won't go for anything exploitative or anything ugly. I'd never watch fisting or that kind of extreme stuff. Just visually and aesthetically, from the cover or the thumbnail or whatever it is, I can quickly get a good sense of whether something might be interesting to me.

One of the things that interests me about what it's like watching porn as a gay man is that, for me, ninety five per cent of the straight, mainstream porn you find on Pornhub feels to some degree exploitative, or if not exploitative, then at least replicating this phallocentric, problematic...

Degrading, I guess?

Yes, degrading, exactly. Which, not only do I rationally object to, but I just do not find sexy at all. It's a massive turn-off. Whereas with porn involving only men made by men for men, I know there're other considerations, but just off the bat it feels like it would be less of an obvious problem?

Yeah, I definitely feel that way. A lot of the time the gay porn that I watch feels like people almost playing. It feels like they would have sex anyway, but they're just doing it on camera. I remember being at a party when Paris Hilton had her porn leaked, and it was on, and people were crowded around laughing, and I remember feeling, Oh, we should not be watching this. It felt really wrong. Really intrusive and gross and just so seedy.

There is a different quality to straight porn. There's obviously tons of exploitation within gay porn, lots of really old men with young men and things like that, but it definitely feels different. I don't know whether that's because I'm gay, or if it's because it's made with a different agenda. So much straight porn really feels like its aim is to make the woman as degraded as possible and end up covered in cum. It's really gross.

I'm sure this sounds like a super naive thing to say, but for me the idea of someone being covered in cum is so far from what should be a turn-on between people who like each other, unless your thing is quite extreme power play. And yet it's not acknowledged as a kink – or rather it's so universalized that it's a society-wide kink. A patriarchy-wide kink.

Yes, I agree. It feels really perverse. There was this website of porn bloopers I found a few years ago. It was really bad, but I remember going through it at one time, because it was also really fascinating. They'd be filming a porno and then something would go wrong. There was one I watched for example, in this fraternity set-up, where it was just one guy having sex with one girl on this pool table and he couldn't get a hard-on. There were, I don't know, a hundred guys on the set – they were all clothed, they weren't jerking off or anything, but they started mocking him. He's there standing up on this pool table saying, 'Fuck you guys! I'm just a human being!', completely naked, with this girl just lying there, and I remember thinking, This is crazy. How on earth would that have felt in that moment?

I remember another one, they'd filmed a girl and she had cum all over her and they'd say, 'Lick your lips,' and stuff like that, then say, 'How do you feel?' And because this was the bloopers, there were scenes where the woman would start crying and say, 'I want to go home.' Just awful stuff, truly the lowest images of humanity you can imagine. Really bad. Really, really bad. I remember one night just going through it, I couldn't stop, because although I'd never seen this stuff, it was exactly what I imagined – actually worse than what I imagined, but also exactly what I imagined. This real human darkness, pure sadism and evil, almost.

I have always found it interesting to think about what happens after people shoot porn. In a physical sense, on the day you shoot a porno and then get dressed and go to the train station or whatever. That in between, it seems so strange. How do you execute that switch? I guess it's like acting or something.

You learn to compartmentalize, don't you?

I think so. I think too, with things like the Rachel Ryan stuff from the eighties, and the *Boogie Nights* stuff – I've actually read a bunch of books by people from that era, like *Traci Lords: Underneath It All*[3] – and it actually sounded as if, particularly in the eighties, a lot of people were in porn because they enjoyed sex and enjoyed the lifestyle. That said, she was underage, so there was complicated stuff going on. That book is in her own voice, though. They were taking coke all the time and it was just a party lifestyle they had.

And there was a lot of money.

There was a lot of money, and the productions were elaborate. In Traci Lords' book, she describes being flown out to Japan, staying in these beautiful hotels. She was treated as a film star.

One narrative around internet porn is that, because it's free, people are watching a lot, and they become desensitized. They stop being turned on by the things that they were turned on by before, and the limits get pushed, and people require more and more extreme stuff. Have you noticed that sort of tendency in yourself?

I don't think so. I'm weird in that sense anyway. I never understand when everyone's excited about someone, a famous person or someone muscled and tanned in a bar or something. I'm usually lusting after the skinny shy one in a Sonic Youth shirt.

3   Traci Lords is a former adult video performer, who used a fake birth certificate to enter into the porn industry two years before the legal age of eighteen. During her brief stint making videos she was one of the most popular performers, but quit two days before turning eighteen. When the FBI were tipped off that Lords had in fact been underage while making her films, those responsible for making and distributing her videos were prosecuted, and all but the last of her films have been banned as child pornography.

That ties into those aspects of the mainstream gay world in Japan that you hate, right? Walking into a gay bar and the first question you're asked is whether you're a top or a bottom.

Yeah. I find it difficult when people casually talk about personal experiences of extreme sex. Especially when I'm out in Tokyo, people will tell stories about a certain person, a mutual friend or something. I've always found it weird that people will share really intimate details about other people we both know. That feels really exploitative and wrong. Even if people say they're just joking and they think it's part of being queer... But I know I'm in the minority here.

How does it happen, just anecdotally?

Just in conversation. 'Oh my God, he fucked all my friends last weekend,' and that sort of stuff. And we'll have just been talking to him. I don't want to know that, Jesus! I'm trying to think of who it was, but someone told me years ago about this friend. Have you ever heard of black room parties? You just go in and do whatever, basically, all in darkness. Anyway, I had a friend who I never even thought of in any sexual situation. I couldn't even imagine it, he was almost actively dull. Then one day I was at a bar with another friend, and the first friend came up and said hi, and then he left, and the friend I was with goes, 'Oh my God, last weekend he was at this black room event and six guys had sex with him.' I remember being really taken aback, in shock for a while, and I thought of the person who told me in a different light afterwards. I didn't think that was his story to tell. Eventually we talked about it, but I remember at the time thinking, A, why would you tell me that? How is that any of my business? I don't want to know that, unless he tells me himself. And B, what is that mindset that you can go to a club, and just, you know... That's so strange to me. I don't get it. I'm sure people think I'm weird for thinking that.

What function is the darkness serving in that club context?

Maybe the danger aspect? Maybe that's part of the allure. I'm sure a lot of it is so you don't have to face up to it.

Is porn much of a topic of conversation? When you've been in relationships with people, have you spoken to them about porn?

Yes. With my first Japanese boyfriend, I was just so interested. There were so many things I asked him, about everything in general. About being gay in Japan, and porn was part of it. He had some porn – not a lot, but a few videos. I remember asking whether he was embarrassed going to buy them, where he'd go and buy them, that sort of stuff. In my next relationship, we talked about it a little bit. Not a ton, but I was interested in what their relationship was to it.

And did they ever say anything that you found off-putting?

No, I don't think so. There was some stuff that was a bit difficult. I remember my first Japanese boyfriend used to show me pictures on video cases of someone who was the complete opposite of what I looked like and say, 'This is my type.' I was young and in a really vulnerable state in retrospect, very isolated, and found that really hurtful and pointedly cruel. For him it wasn't that at all.

He would always say, 'No, no, that's just for sex.' And I'd be like, 'Well, you know, that's sort of a strange thing to say to me...' But other than that, no, not really.

With my second major relationship, I found a lot of his sexual history really difficult at the time, which I wouldn't now. I was really naive, in retrospect. He would go to glory holes when he lived in America, when he was quite young. I remember he told me about it so casually. The idea of him going into the back of a porno shop in the middle of Hell's Kitchen to use a glory hole. It seemed so dangerous, I couldn't imagine it. Now I don't think I would react in that way. I think I'd just be more interested. But at the time it felt like, Oh my God, I don't really know this person. It didn't sit well with how I saw him. Do you talk about it with people you date?

I always want to and I'm always scared to, at least with men. I think for a large majority of heterosexual couples, the pretence is that nobody watches it. If you don't speak about it, you can pass as someone who doesn't watch porn. That feels odd to me, because it's very clear that the vast majority of men and quite a lot of women do watch porn, so why don't we speak about it? Part of the reason that people don't speak about it in heterosexual relationships is because such a large proportion of the porn is degrading to women to some degree, and that makes people uncomfortable. Yet it's happening, and I would rather speak about it than just have it as a sort of untouchable zone in the relationship, because any kind of untouchable zone immediately makes me feel nervous and I think about it obsessively. But then actually having that conversation often doesn't go down well...

There's one particular conversation with an ex that's really stuck in my head. We went for two nights to this amazing hot spring in a snowy part of Japan, in the depths of winter.

Things were not going great with us at that point. On the second evening, we'd spent the whole day in the baths, and were sitting in our room, having a beer before dinner was arrived. It was this grand dinner made up of a gazillion tiny dishes across several courses, and every night they served bear soup, which was a local speciality. You could request not to have it, which we had done, but the previous night they'd brought it anyway, and it was even worse because there was this cage really close to the open-air baths. There were lots of wooden signposts around, and one of them was 'To The Bear'. When we first got to the hotel we'd followed it and found this cage with a single, very small bear in it. It was really upsetting, and inevitably, when we'd been served the bear soup that night, all I could think about was this lone, sad bear, and wondering if she was what was sitting in a bowl in front of me.

Anyway, for some reason as we were sitting having this beer, the topic of porn came up and I asked him, 'Do you watch it?' From various things he'd said in the past, I'd formed the sense that he had a relationship to porn as something that he shouldn't do but he did anyway, and lo and behold, this transpired to be the case, and he admitted to watching it, not regularly, but sometimes. The problem was that the moment he started speaking about it he became visibly ashamed, and I sensed this palpable reluctance to speaking about it, which translated to me as secrecy. I honestly think that if he'd come out and said, 'Yeah, I watch porn sometimes, I don't feel great about it,' and we'd had a discussion about it then, it could have been good for both of us. But there was something about the tenor of the discussion that I found immediately troubling, and obviously linked to what was going on with us. He took on this hangdog expression, and I felt like I was interrogating him about this crime that he'd committed. I don't know what the emotion exactly was that surged up in me, but it was

69

somewhere between anger and disgust.

Because of his way of talking about it, or because he was watching it?

Because of the way he was talking about it. As though he didn't want to tell me, and I was forcing it out of him. It was weird, I had a really strong physical reaction. I could feel all this blood surging into my face. I felt a little bit like I'd been possessed, just beside myself with fury. The whole conversation had this strange confession-box tone, I think he even said, 'I won't do it again,' and at exactly that point there was a knock on the door and they started bringing in this set dinner with the fucking bear soup, setting the table and bringing in course after course, when the last thing we could think about was eating. It was one of the worst evenings of my life. So that remains a benchmark of how bad it can get when you open up this can of worms. The thing is – and I'm not sure, because we didn't go into it that much and I wish that we had – I don't think that the sort of porn he was watching was particularly exploitative.

It was enough that he felt shame about it.

Yes. It made me think, that's where the barrier is. It's not really the thing itself.

THREE

Three is a straight man in his thirties.
He has been with his partner for years.

POLLY BARTON — *Have you had many conversations*
about porn?

THREE — No, it's not come up. But I'm not the most
open person and, emotionally speaking, I haven't been
the most open person for a lot of my life. Then, with
porn, there're a lot of societal and other reasons why it
doesn't come up. I'd be curious to know the percentages
on that. I'm guessing it's a generational thing, and that it
has probably changed recently.

Is porn absent from conversation entirely? Or does it only get
referenced, rather than being the main subject of discussion?

In personal conversations with friends or acquaintances
or people I've slept with, it's not come up and it doesn't
get referenced. Not out of prudishness, so much – it's
more that, if you were going to make references to porn
which aren't serious, it might be a passing comment
or ribbing someone, and that doesn't seem to happen.
Then, online and in forum communities – mainly the
latter, because I've never done Reddit or the chan boards
and all that sort of stuff, but I grew up in that orbit – it's
been a constant presence, from when I was fourteen
onwards. So there's definitely a delineation between the
online and the real world.

What forums?

I was on one called Something Awful. It's kind of the ur-forum, and Reddit and 4chan – and therefore 8chan as well – were born out of it. I think it started in 1999, but I started reading it in 2000, when I was fifteen or sixteen. It had a front page with funny articles which were pretty tasteless, but fun when you were a teenager, and then attached to it was a forum, back when forums were still a thing. This was when MySpace and MSN messenger were still a thing, and you had mIRC, ICQ, and gaming[4]. I came to SA via gaming because part of the forum would be about organizing servers for that. It was an example of gaming culture leading into porn culture, part of the whole package of being a teenager on the internet when it was a new thing. Pornography was just one part of growing up with the internet at that time.

When internet porn was in its early developmental stages.

Exactly. I have a particular perspective on this topic because I'm a man in my thirties who grew up geeky enough to be exposed to a lot of the early internet. The context is that you're fourteen and the hormones start going. You realize, Wow, masturbation is fun, but the access is not good, you're still too young for the embarrassment of the top shelf of the newsagents. So you're passing around a magazine between mates a bit, but you're not enough of a jock for that to be a big thing either, and you have precious little visual stimuli... Then the internet comes along, and there's a load of fourteen- or fifteen-year-old kids who know more about what they're doing than their parents do, and communicate with each other constantly.

4   mIRC is an Internet Relay Chat client and ICQ an instant messaging service, both of which were widely used in the late nineties and early 2000s.

I had early access to what pornography was at the time, 56K modem JPEGs loading very slowly. More softcore. It's interesting to talk about the softcore and the hardcore distinction back then, because hardcore at the time was more for the absurdity of it. It wasn't a sexy thing, it was shared more out of disgust or 'what the fuck' type reactions. Someone saying, Check this out, and the other person being grossed out in a very puerile way.

Like how people look at hentai with octopus tentacles?

That was also passed around at the time, because it was gaming culture and internet culture, before there were things like Rickrolling[5], or Goatse-ing.

What's Goatse-ing?

The link was goatse.cx, so it looks like goatsex. It would take you to a single image of this guy bending over so you just see his ass, and he's got a really distended anus that he's pulling apart with his fingers. It's really horrible. Anyway, it was the default disgusting image that people would use to trick people. You'd 'goatse' someone, which meant you'd say, Check this link out. You'd try to do it to people at work, to make them open it in front of their boss or partner or whatever. That was one of the early internet pranks, and it was sexual in a way, or adjacent to that, but it was mostly about disgust. That kind of thing gives you a flavour of the scene at the time.

I'm interested in the hardcore stuff being passed around out of curiosity or because of the wildness of it, but presumably

5   Rickrolling is a set form of trolling someone on the internet by linking them to the music video for Rick Astley's 1987 hit song 'Never Gonna Give You Up'.

there's a pretty blurry boundary between the wild hardcore stuff and the arousing hardcore stuff, right? It's not a hard divide, as it were, and it differs between people.

For sure. But there is a boundary that's always existed, like you said, with the hentai and tentacles. As time has gone on, the delineating of that boundary of what arouses people and what disgusts people has been really well mapped out, but at that time it wasn't, and it was all teenagers who were in the process of delineating that for themselves. In that sense, my exposure to pornographic material was incredibly broad – unbelievably so, comparative to previous generations, but compared to now, probably not so much. Yet it was also extremely narrow in the sense that it was incredibly male-gaze, objectifying of women. It wasn't feminist in any way.

Have you witnessed a change in that over time?

It's changed massively. For starters, free pornography used to be hard to come by – unless you were torrenting stuff, which for some reason I never got into – so it was always about trying to find free porn. There were always paid porn sites but I had no access to credit cards and no wish to spend money anyway. So back in the day, you'd get JPEGs off free sites and so on – that's before you could torrent them. As soon as you could torrent porn, though, you had bad quality proto-Pornhubs springing up. There was an escalation of content or the type of content, although mostly I think that had to do with internet speeds going up because streaming any video on a 56K modem was impossible. Then, with ADSL, it became a possibility. So, as always, it's really the technology that changed everything.

The biggest change by far, though, has been in terms of who is making pornography – the fact you can now create porn as a small business. In order to film anything in the early two thousands, you needed massive lights because the camera resolution was so shit, and a camera which costs a bomb, and then you've got to edit it using specialized editing tools because you're still working with mini DVs rather than flash drives. Everything cost a lot of money and the people that had money were blokes in San Fernando Valley making very gross – or not even gross, just gross in the sense that it was just very standard – porn. So the biggest revolution has been the Pornhub one, where the development of broadband has made possible those kinds of video pornography aggregators. Now there's a second revolution underway, which is that of DIY pornography, with the emergence of OnlyFans and the like...

Do you think that's generated a new normal in terms of what the standard porn film looks like?

Absolutely. Since it's now easier to make pornography, and dirt cheap, all of a sudden it's become commercially viable to make porn around fantasies and kinks and sexualities that weren't served before – all that stuff now exists. Back in the day, there was only one kind of straight porn and it was hulky guys and women with fake tits, and it was very perfunctory and unpleasant and base, and now it's just whatever you want... Kids these days, they don't know how good they have it!

But it's not like there weren't horrible things to look at back in the day. There were a load of horrible things to look at, and you would probably look at them more than you would now a) because of the novelty and b) because it was a different ecosystem. Whereas now, in the privacy of your own home, you can say, Well, I'm queer identifying, and there's something available for me.

A lot of the tension that I have around this subject comes from an understanding of that diversity, and wanting to celebrate it, standing in conflict with the pressure that standard straight porn – where the man is dominant and the woman is treated quite violently – puts upon what it means to be a sexual person in the world.

I spend time looking at how I've been shaped by my past and the continuous presence of those influences, and feeling: Well, that's a load of shit! It'd be nice to be experiencing certain things in this environment rather than in the one I did. I don't know whether that's just one of those generational malaise things.

So you actually feel quite positive about kids who are growing up with porn these days?

Much more positive than I feel when I look back at what I grew up with. It's night and day.

Did looking at that stuff when you were fourteen shape your expectations/feelings about sex and women and so on?

I can't say no. I'm sure it did. But at the same time, I knew it to be theatrical bullshit, though I don't know whether 'theatrical' is the right word.

A performance?

Yeah, a performance, and also because you're online, in

76

an environment where it's taken with plenty of irony. You know it to be made by assholes, and that women are not like that. It's interesting because SA was the birthplace for a load of the worst things on the internet but as these things have split off from it, it's now become a massive leftist hub. That part of it also existed back in the day. Communities change and people grow up. All of which is to say that what you were seeing was taken with some nuance.

That said, there were forum projects that would happen every now and again, where things would be crowdfunded before crowdfunding existed. The most infamous one of those was when someone found some South American porn producers who would produce porn to spec, and said to the forum users, let's commission our own porno. And because of the context of the time, what they came up with was horrifically gross, involving scat play and so on. It got made and it exists, it's now one of those horrible artefacts of the internet. I don't know what I think about that. It happened, and it's hard to say how it was taken at the time, but I know nothing like that ever happened again.

It's interesting to hear about the forum serving as this meta space, almost. As though, if the porn is the show, then the forum is like a green room where you can give perspective on it.

Yes, but I don't want to make it sound as if SA was a porn forum, because it wasn't. Porn was completely at the fringes. It was an aggregator in a time when you didn't even have Google.

Where do you sit now on the ethics of it? I suppose I want to ask about two things which are linked, but probably not as linked as they should be – or rather more complicatedly so: your rational, ethical position on it; and then, also, to what extent you feel shame about it or have felt shame in the past.

Are we talking pornographic material in the abstract, or pornography as it exists...?

Both?

Famously, pornography has always existed, so it does feel as if there's something natural in people that it appeals to, and we are, if anything, a visual species. I don't have any problem with it per se, because getting horny and looking at horny things seem like two great tastes that taste great together, you know?

Then it becomes a question of who makes the porn and what power dynamics play out. Starting with a potted history – a personal one, but one that also takes in an aspect of the history of pornography on the internet – was to give some context for how I ended up with this hopeful, positive feeling about it. I'd say pornography now is 10,000 times better and more ethical in terms of power dynamics than it has been.

Because of its diversity?

Because of who makes it, yes. It's not just big porn conglomerates that are saying, Hurrah, I'm going to start making queer porn now because there's money in queer porn. It's queer people saying, I'm going to make porn with my partner, because we feel sexy, and we're going to film ourselves, and make some money from it, cottage-industry style. The thing that comes with it is people being forced into sex work and cam work for organized crime gangs and that sort of stuff. That certainly has been and is a thing, and that's really hard. And that's the sort of thing happening to all sorts of people everywhere anyway, so pornography isn't special in that regard. The fact that the potential for ethical pornography exists is a massive step. I am so glad that that can be a thing.

Is that something you personally endeavour to do: watch only ethical porn? Or is it that the democratization of porn means that the whole field is more ethical?

I'd say for sure the second, and then yes, ish, to the first. It's tricky – here comes the hypocrisy of it – because I don't want to spend that much time thinking about pornography in my head. I'm not signed up to any porn sites or OnlyFans, which I guess would be the thing to do if I wanted to be more ethical about it.

Why do you not want to spend time thinking about it?

I don't know. It's an amalgamation of things. There's definitely a residual...thing. The idea of putting my details into something attached to any kind of pornographic content makes me feel uncomfortable, however ethically respectable it might be. Maybe it's a continuation of how I've never kept a collection of porn.

Do you have a discomfort with thinking of yourself as a user of pornography in some way? Or is it that you want to maintain the casualness? Or do you only want to think about it when you want to use it and then forget about it very quickly?

It's a bit of the second and a bit of the third. That's what

I meant about the users, because another thing that's changed a lot, especially with Pornhub and OnlyFans, is the connection to performers. All of a sudden, they're social media people or even acquaintances of yours. A friend of a friend does OnlyFans, and sex toy reviews and things. I'd be interested to hear what other people, maybe younger, maybe my age, who knows, say in terms of following specific people. You know: 'I just love to see these two performers have sex, that's my thing.' Or maybe: 'I don't even get off on it so much anymore, I watch it for X, Y, Z...' Who knows? It's starting to be used in different ways. I suspect people of different genders and sexualities might have a very different relationship with performers.

Does that make you feel uncomfortable, the coming together of those two realms?

No, I don't think it does. If it does, then it's a feeling I don't feel I should have, in a way. If you're talking about ethics and power dynamics, that feels a much more rounded, equal, reciprocal thing that's starting to happen. Good for those people. I'm just too old and broken from previous things.

I'm fascinated by masturbation, the privacy of it, and to what extent that necessarily needs to remain a private world, and to what extent it needs to out of some latent sense of shame. This ties into assumptions about when you're in a long-term relationship: to what extent is masturbating and watching porn taken as read, and okay, and unthreatening, and so on. Where do you sit with that stuff?

In the broad: live and let live. I know my partner doesn't

80

watch porn. She's an interesting one, she's very private sexually. Even having sex is a little bit private for her. She's a one and done, kind of. She enjoys it, but then it's over. Before doing this chat, we talked about it, but before that, we never had. She didn't ever seem curious enough to ask me about it. And from my side I was pretty certain she didn't watch porn. I could have been wrong, but it turns out I was right in that assumption. I don't think she masturbates much, even. She doesn't have a big sex drive. Eventually she feels, I really want sex now, as everyone would, but that would be it for a few weeks. Ultimately I have more of a sex drive than she does, I guess. Sometimes it's kind of unsatisfying just to be masturbating, but it's also part of my life, you know? And sometimes I don't for days and days and days, and then sometimes over two days I masturbate twice. It comes and goes, but it's always present in my life.

Have you ever felt weird about the fact that you don't discuss that with her, or does it feel private?

I think it's private. If I felt there'd be something for us to gain in our sexual life from sharing it then I would, but I don't think it would add much. Also, I'm not feeling great shame from the things I'm watching. It would be different if there were some aspect of my sexuality or my kinks that wasn't being met by my partner. I'm quite vanilla in that sense.

In relationships I've had in the past, it bothered me that I shared every aspect of my life with a person and talked about so much, and then at some point I find out they've been watching porn. This is back when I never did. It doesn't seem to me like just an accident – it's clearly deliberate. I'm intrigued to

*hear whether other people feel that that's odd, too. Not odd for
those exes, but just odd for us as a society. For you it sounds as
if that feels a relatively natural omission.*

Yeah. I would assume that someone I was in a relationship with would assume that the guy would on occasion
be watching pornography and masturbating.

*In principle, if I'm with a man, I have no issue with them
watching porn. But maybe one of the reasons I don't bring
it up is that I'm concerned that the type of porn will be
gang-banging a slut who was gagging for it, etc. I go through
this thought process in my head of, Hey, wait, I thought you
were a feminist, how can you be getting off on this? And that
whole can of worms sometimes feels too wormy to open up, if
you know what I mean.*

Yes, for sure. Not to say that I've never watched gang-
bang porn, because I have.

And do you feel guilt about that now?

Yes. But I feel guilty about a load of stuff in a way. I think
there's also an aspect to it where, because I'm not the affected gender, I can mute it, in the same sense that I feel
guilty about all the stuff I do by not dealing with climate
change. I feel guilty buying some horrible person's music
when they're assholes. It falls into that kind of category,
where if I was a woman, and I was watching it and getting off on it, then I'd feel guilty in a very different way.

*Let's say you were in a relationship with someone who had
a similar sex drive to you, would you be perfectly happy not
watching porn and masturbating? Do you feel as though*

82

that's a separate part of your sexuality that you'd want to preserve, or that would be there regardless?

It's hard to say. I haven't had that much sex regularly, so I just couldn't say. I guess if I wanted to feel virtuous I'd say no, that I'd be perfectly satisfied with my incredible powerfully sex-driven partner. In reality, I'm not sure. It's a different box thing.

At the moment, we read a lot about porn addiction, and porn-induced impotence and so on. What's your take on all that?

That feels like another aspect of the internet nature of it. You're going to find addicts wherever something gives a dopamine hit online – there's pornography, but there's also gambling and social media and cryptocurrency trading. It's part of the problem of the technology.

Even with things like Instagram, when I find that I'm checking it too much, I feel really angry with myself, as if I'm becoming this passive entity. With porn, on the times that I have watched it, that feeling is tripled, as though I'm really lacking in agency somehow. It's strange. Although I watch it so infrequently that I should have far more agency than, say, with Instagram or emails.

What's your use case? You're on your lonesome and you get horny and want some visual stimuli?

Yeah, and then afterwards feel, Why was I doing that?

How have you found the Pornhubification of content? Can you find something for you there?

Kind of. I can't find the dream stuff at all, but I can mostly find something that just about does the trick. I go on and search for something quite specific and then come away again, all the while trying desperately to not encounter the kinds of porn that make me feel quite weird. Just the fact of being on that forum and an awareness of the other ways in which it's being used makes me feel... queasy is a good word for what I feel. Then I am troubled that it feels like such a good word because I don't want to be a prude and I want to be sex positive. It's this real big soup of issues. To come back to your question, it doesn't feel made for me. And yet I know that there are many women who watch porn and like it a lot, so maybe the 'me' there is not just about being a woman, but something else.

It's still heavily male used and, because it's serving algorithmically, like YouTube would, the home page of Pornhub is going to be full of not the most feminist things. You might do well to get a login for Pornhub and having the algorithm learn what to serve you, and bubbling yourself into your stuff.

You don't do that?

I don't. Again, maybe a social shame thing. I don't have an account for Pornhub.

Is that partly because you are served by the main page stuff?

I don't think I'm served by the main page stuff. I'm not really looking for the stepsister wants stepbrother's dick stuff, which seems to be a blight upon the whole thing, but it's quite easy to find what I do want.

Do you ever think about ethnicity in porn?

I do. I think about the exoticization and ethnicization
that goes on. But I don't really watch porn with non-
white male performers, or very rarely.

*I've spoken to quite a few men who suddenly become experts
about Japanese culture when the subject matter is porn and
I find that upsetting. I remember, once, a friend and I were
talking about someone called Haruka, and he said, Oh no,
you can't call your kid that, that's a porn star name. I was
thinking, Well, it's also a very regular name. That friend was
white, of course, and that made me feel uncomfortable.*

*But let's say you reach the stage where you've identified
that you find yourself to be turned on by some very broad
ethnic group – Asian or Caucasian people – more than
others, what do you do about that? If you were searching for
porn, would you ever put the word white in? Or does that just
come up naturally?*

Yes, it assumes the user is a white male. Same as how,
when I was a kid on forums, everyone was assumed to be
a white male kid. Even when, you know, they turned out
to be girls or people of colour or whatever. That's still
the case on the internet: anonymity comes with assumed
whiteness.

FOUR

*Four is a queer woman in her mid-thirties. She is
married to a woman and lives in the United States.*

POLLY BARTON — *Is porn something that you talk
about with your friends or people around you?*

FOUR — Not really. Probably a little bit more when I
was single. When you're single, part of the bonding ritual of friendship is talking about being single with other
single people, and so the question of libido and how you
deal with that comes up in a way that it rarely does now.
I've had some more abstract, philosophical discussions
with people about porn and how it influences how
we view sexuality, but not in a way that's informed by
personal experience.

And when I've had conversations that *have* been
informed by personal experience, usually it's been
prompted by the other person. I'm someone that people
often confide in. When people want to have the 'I'm into
this thing, I feel like it's weird' conversation, I'm usually
the go-to person who will say, Well no, it's not weird,
go do your thing. So, pretty limited, in terms of porn
factoring into conversations.

*That's my experience too: that the conversations dealing with
the philosophical aspects of it are separate from the sort of
conversations that are informed by personal experience, and
that it's very hard to have a conversation where you're doing
both of those things. When I've talked with people about it
from a theoretical perspective, everyone involved is more or
less pretending that they've never even seen it or that it plays*

any role in their life at all. It seems odd that we have to do that. And yet I'm as guilty as the rest.

Yeah, and talking about sex itself is not dissimilar. Often it turns into this supposedly theoretical exercise, where people aren't very forthcoming about their own personal experiences.

With porn, and with sex to a certain extent, talking about it has been regarded as shameful for so long that it has almost become discredited as a form of discourse. You can't wear your philosophical hat and your porn consumer's hat at the same time, because the respectability levels are so different.

There's such vulnerability, too, because it's hard to predict where people are on the spectrum, from condemning to avid consumer and everything in between. So people are afraid that if they reveal something, people are going to draw conclusions about who they are as a person, judge them, and so on.

Sometimes I get the sense everyone operates on the assumption that everyone feels the same as them about porn. Or, at least, assumes that attitude as a kind of shield. I've mentioned porn in the past to women who are quite straight, in both senses of the word, and they immediately jump to talking about porn as though it's something that only men consume, that their role in it is totally passive – as people who are affected by men's porn consumption. I always want at that point to probe them a little bit, because I'm genuinely curious, as to whether that's coming from a real place. Whether that's genuinely how they see it, or whether that's the default assumption that you have to play along with to avoid ostracization.

It's probably a little bit of both. It's the same with fessing up to being into anything resembling kink – that's also something that people only ever bring up jokingly in the abstract. I personally like to shoot that down, because you see people's faces falling. Like: I'm sorry, what?! Then in the queer community, it's almost the opposite. There's this assumption that you're going to be into porn, and there's an assumption that there's a specific type of porn that you're going to be into, which is that body-positive, naturalistic, Crash Pad-style, basically amateur or glorified amateur stuff, which I find super alienating. That's just as alienating to me as people assuming that porn is for dudes and irrelevant to women – I can't relate to either of those assumptions.

Are you familiar with Crash Pad? It's super popular with queer women. It's amateur – I don't think it's ever professionals – and it's people in their bedroom, but it's pretty high definition. I guess everyone has good amateur recording equipment these days. It has this inclusive, body-positive ethic, so you will see bodies of all shapes and sizes, and it's racially diverse, but at the same time, I don't connect with it because I feel it ends up being normative in its own way. It's all women with lots of tattoos and blue hair. It purports to be inclusive, but it feels very narrow in what it offers. It's interesting that that's the sort of porn that's lauded and celebrated in the queer community. Autostraddle, the lesbian website, will do this weekly mailout called NSFW Lesbosexy Sunday. It's a round-up of links that are vaguely porn, erotica, and they always intersperse those with stills from Crash Pad movies, so most of my exposure has come through that. Every time I see those pictures, I think about how it's not the glamorous fantasy that I want, that I'm always hoping for in porn and just don't ever find. I much prefer the erotic thriller genre, which is always trying to be a glamorous fantasy. Those women are always super high femme, over the top, super in charge, no one's ever awkward or insecure or fumbling. I like that, you know? I don't necessarily want realism in my porn. I want some archetypal thing.

This is more of a general observation that extends wider than just porn, but I feel that in the queer community – or maybe I should say among millennials and gen Z, because it's just as much of a generational thing – the backlash against sex being taboo, and against unhealthy beauty standards and all that, has been to make it this friendly, approachable thing, and I don't really like that either. The thing that I have an absolute loathing of is sex workshops. People go to fisting workshops! I honestly think that's unhinged. Sex is not a group activity! It's not recreational, you can't learn fisting the way you learn to play volleyball, you know what I mean? I just think it's crazy. But yes, I feel like there's this push for that to be the new normal. You know: let's not make anything taboo anymore, let's not make anything private anymore. It's now this social thing, and that doesn't sit right with me either because sex is still something intimate.

I feel the same. And then I try to unpick where that aversion comes from. The thing that immediately springs to mind is: but it's not sexy! I suppose the thinking is that you learn to do the fisting or whatever in the workshop context and then use it in a context that you do find sexy?

Every time you have a strong aversion to something it's worth examining where it comes from. I'm very suspicious of group dynamics, because in my life they've often been harmful. I find it hard to see how you could create a healthy group environment in which to teach or be taught anything sexual. It's so easy for that to become predatory in some way, whether it's about inflicting sexual harm upon others or just about some sort of power trip, empowering someone while disempowering someone else. A big part of where my suspicion comes from is that I tend to look at the people organizing these things as sort of snake-oil salesmen, basically.

That makes me think about these blues dancing classes I started going to when I first came to Bristol. The prevailing ethic there was this pressure to be cool about having quite intimate physical contact with people without any kind of emotional or even social intimacy. So if, like me, you aren't immediately comfortable with touching another person, or touching everyone in that way, then you end up feeling ostracized. I found it interesting to feel that even within this environment that was presenting as being so accepting and cool with everything.

Yeah, that's the 'survival of the fittest' element of group dynamics that I really hate. Someone always ends up feeling shamed for not being able to conform to whatever the median standard of behaviour is, and it's easy to see how, in a context where it's about physical intimacy, that could become harmful.

That's also what happens in sex or porn conversations, in terms of people's assumptions that you are X, Y, or Z. To come out and say, No, I'm not, sometimes means going through the shock of that ostracization.

For sure. And you often wonder, what's to be gotten out of that? When other people's normative expectations already set you up to believe that you're not going to be necessarily seen or understood when you disclose something really personal, you think, Well then why bother?

Yes. You're making yourself vulnerable when the other person is staying behind that kind of comforting safe wall of 'the norm', regardless of whether that's reflective of their practices. Is porn something you've spoken about in relationships in the past, and with your current partner?

Yeah. Not to incredibly great lengths, but along the lines of, What have your porn consumption habits been in the past? What role has it played in your life, or does it play in your life? That whole thing. Most people I've been with have been much bigger porn consumers than me. I tend to be the outlier in that regard. I've never had detailed discussions to the level of, What's the specific thing in porn that gets you off, or whatever. That's come up organically sometimes. The discussions I've had have not been these probing, exploratory discussions, but more feeling out how big a thing it's been for someone.

When you've come up against that repeated fact that it's more a thing for the person you're in a relationship with than it is for you, has that ever felt problematic?

Yes and no. On a certain level, it's hard for me not to judge people for getting off on things that I don't find hot, and that I even find, in some cases, crass or offputting. There's this knee-jerk judgment of: Oh, if that gets you off, you must be a really uncivilized character, you know? That's ultimately just as informed by societal attitudes and handed down ideas as anything. On the other hand, part of me kind of likes it because I've tended to be drawn to people who are more sexually experienced than me. You have to get there somehow, and exposing yourself to a wide range of sexual flavours is part of that, so it's logical that porn would be part of that. So it's a mixed thing. I find a lot of porn so alienating that the idea that someone I'm with finds it hot is a little bit mystifying to me, because you expect sexuality to be at least to some extent shared with the person you're with – to some extent, you have to be on the same page. But then there's something about that difference that I also find alluring.

That feels true about how I think, too: in order to enjoy having sex with someone, you must have some shared sensibility or feel like you're on the same page somehow sexually. So then to find out they have tastes in porn you find really out there – how do I reconcile these two things? You mentioned finding their tastes off-putting...

Well, it's not even about the specifics of taste, this one thing they're into. It's really just the fact of porn, because I've tried with mainstream porn, but it's never really done it for me. Or I should say I've never found anything that could do it for me. When people tell me that it's something they go to or have gone to all the time, I automatically assume that it must be the same stuff that I've seen and been totally perplexed by. The gender and sexual orientation of the person makes a real difference in how I perceive their porn consumption too. I remember that part in *Fifty Sounds* where you talk about having that sinking feeling when you are confronted with a lover's porn habits, and I really recognized that. I recognized it from dynamics I've been in with straight-identifying men, because the moment I'm confronted with their porn consumption, I'm like: Oh, that's the thing you're going to expect me to conform to, and I immediately feel I'm being pigeonholed. It's only a matter of time before I'll be requested to behave in a certain way that doesn't come naturally to me. I'm expecting personal implications and they're not going to be good.

Yes. I feel that, and then I also feel like it's the more essentialist thing of: Well, I'm never going to beat that. It's so clear that what is going on there is not me, and so what is going on, then, with us? Because if this is what you want then you shouldn't be with me.

Also a feeling of, are you settling for me just because I'm around? Because I'm obviously never going to be able to deliver on any of that.

Can you talk a little bit more about feeling alienated by 'mainstream' or regular porn?

I don't necessarily need a whole storyline, but I need a scenario that feels lived-in and plausible, and that's where it usually falls flat for me. Because the acting ability is minimal, and I often feel like people aren't present in any real way, you know? That causes me to reflect on their working conditions and wonder whether they even want to be there. And then it just becomes depressing, like I'm objectifying them in a way that doesn't feel good. Again, the closest thing I have to porn is usually erotic thrillers. They're one of my favourite movie genres anyway, because they're ludicrous, but also, the sex scenes in those movies are the only thing that I experience as visual material that will turn me on because there's a run-up to it, and there's some sort of characterization. The person feels like a person by the time the sex happens. I'm inclined to say that the fact that it's suggestive sex more than, say, explicit close-ups of genitalia is part of it, but I'm not sure if it is. I don't know if I'm necessarily opposed to seeing sex acts in close-up. It's more that I've never seen that presented to me in a way that I liked.

It's the kind of directorial spec, more than what is being shown and what isn't. When you first said 'erotic thriller' I thought you meant of the book variety. Which reminds me that the first thing I used as porn – although I don't know if it counts as porn or not – was books.

I spent many years of my life jerking off to fan fiction.

It's such a cliché, isn't it, that women go for books and men hardcore vids. But I often feel that it's more about what isn't there. The absence of the real turn-offs.

Although I've gotten pickier over time with fan fiction too. When I was younger, pretty much anything would do it for me, partly just because of the novelty of it. But also due to basic things, like the fact that my sensibilities as a writer were not yet honed to the extent that certain words would immediately make me cringe. Now there's a whole list of words for genitalia that are an instant turn-off, you know?

Out of interest, I've looked up some fanfics that I remember very fondly and have been just horrified. One paragraph in and already I'm thinking this would never do it for me now, which is a shame because it reduces the pool of potentials. I mean, I pick up pulp lesbian fiction whenever I see it at flea markets, because I find it interesting. For a long time it was this underground outlet for queer writing. And some legit writers such as Patricia Highsmith wrote pulp fiction, although in her case more thriller-type pulp, rather than porny stuff. That's interesting to me anthropologically, in terms of queer history, and if there's a teacher-student scenario, I will always pick it up. But does it ever actually turn me on? Not really. The teacher-student thing is a trope that does work for me, even if the writing's really shitty – to the point where I'll feel mildly aroused reading it, but does that then inspire me to masturbate? No. It's more like, Okay, that was interesting, moving on. That said, if I wasn't in a relationship, I'd probably be searching harder 'cause I'd be looking for ways to meet my own sexual needs more.

Something that intrigues me is how people conceive of masturbation within relationships. One of the default assumptions that some people operate with is that, if you're in a relationship, ideally you wouldn't jerk off at all. I don't think that's how I have been, but then I've also never been in a relationship that felt like it was serious or long or fulfilling enough for that to be something I gave serious thought to. For some people it's a domain where they want something private for themselves, and it operates quite separately to what's being had with their partner. Where do you feel you stand on that?

Somewhere in between. I recognize the feeling that ideally you shouldn't need it, and I feel that idea sort of lives within me too, but it's not the reality. Part of it is that there isn't always a match in libido in a relationship. That ebbs and flows for both people and you're not necessarily on the same track. For much of the past year and a bit,

I've probably had more of a sex drive, so I've taken care of myself more. There's also the fact that it's honestly one of my oldest ways of engaging with myself, physically and just generally, and it's a mood regulator. And, you know, it's really quick. Whereas sex – especially lesbian sex in my experience – is never quick. It's usually quite a drawn-out thing. Sometimes I don't necessarily have the emotional energy to engage with someone else, but I just want to get it out of the way, or even just relieve tension. I notice sometimes when I'm really stressed about something – I've noticed this especially in the past year of the pandemic – that I'll get turned on, and it's a kind of body-regulating thing, where I can do that and it *is* a sort of stress release. In that case, I wouldn't necessarily try to channel that into sex because I know that my mindset is angry and solipsistic and frustrated, and that's better dealt with the quick way.

I was reading recently about different ways that stress affects libido. For some people, it does exactly what you just described – feeling anxious and tense makes them feel horny, and having an orgasm is one way of relieving the stress. For other people, the exact opposite happens and stress takes away the libido.

You mentioned watching porn and sometimes wondering whether the performers are enjoying it and therefore whether they want to be there. Most people around me are sex positive and keen to support sex workers, and that feels really important. At the same time, I occasionally worry that the overwhelming desire to present as being supportive of sex workers means that we can't talk as freely as we might otherwise about exploitation. Is that something that you contend with?

Yeah. I'm reflecting again on questioning whether the porn actors want to be there and realizing that what I've seen of the behind the scenes of porn completely dispels those anxieties. Something that comes to mind is that I went to this live storytelling event here. It was some sisterhood event for women, and one of the people doing the storytelling was a porn actress who was apparently quite well known, and she told this story about giving birth. I don't really remember many of the details, but it was about a shift in her relationship with her body, and one of the things that was super interesting was that she talked about pain thresholds. I remember her saying, In my line of work, we're all sort of extremists. We like challenging ourselves, and all this really intense stuff like double penetration. The point that she was trying to make was that in a healthcare setting when you're giving birth, tolerating pain in a very extreme way is not necessarily the approach the situation calls for. It made me think that maybe doing porn is just doing a physical thing, and some people have an interpersonal ease that allows them to do that. For me, it's inconceivable. For me, sex is an emotional experience. But then I don't know to what extent that's about who I am innately and to what extent that's just about the direction that life has nudged me into, and it could just as well have been differently if I'd had different encounters and different opportunities.

I watched this movie a while ago – fictional, not a documentary or anything – called *Starlet*, which is the name of a dog in the movie. It's about a young woman out in the Valley who's a porn actress, and she befriends an older woman in the neighbourhood and is trying to help her. It's a really good movie. It shows her going into work, and she lives with co-workers and they're kind of a mess – there's substance abuse going on and stuff – and it shows her doing these porn shoots and then they take a break and just smoke a cigarette round the back, you know, and there's this instant shift from having sex with someone to just being buddies and shooting the shit. That gave me a different perspective. I can't imagine having that attitude, just as I can't imagine doing sex work, but I can imagine how someone else with a different psychology would be able to do that and find it quite enjoyable.

I was listening to a podcast today hosted by three Jungian analysts who were interviewing a sex worker about her experiences. She was talking about how there're days when it's great and days when she's just not really into it, and saying that the fact that it's her job and transactional in nature doesn't make her feel like doing it on those days, but it does mean that it doesn't feel scarring in the same way as it would if she was not into it, but being forced to do it by someone she was in a relationship with.

The idea that different life experiences could mean you'd have a relationship with sex that's less emotional is fascinating. Owing to the way I've been brought up, I have a preconception, a kind of snobbery in a way, that that kind of emotional relationship to sex, one that's based around intimacy, is the best way to feel about sex.

Yeah. I have a little bit of that too, though in my case that's partly feeling defensive about my relative inexperience compared to many of my peers.

Do you feel your peers are much more experienced?

Yeah, probably. Not necessarily in terms of variety or

how out there it gets, but in terms of number of sexual partners, absolutely.

When I was growing up and a teenager and then in my twenties as well, I worried a lot about my sexual inexperience, and whether I could 'do sex' properly. Into my thirties, I feel as if that's totally gone, and I operate with this default assumption that we're all on the same sex-page. And then, if I have a new partner or whatever, that worry suddenly pops up again. Which is just to say, the imbalance between people's experiences is definitely there. That's an interesting thing about porn as well, that it serves an educative function as well as being just a tool to get off to, and perhaps gives people the sense that they've seen it all, whereas actually porn is very different from real sex. And watching something over and over again is not the same as doing it. There's also that thing of people who see things cropping up in their sex life and feel fairly sure it's come from porn, and the sense of discomfort that comes with that.

Yeah, I recognize that too, from experiences with men.

How did that make you feel?

Sad? It's that sinking feeling, where you think you're being seen, or at least you think you're trying to figure something out together, and then it turns out there's an agenda on the other person's part. It's hard not to then judge them as misled or brainwashed, even though that's not really fair, because we don't necessarily choose what shapes us sexually. You're exposed to things and you take away some things and discard others, and I don't think that's a conscious process.

You used the word 'agenda', which could manifest in two ways – as a specific, conscious, sense of 'I want to do this thing that I've seen,' but then also in the sense of a wider conception of 'This is what sex is, these are the boundaries.'

What I balked at in those situations was that it felt restrictive. It didn't feel as if it opened something up. If I'm being honest, I usually have some sort of agenda in sex, too. I have a pretty clear sense of where I want it to go, which is pretty individual to me. But that sense of recognizing the influence of porn is more about it leading to being asked to behave in a certain way that doesn't feel authentic.

I sense there are people for whom porn has widened their sense of what sex is, suggested new possibilities and new things to try, new ways of being, new types of bodies to find sexually attractive, and so on. I think I've always felt the opposite. I don't watch much porn at all, but when I have watched and do watch it, it feels like it's a shutting in rather than an opening up, which is probably more about the perspective, the feel of it, than the acts themselves.

It's interesting how the different types of porn interact with one another, because there is now a huge diversity of stuff out there, and people talk about the democratization of porn, but I do get the feeling, and maybe this is unfair, that people are quite narrow in what they watch. Pornhub people will have their favourite categories on Pornhub, and people who are into kink will watch that on a specific site. Yes, there is interesting and thought-provoking and boundary-expanding stuff out there, if you look for it. But my fear is that most people don't, they just get horny and go on Pornhub and look at the first thing that seems like it'll do the trick.

The nature of the internet means that you can't really rule out seeing visuals, even just the stills, of things you don't like at all. Things like gas masks – you know that whole kink thing where there's the electric chair and that whole sort of medical, institutional, fetishization – that is super off-putting to me. I've had times where I've been looking for other kink stuff, and the moment I see that in a thumbnail, I'm done, and there's no way to stop that from happening. Just as I haven't found a way to look for mainstream lesbian porn without immediately getting five pop-ups with fifteen penises in them. Part of what's super off-putting is that there's no way to go straight to what you want. Or at least maybe if you do extensive research and really hone your algorithm, but I wasn't really willing to put in the hours to that extent.

How do you feel about mainstream lesbian porn?

I find it super unconvincing. The last time I tried to watch lesbian porn was when my partner and I were long-distancing and I was back in Britain and very sexually frustrated. I watched some tickling porn, partly because it's playful. Have you seen that fascinating documentary called *Tickled*, about this nefarious tickling-porn mogul? Anyway, I'm interested in being tickled as an organic reaction that you can't fake, so I thought, Okay, that's maybe plausible. But the women were these nasal Barbie dolls and the way they behaved towards one another was so fake, and I immediately didn't believe that they were into women, which I know is kind of a sexist thing to say. It's not as if a woman who looks like a Barbie doll can't be queer, but it immediately felt like it was appealing to a straight gaze. And all the activities that led up to the sex... The run-up to the sex

101

is always too brief for me, but also just not plausible. Raking each other with long fake fingernails is not something that I've ever known women to do. And then, again, because the run-up was so absurd, when the actual tickling-plus-sex part began, that just made me sad. You've expressed so little enthusiasm towards each other and now I'm supposed to believe you're super into each other? I don't buy it, you know? So then it doesn't go anywhere.

You were saying that when you're looking for lesbian porn you bump into thumbnails with penises – I feel as if even within the videos themselves, you feel the invisible penises surrounding it. This wall of invisible penises. It makes me think of the sex scenes in Blue is the Warmest Colour.

You know, I liked the sex scenes in that movie. I've often seen the discourse surrounding that movie as symptomatic of the policing that goes on in the queer community. I'll often hear that movie being referred to as an example of something nobody could ever find plausible or hot. Or, what's even more frustrating, and I've heard numerous people say this: 'Everyone knows lesbians don't scissor.' Excuse me? What? That's somehow become the default reaction to that movie. I don't recall finding the sex scenes particularly hot but that's partly because I watched it with someone else. When I'm watching a movie with a sex scene in it in someone else's presence – even when, as in this case, that someone is my wife or my then-girlfriend – I'm so aware of their presence and their awareness of me that I couldn't possibly get turned on. I didn't find those scenes particularly hot, but I was very taken with the movie as a whole and the dynamic between them, so I completely bought it.

I was also taken with the movie and the dynamic – before I read about all of the stuff with the director – and I was quite excited about what the sex would be like between them, but then when it cut to it, it felt too male-gazey, too porny. Overly flawless, to the point it just wasn't plausible. I can also see how that scene might be used to police.

Yeah. There's this consensus about that movie. Of course, what people know about the abusive working conditions hasn't helped, because now people feel they have a moral obligation to condemn it. I found it to be probably a little bit better than most of the lesbian movies out there.

I'm trying to think of lesbian films I found more credible. Carol?

Carol is great – because of the age difference, that movie is extremely my jam. But it's also much more artsy, right? It's not very sexually explicit.

FIVE

Five is a straight man in his early twenties.
He is recently single.

POLLY BARTON — *Can you describe your current*
porn-watching habits?

FIVE — It's not something that's set in stone. I probably watch it more in the morning than I do at night. I find
if I do it in the morning then I can just get on with my
day. If I gave an estimate of how often, it varies on how
I'm feeling, but say two to three times a week.

Would you ever masturbate without using porn?

I have done, but if porn's available, then I'd probably use
that. It's more stimulating than my imagination. I'm fine
with pictures, but if we're talking videos, then these days
I just use Pornhub. I tried a few different sites when I
was younger, but Pornhub was the first one that I used,
so maybe that's why I've stuck with it. As far as ease
of use is concerned, it's pretty good. When it comes to
safety, viruses on the site and so on, it's actually one of
the better ones too.

What would you be watching on there? Do you go for the top
page stuff?

I'll look through the top page first, and if there's anything
there that catches my eye, I'll click on it. If I was going
in looking and searching, I don't search for anything too
crazy, to be honest: maybe anal or orgies or something

like that. Something maybe that I wouldn't do in my own life. I don't go out of my way too much. If there're things on the first page that aren't too bad, I'll watch them.

What would catch your eye on the top page?

Sometimes it is to do with finding the performer really attractive. That certainly would merit a click. Otherwise if it was something that's the full experience: something that's of a reasonable length, and does everything – foreplay all the way up to normal sex, and then whatever else. If there's something like that, it will catch my eye.

Do you have an ideal length?

The thing is to make sure it's not too short. Depending on what it was, I could maybe swing for just over five minutes, but under five minutes is definitely too short. Saying that I don't sit and watch the whole video. If something's happening and it's good, but it seems as if it's going to be the same thing for the next four or five minutes, I'll just skip forward. Which is probably why I'll go through a few videos. If it's a half an hour, you maybe only watch a third of it.

You said you tend to watch things that are things that you wouldn't do in real life. Can you talk me through that?

Yeah, not as much with anal, because obviously I've done that quite a bit, but it's not something that you do all the time. With orgies and threesomes and all that kind of vibe, it's not that it's taboo, but it's something that you don't normally experience. So it's living vicariously through that lens.

105

The full fantasy experience?

I don't know if it's my fantasy. I'd probably be down for a threesome, but with the orgies, I don't think I'd actually want to do that in real life. It's more that the chaos on screen of everything happening is quite stimulating. I wouldn't choose to watch a porn of myself, basically, because I've got lived experience of that. Not that it wouldn't necessarily be stimulating, but I think if you're going to go to that effort, you watch something that you're not going to do yourself.

Is there anything that you find a real turn-off or no-go in porn?

There are a lot of things that I wouldn't click on but I'm not absolutely outright disgusted by. The one thing that springs to mind, though, is the stuff where people dress up as babies. I see that sometimes when I'm scrolling and it just knocks me sick. I'd ban that if I could. Similarly, something I can't stand – not just in the bedroom but also in my personal life – is the 'daddy' thing. That turns me off something rotten.

Where do you stand on violence, and rough sex and that whole aspect of porn?

Some people are into being a bit more rough, and I am as well, both watching and in my own life, but at the same time, there's got to be limits to that. I'm not into people getting slapped in the face, or pinned down by the neck, or kicked. I get that maybe some people are, but to me that doesn't seem enjoyable. A bit of choking and a bit of slapping is fine as long as both parties are in agreement.

106

Whenever that is happening in real life, you talk about it first and have safe words so you know that that's what you want. In regard to porn, even the taglines for porn are worded in a way that fantasizes violence: 'small white girl getting brutally destroyed' and stuff. I do think that porn has created a fantasized ideal in people's heads about sex, and the physicality can bleed into people's lives. If you've seen James Bond jump on a fucking train in a film, you wouldn't then think, I can go and do that. But with porn, even though it's all scripted and specially cultivated in such a way that that's what the end result is, people take it too literally, and I don't agree with that.

Is it clear to you where the line lies between the fantasy violence that exists only within porn, and real sex? You could be confident you wouldn't take that into your sex life?

I think so, but I don't know if that's the general consensus. I can definitely see the clear line. I know I'm watching a film and it's not real. A lot of people don't know that, but I think that comes down to social interactions. If you don't have a lot of or any experience to base against it, then what else can you draw from? So it becomes foundational knowledge, almost.

How old were you when you first saw porn, and how did it happen?

My first experience of watching porn was when I was in first year, so I would've been about twelve. It was my dad who showed it to me. He was on this group chat and one of his pals had sent these two videos. One was just normal sex and the other was called Super Squirter – you can guess what happened in that. They were both

107

short: one was maybe two minutes and the other thirty or forty seconds. He showed me them on his phone, and I was like, This is great shit, so I asked him to send them to me. Then I took them into school, showed all my pals. From there I just started searching myself – the thing with my dad is the part I vividly remember. As much as I probably wouldn't send porn to my kids, I also think that when you do that, it opens up a dialogue. We were able to speak about things like that from that point. I'm quite open with my mum as well, so I don't have any issues talking to her about relationships or sex or anything like that. My dad doing that made a difference. It makes a difference when you're able to talk about the same things and you laugh and enjoy it. As weird as it seems now, I think that did help to make it okay to talk about sex.

At that age, were you already feeling sexual arousal?

Yeah. Growing up, a lot of kids find the opposite sex icky until they get into high school, but I wasn't like that at all. I was always into girls and I always enjoyed chatting with them. I first got with a girl when I was in the last year of primary school. I couldn't pinpoint exactly when I first masturbated, but I'd say it was around the time of those videos. I don't think it started because of them, but that happened during the six-month period where that all started kicking off. It was the start of high school when you start hurting your wrist.

You said you showed it to your friends. Was the dialogue around that all quite open?

Dialogue, yes, but when you're that age, people just talk rubbish. People are always trying to act bigger than they are, when the truth is that the majority of people haven't even held hands with somebody. Among my close friends, especially my best mate, there's nothing that we wouldn't say. We're very open about things that have happened, including things of a sexual nature. It was always fine for boys to discuss masturbating and porn and sex, but for girls, it was so stigmatized, which never made any sense to me. I expressed my opinion about that to many of my female friends at the time. Some really appreciated that, and we chatted at great length about it, because they were doing the same thing. I never came over either weird or creepy, or trying to ridicule them for it. I was just like, Why can't you just talk about it? That doesn't make sense to me. Some just outright denied it. But again, even with sex and stuff, the whole culture of society makes it fine for boys to talk about it, to be like, High five! Whereas for girls it's shunned. That's caused a lot of issues with people not being able to communicate properly in regard to what they want sexually.

I have the same experience of talking to girls about it at that age, and them denying it outright. And you know, maybe they just really aren't? That's what I thought at the time.

There are a few who definitely didn't. There were some who were so overtly against it. At that age, when you're just getting used to your body, I do understand that. But let's say I asked ten people and two had said, Yes, of the eight that said, No, I think at least half of them were lying.

It sounds as if it's never been something you've felt embarrassed about.

Certainly not to converse about it with people you're close to. I always think that's a healthy way of dealing with any issue. In regard to actual sex, speaking makes things better. Being embarrassed just breeds more embarrassment for everyone else. If I feel embarrassed and I'm embarrassed to talk about it or I'm embarrassed when someone brings things up, then that says to other people, Well, I should feel embarrassed then. Whereas if you're open and honest and understanding of the fact that everyone's different and everyone's experiences are different, then I think we could all be a little happier.

For me, the key is accepting you're going to feel a little bit embarrassed at first, but pushing through and talking about it anyway.

There's definitely all kinds of things that happen where you think, Oh fuck, I can't believe that happened, and you feel that bit of embarrassment. I've had many of those experiences, and it may be slightly embarrassing in the moment, or discussing it later on, but it's not the overwhelming feeling and I don't think ever should be.

Are porn and masturbation things you've talked about with partners?

Porn has come up in quite a lot of my relationships, because you get into the question of what you're both into. I wouldn't say masturbation comes up too much nowadays. From maybe seventeen onwards I haven't really cared, I don't need to know when you're doing it, you don't need to tell me. I've watched porn with two partners as well. It was alright. It was its own experience, but it's not something I would be dying to do again. It's not something I'd push for, but it's nice for you both to get turned on at the same time by an external force that isn't going to breed jealousy in any way. Sometimes you see some weird things that make you think, Let's try that, that looks fun. Otherwise, I think it's fine if it's just giving you ideas and a bit of foreplay, but I'm of the impression that sex should just be quite intimate. So I'd happily put some music on, but I wouldn't be rushing to put porn on.

It's interesting that you said that porn is something that doesn't breed jealousy, because I think a lot of people don't see it that way. Among people of an older generation especially, there can be an idea that it's infidelity in some sense.

I understand what you mean. I said what I said in the context of being with a partner, and there's an external, digital force turning you both on. It's not as if there's somebody in the next room getting changed and you go, God, have you seen them? Porn could be emotional cheating, though. If it's just something you're doing in your personal time to get off, I think that's fine, but if it became an issue of preferring to do that than spending time together, then there's an issue. It's probably naive to think that people don't get attracted to other people, though. That's maybe stating the obvious.

Regardless of the kind of relationship you are in and how good the sex was, would you continue to use porn on the side?

It's totally separate. It's a means to an end, almost. Masturbating lets off steam. It's not as if I'm choosing to not speak to you in order to go and do this. It's when nobody's around. But moderation's a big thing. If I were doing it every day and it became not so much a habit as an addiction, then that's dangerous.

Has the moderation come naturally, or is it something that you've achieved?

When I was younger, when I first started getting into it and falling down the rabbit hole, I was masturbating a few times a day for the full week, just thinking, Oh my God, this is amazing. Once I started having sex, though, the realization came that it's a really different ball game. Between the ages of fifteen and seventeen, when I started having sex and understanding more what sex actually is and what's involved, my porn usage really died down. It became more like I'm describing it now: a wee external thing for yourself. I would hate to rely on it, I'd hate it to be an end in and of itself, to think it's better than the real thing. Maybe the first few times you have sex, it probably is. But then that brings up the question: how can I have better sex? That's more of a task, it's more interesting.

When you realized sex was a whole different ball game to porn, was there an element of disappointment?

Not necessarily, because the emotions and adrenaline you feel when you do it for the first few times override the excitement of watching porn. The first times weren't that great, but I don't think I was disappointed that it wasn't the way it was in porn. I think I was also under the impression that the first time isn't going be great. It's the same as anything: you don't lift a hundred kilograms of weights the first time you go to the gym, you lift five. I knew it would get better. I didn't know if it'd get to some sort of fantasized version of what you see, but I did know it'd get better. So I wouldn't say I was disappointed. There's a whole different level of feelings and emotions that come with having sex that porn can't match up to. Porn's just a quick little fix to get off. There are no emotions attached to it, no intimate feelings, no actual desire. Emotionally, there's a real difference.

The way people view porn is changing, and things like OnlyFans foreground the idea of getting to know performers, and generating a certain intimacy. I wonder whether, when there's a particular porn performer whose OnlyFans you subscribe to and who you watch a lot, that simulates the emotional connection you're describing.

It's made to simulate that, a hundred per cent. Regardless of whether you feel it's genuine, it's probably not. There's a script, they're playing the game, they know what to do and say to get you emotionally invested so you'll say, 'Here you are, take my money.' That's the thing with virtual encounters. Even if you were texting somebody that you actually did know, you could still be aroused and want them, but physical proximity is a huge thing. Being in a space with somebody and feeling that energy is huge. Is it eighty per cent of body language is non-verbal? All the feelings that you have are less to do with what's being said. That sense of intimacy is definitely what OnlyFans is trying to emulate. I get it, but it's fake.

Have you ever looked into any of that stuff?

I was interested at one point to see what it was, but I didn't bother, because I don't see why I would pay for it when it's not real. I could just go and watch porn. Why have a pretend conversation with somebody and give them money to do the same thing that I could just type in on Pornhub? It just feels like a lot of extra steps and a lot more money for the same end result. I know that I'm not actually going to get anything emotionally from this. Once I finish there's nothing else to this. It's just a different recipe for the same meal. That doesn't appeal.

How do you feel about the idea of making your own porn, doing amateur stuff?

It would depend on why I was doing it and what it was for. If it was for someone's OnlyFans, probably not. If it was just for me and my partner's private use, I have no issue with that at all. I've done a couple of short videos when I was younger, 'cause somebody said that was what they were into, but it's not something that entices me particularly. Mainly because the positions and the way things are in the videos isn't how you have sex. The way they try to get their face in it all the time and sit at an angle just to capture something. I don't think it would be natural and fun the way that sex normally is. It'd be more like, Oh right, we do this, now we do this and we do that. That feels a bit like killing the feeling.

I watched a programme about couples who've started doing OnlyFans, and it's harder work than I thought. There's so much planning, a lot of them seem to choreograph it before, and every time someone gives them a tip you have to mention them by name...

It's not just taking the mick, it's not just sitting in front of a camera. I'm not discrediting it. It's just not something that I would do. I don't think I could be with a partner

114

that was an adult entertainer, either. That's a different form of jealousy. I know that the person who's looking isn't in the room, but that to me is a level of intimacy that should be between the two of you.

How would you feel if one of the videos that you filmed found its way onto Pornhub? Would you have worries about people finding it?

I feel fine about it, purely because my face isn't in it.

The face is a game changer?

I'd say so. I'd be more concerned if my face was in it. Not that many people would be searching for 'Scottish young teen', but still.

It used to be that finding someone's old porn tape or nude photos they'd had done when they were eighteen was the biggest dirt you could dig up on someone. We've moved into an age where it no longer feels as underground in a clear-cut way, with people sending nudes and sometimes posting nudes or semi-nudes quite openly online, and yet it's not totally the other way. It's not shame free. As revenge porn illustrates.

I don't think it ever will be shame free, because it has the air of being a private thing. If people are choosing to make the private thing public, that's their call, but it's not something you would advocate for people that you care about to go and do. I wouldn't want my little sister to be going on OnlyFans. But if somebody showed me a video of someone else on OnlyFans, I'd watch it and say, Okay, no bother. I don't know if that's hypocritical that you'd watch a random person's sister but you wouldn't want your own sister to do it. I think the media has really affected how sex and OnlyFans and porn are viewed. You've got shows like *Naked Attraction* and all these different shows that are – I don't want to say dehumanizing – but certainly desensitizing our sense of what sex is. It's almost treated as a novelty on the telly. 'Pick which one of these six guys you like from their dick.' It's absolutely horrid. I hate the thought of that. I've never looked at a woman and gone, Hmm she's nice, but her pal's got bigger tits so I'm going with her. It just doesn't make sense to me. If you speak to someone and you go, You're quite nice, I quite like you, and you start to feel attracted, then you might think, I'd like to have sex with you. I'm not saying it has to be all that much for that attraction to develop, but the idea that I'm going to look at you naked to decide whether or not I want to have sex with you is such a judgy, horrible, toxic thing.

You could make the argument that porn encourages people to see especially women like that. With porn, you are watching it for the most part to get off, and so you are going to go for the person you find just most sexually attractive in that moment. I wonder if that doesn't then leak into the way people see women as sexual tools in a sense.

I wouldn't say that I go in and look for the one that's the most attractive. If I'm scrolling and there was somebody that really stuck out, someone who made me think, I want a bit of her, then I'd maybe click on it, but if I've seen a few videos that would do the job, I wouldn't be that judgy with it. In the same vein, if there was someone that was absolutely stunning and really did it for me but the video itself was something that I'm not into, I wouldn't click on it. It's content over aesthetics. If you can have both, then wonderful.

Do you feel porn has helped you know what you like in bed, and to talk about it with people?

I don't want to give it the credit but I'm going to say yeah, I do think so. If anything, it gives you the language to explain and verbalize things. You see things in videos which make you think, That seems quite interesting, maybe I'd like that. It all comes down to doing it, but porn did help in giving me the vocabulary to be able to express it. Take how vocal people are in porn. I can't speak for all guys, but I know that there're quite a lot of girls that aren't that vocal in real life. I'm not talking about screaming in my ears, but just something, anything at all. That's what gets people off sometimes, that's what people really like. Even just moaning in somebody's ear can go a long way. It has helped me to be able to understand that. Let's say you do see something and think, That looks good, I'd like to try that, I have the vocabulary to express that, you've still got to approach it with the understanding that, one, your partner's got to be into it, and two, that it's not going to be what you've seen on screen. Even talking about it is difficult, especially when you're younger and you're just starting out. When I was younger, I was in bed with girls who wouldn't take their tops off because they felt insecure. You can even go as far as having sex with somebody, and there's still that stigma, especially when you're in your late teens. To be able to talk about things, you have to feel comfortable. Everyone wants to talk about things deep down, but they find it difficult. Especially if it's a newer relationship or if you're sober, people really struggle. If you're in a committed relationship, it becomes second nature to discuss

117

things. If you don't then your sex is doomed anyway. The more you do it, the more comfortable you are with talking, and if you're comfortable then other people are comfortable. That's the main thing: having a really good space to speak and to be judgement free and to be like, I want you to feel pleasure the same way I feel pleasure. Being able to comfortably speak about that is something that's not stressed enough, especially in sex education. It needs saying far, far more.

Something that's shocked me as an adult is how few people are comfortable with themselves sexually. Maybe it's just the ones I attract, but I feel as if people are a bundle of insecurities about stuff, in a way I thought might disappear after adolescence, but just didn't. There's a negative feedback loop at work: you don't discuss it, so it doesn't go well, and then you feel more like a failure.

I don't think that's wrong. A lot of people still feel insecure about a lot of things, and some are far worse than others. If you're going to have sex with someone, you're going to a different level of intimacy with them. If you've both said you want to do that, then any insecurity should be null and void, because you've disregarded it. You're not going to go, Right, what can I pick out to ridicule about you? I'm here to be with you and to have fun, I'm not trying to make you feel bad. If anything I'm trying to make you feel good. I do think there's still a bit of that. It's something to do with social media and body pressures.

Do you think you've ever felt any insecurities that come specifically from porn?

118

The dick size in porn is just absolutely unrealistic. Half of them are the size of my arm: not even to the elbow, the whole arm. Especially when I was younger, that was something that I was really aware of. Again, once I started having sex, getting a bit more experience in it and understanding what people actually like, that went away very quickly. I can see how people could feel insecure about things. There are a lot of girls who are insecure about their boob size or if they've not got much of an arse or whatever, and that really upsets me, because everybody's beautiful in their own way. There's no need to compare everything about yourself to other people. I'm not saying you need to love every-thing about yourself, but the idea of wishing this was bigger or that was different – that's quite an unhealthy mentality. That might come down to being with people who have said something. Even passing comments go a long way. School is incredibly toxic for it. I was only in high school for four years, but that was during the time when everybody's bodies are starting to change, hormones are starting to surge, some people are starting to develop, some people are ahead of the game, some people are served alcohol because they look old enough and there are others who haven't yet developed. Porn's racist as well, all this 'big black cock' stuff. You don't see that written about the white cocks, they don't get fucking objectified in that way. It's a strange world. It messes with your head if you don't have any perspective on it. I don't think porn should be banned, but there's moderation needed. Ultimately you've got to moderate it yourself. That's the thing.

SIX

Six is queer and in their late forties.
They live in Japan, and are in a long-term relationship.

POLLY BARTON — *Is porn something you talk about*
with people around you?

SIX — Well, leading up to chatting with you, I went
off in all kinds of directions thinking about it. I made
a Venn diagram, I was all over it. One of the things
that really interested me was a presumption that I'm
part of a community that's all about sex positivity and
body positivity, where we happily and freely talk about
various sexual things at the drop of a hat, nobody's shy
at all, etc. It's not necessarily true. I've got these random
memories of porn-related incidents or conversations in
my various queer circles, and aside from those related
to my partners, none of them feel really deep-down. So
I was thinking: Maybe I don't really have a relationship
with porn, fuck, what kind of a queer am I? That sense
of disconnect goes way back.

When I graduated from university, all the cool lesbians went on a camping trip. They went in their cars up
into the mountains, and for some reason I got to go with
them. There was a hailstorm, it was really atmospheric.
The cool liberal studies graduates were talking about
sex, and one girl, whose cool mechanic girlfriend Dusty
was right there with her, was saying, I just got Dusty to
let me touch her perineum for the first time the other
day, and everybody was having this conversation. I was
there thinking, Ah, that sucks for Dusty. If she hadn't
had her perineum touched before, maybe she didn't

really want to talk about it either. There's a coolness
that doesn't always go with checking everyone's comfort
level. I've seen that a lot over the years – people are
happy to talk about sex while also not talking about it at
the same time.

*Most people I'm friends with are sex positive and body posi-
tive and so keen to register that they're down with anything
and supportive of everyone. That, for me, is a positive thing,
but I often sense that when we're talking about things that
are hard to talk about initially, such as sex and porn and
intimacy, and what we feel comfortable doing or sharing or
watching, because we don't have much practice, that need
to be 'cool' can present a barrier. There's an echo of the way
people worry about political correctness in this pressure to be
pro everything.*

'Well *of course* we're fine with all of this' – that becomes
a given. As you say, in most circles we haven't really got
the language. That's why those sex toy videos I emailed
you about are so great: 'I'm just sitting here talking in a
very normal salesperson voice with a little bit of extra
softness about something I'm suggesting that you'll
really enjoy putting in your anus.' The disconnect that's
there is fantastic.

*Does it feel jarring to you in any way? Is the jarringness part
of the fascination?*

They assume that we're all fine with it and build a world
there. I find that really charming.

*When you haven't got a language around something, how do
you go about developing one? Does learning to speak that*

121

language then better shape what you think and feel? At the start of this project, I didn't feel comfortable talking about porn or masturbation. It was absent from my life.

Your spoken life.

Exactly, from my spoken life – the distance between the discourse and what's actually going on is odd. When we're forming a new language, does it have to be a kind of 'fake it till you make it' thing? Do we have to seem totally cool with things and say of course we're all fine with this, or can we be really awkward? It sometimes feels that if you can't manifest that total coolness, it's quite hard to get a toe in.

And that means that you can't have the meaningful conversations that you need in order to get comfortable with it, to get in there. Before I moved back to Japan, I was living in the countryside for eight years or something with a bunch of back-to-the-landers. I left my very queer Japan life and went to the middle of the English countryside where maybe some people had *some* kind of queer consciousness before, but most of them didn't seem to centre it at all. I'm really dating myself here, because it is oh-so-generational. In my experience there's a break between hippie identity and queer identity, unless you're talking about fairy communities that live off the land and that. For the most part, back-to-the-landers in this story are all about making families and cycles of nature, in a very male/female way... It's all changing now, but I was living in a field when concepts like cis-gender were coming into the discourse, and when I heard that term used for the first time, in a field, I almost cried. Those words that you've read, that are important to you, but nobody ever says them out loud, it's a special kind of

loneliness... That experience was paralleled in a way by
a friend I had out there who lived in another field and
had these unfortunate relationships with smelly men.
No disrespect to smelliness meant – most of them were
not very kind to her, and I'm inclined to call them names.
As I recall it, she had a classic seventies woman sexual
awakening, where she went on a retreat, and probably
looked at her vulva, you know? When she came back,
we talked about perineums, and prostates, and so on. She
would say things like, I just want to be able to squirt, how
do I do this? I hadn't been having sex conversations with
people for the past five or six years, unless it was about
sheep reproduction or prolapsed cows, so that was really
cool. She wasn't ashamed or embarrassed about it. It was
all just, This is a natural process and I want to find out
more. We tried to find her some responsible BDSM sites
and that, where no one would be taking advantage of her
and she could try out different things. But most of that
was in the cities, and the stuff closer to home felt quite
dodgy and scary, and I worried. So there's that, too: you
can find a language, but it might not be spoken where
you are.

I sometimes feel envious of people who have sudden awak-
enings, and are then able to be very straight up about what
they want. That process has never been sudden for me, in any
realm, it's always felt more muddy and drawn-out.

In her case, it wasn't a happily ever after situation.
She would start being a lot more vocal about what she
wanted and the straight cis men that you can pick up on
whatever those apps are in the area aren't necessarily
going to be going for that, or at least not necessarily in a
way that respected her. The lovely thing about it, though,

was that she was having the scales removed. She was learning for the first time about the different things her body could do.

There's good porn and bad porn, right? There's the kind that doesn't really reflect me or anything that I want to see, and then there's the stuff that is really right on. I don't think that she had easy access – I don't think a lot of people have easy access – to really right-on porn.

Do you think there is something objective about what constitutes good porn and bad porn?

I feel like it's hugely problematic to be the one deciding for everybody what good porn and bad porn is. I can remember watching porn with an ex, because there aren't that many of these stories in my life, but there was one time back when we were together when he wanted to watch some porn, and so he had it on. It was something about this blonde Barbie doll-looking woman and this old playboy-looking man, and she was getting lots of piercings. And she was saying 'Ow', and I was saying, 'Wait... Her pain being titillation for this other person, and I don't find either of them attractive in any way, why are we...?' And my partner was like, 'Nah, it's all put on, she's enjoying it, she's loving this.' And I was like, '*You're* loving this, I'm not convinced about her.' And he was loving it. So I think it has to be subjective.

It's fascinating that two people in a relationship can be watching the same thing, and one of you thinks the woman is hating it, and the other thinks, No, she's loving it. What is the different information there? If you did find it more arousing, would you be more inclined to make yourself believe that she was?

124

It was hard for me not to think that. It spoke a lot to the relationship as well. We were both watching the same porn and having completely different responses and finding each other sort of ideologically unattractive because of it.

Did he find your lack of interest in it unattractive?

Oh yeah. I think he'd say so, too. This was my first trans male partner. He had a chequered past and knew city things, from the streets. He knew how shit was, and how the hardcore city queers live. Whereas I didn't, so I just had to take his word for it. Every once in a while, the nineties Women's Studies dyke still in there somewhere was saying, Uh, wait a minute, this doesn't feel right. About a lot of things. Some of it I was wrong about, and some of it... You know, even if she *was* enjoying it, I couldn't put myself in a position where I found that sexy either to be her *or* to be watching it. I don't know how porn works outside of those two positions of actor and viewer. Does it? Is there a narrator role in porn that also gets off? There probably is.

When you're watching porn, do you always identify with one person rather than the other? Or can you be sort of switching, or are you just finding the whole set-up attractive?

It has to be all of the above, right? Do you have a clear answer to that?

I don't think so. It depends so much on what you're watching.

I've got to admit, I don't do much watching. The piercings video, or another one around that time, broke the family computer. This was back in the day when we didn't have firewalls and internet security. My partner broke the house computer, streaming porn illegally off the net, so that put me off trying to find it. I didn't have videos and I didn't really put in the work – I tend to count on other people for good music too. I have my things that I know about, and then I have specialists around that I can count on. If I ever needed good porn, I would probably just go to someone and ask for it, because it's not in my personal library. What I tend to have – and even this is from a partner – are smut books. I have porn books. Because people have different porn media preferences too, hey.

Going back to the question of whether you have to identify with someone in porn, there's a thing about gay male porn, isn't there – lesbians who are really into gay male porn. And who are you in that? If your identity is as a lesbian, and it is set up as and defines itself as gay male porn. I don't know. But then it's play-acting, so there's that.

That makes me think about BL [Boys Love manga], which is mostly written by either lesbian or straight women and read mostly by women. Gay men read it sometimes, I know my gay Japanese friend is a fan. I think it's used in place of porn by a lot of women. Again that raises the question of, who are you identifying with? I read it and definitely found some of it a turn-on, partly because it's removed from the problematic depictions of women that I find so oppressive and which constitute an immediate brake. For a long time, whenever I was looking for things to be turned on by it was always books, at first just random passages I stumbled on in whatever fiction I was reading. Partly because it's using the imagination, and then because it doesn't have the problematic aesthetic elements that I find in most of the 'bad porn' that's readily available.

Bearing in mind that we still haven't defined what bad porn is. But, yes, what you said about the turn-on brake, that's definitely a bad-porn quality and a lot of it is, 'I'm uncomfortable with this because it makes me feel uncomfortable about myself and that doesn't turn me on.' Bad-porn-for-me. But maybe not damnably bad?

Do you and your current partner talk about porn?

My partner is just getting over a bout of the dread virus. It's been really rough, and he went away for a while to self-quarantine. We've been talking on Skype like we did back when it was a long-distance relationship, when I was still in the sheep field. Yesterday I told him, I get to do the porn chat tomorrow, and I was asking him what he would say his relationship was with porn. He said that, right now, the virus has killed his libido, he has no energy for anything. The idea of sexual things right now is still up there with, um, what was it? Chillies and caffeine: things that he's not quite ready for yet.

Back in the day when I was in the countryside and he was here, we would read porn to each other. Send each other little videos of readings, or read to each other live until my laptop battery ran out in the horsebox. I don't remember what came first, but there were also wanking videos sent back and forth, on memory sticks. We had our own little poor-relation Pornhub going on. I'd forgotten about it until I was thinking, Let's see, porn, porn, porn... oh yeah, there was all of that. When I first started reading *Fifty Sounds*, I was crying and laughing and going crazy about it, and I thought, I can't go through this alone, so I made him read it. But it was taking him forever, he never had time to read. Then I realized that, because he's away from home, we can do it like porn! And I started reading him a page a day on Skype. You've joined, unwittingly, our porn dialogue.

I love that. In the beginning, when it was 'real' porn, was it stuff that you had written yourself?

No, we never wrote each other smutty stories. It was mostly books that he already knew, or that he'd introduced me to. We did have a whole bunch of journals that we posted back and forth, and there was some smutty stuff in them, but I don't think we ever read those out loud. An opportunity lost!

Do you feel that what you are turned on by with him is more closely matched than with your previous partner? And can you conceive of anything that he would admit to being turned on by that you would feel like, 'Oh, whoa there.'

'That's disgusting!' Of course there is always that possibility. One thing that happens that's quite exciting is that you can – I'm going to sound like a sex therapist now – leave yourself open to it? If there's something that they're interested in, you can try it and see if it works for you. But we knew from way back that we were into a lot of the same stuff so maybe there weren't any real shockers. The interpersonal dynamics with porn are interesting. Like there's some risk or threat? When you're afraid of someone not wanting you anymore, or it not working anymore, or doing something that breaks the magic. See, he identifies as a homo, but then there's me, right? So he likes a lot of gay male stuff. In the beginning of the official relationship, when I was needing some affirmation that the fact that I haven't got any boy parts is going to be acceptable, then yes, there was some difficulty for me there in embracing his enthusiasm for lots of boy parts. That was tied in with embracing his inability to even believe that monogamy exists in the world, and all the other bits of an open relationship with someone who identifies as being attracted to something you're not... We worked through all that, so it's fine now. Ahem. I think everybody who does porn with somebody else, or maybe not everybody, but a lot of people will have some version of that insecurity.

When you say 'does porn' do you mean watches porn or makes porn or both?

Both. People who make porn together probably have as many variegated worlds to live in as everybody else. Actually, we made a little video, using our videos back and forth to each other from that time, and sent it in for an online screening of pandemic porn. I don't know if we made it in, because it was three o'clock in the morning here when it was playing in the UK and we couldn't get the link to work.

Did they not send you an email saying whether it had been accepted? You just had to watch and see?

I suspect that if we'd definitely been in it, they would've told us. They did seem to have a whole lot of submissions, what with everyone there in lockdown. I'll probably die not knowing. Or maybe someone will come up to me one day on the street and say, Oh my God, was that you in the sheep field?

*Do you have any anxiety around that? I'm incapable of
sending people videos or nudes or anything of me, because the
idea of them getting out is terrifying in quite a non-specific
way. It's not a particular scenario based in my head. It's just a
sense that I need to not do that for fear of... something.*

With unknown fears, it's not *what if this happens* – it's
something could happen. But, people on the street, maybe
not so much.

There's a really cute lingerie company called the
underargument. They have a tag for each design, like
'my body, my rules', things like that. You write a little
essay and then you do a little photo shoot in the underwear, and then you're one of the models. That's their
marketing. The website's full of these people in beautiful underwear talking about their relationship with
their bodies. Which is cute, right? So I did that. And I
realized I wanted it to be anonymous because if it was on
my Instagram account my sister-in-law might see it and
judge me. Then I heard myself thinking that and wrote
to the woman who runs the company and said, Would
you please put my name on the damn thing? Because
this is my sister-in-law I've not seen in years, and she
hasn't even contacted me directly since she followed me
on Instagram. You know when someone follows you
and you say, Oh hey, and then they write back, and you
have a conversation? She didn't write back. I've got this
whole thing about how she's following me just to see if
I say anything that might corrupt her children's minds.
Weirding myself out about family dynamics, mostly in
my head. But when I think about people seeing me on
the street... Honestly, I think our little video is so funny,
I don't mind anybody watching it. Hell, my sister-in-law
can watch it, any number of times.

When I was living in the city a long time ago, whoring, often I'd be thinking, What if I'm walking down the street and one of my johns sees me and says hello? How funny would that be? How weird would that be? What if someone who's only ever seen me naked sees me now? But that wouldn't really be any different in terms from one of my clients from the English conversation company I work at now seeing me in my not-work clothes. There are so many ways in which that work, selling my full attention and all of my words for forty-minute sessions one after another, feels more distasteful and more dishonest than selling my body for money. I'm pretty sure I think that, anyway.

Obviously the way porn and misogyny and patriarchy interact is massively tangled and anything but unidirectional, but I do find myself wondering about how porn radiates outwards, in terms of shaping sexual practices and the things that people – particularly men, I suppose – want to enact in the bedroom. In your experience of doing sex work, did you see that play out, or see things that were clearly from porn? I know that's a huge question.

You can't not go there, though. That's the dark side, right? That's the not sex-positive or person-positive side. The truly sinful side. I was only doing sex work for maybe four or five months. It wasn't legal, I didn't have a visa for it. It was how I was making a living, but it was also something I had chosen to do out of interest, something I wanted to know the experience of. When I thought about it in terms of temple priestesses, say, when I went Ancient Greece fantasy with it and was like, This thing that I'm doing and this service that I'm providing for this person is holy, and if I was with someone from

131

whom I could get that sense of gratitude for the profundity of what was going on – because some people were like that, and that was amazing– that was pretty right on. Others were very clearly not like that – some people were doing things that they wanted to try out because they'd seen them on TV and they weren't nice things. Or they saw it that way. You can feel it. You can feel it in any situation when somebody is not seeing you as a human being. And that really sucks when you're naked and you're sucking their dick.

Did you have a sense before you got to the being naked and sucking their dick part – would you know which way the interaction was going to go? Or did things come out once it turned sexual?

There are probably a lot of people in the world who have better risk antennae than I do, but even I sometimes would walk into a room and think, Oh, this is going to be one of those. Sometimes I'd be wrong, and it would turn into something everybody could get something good out of. Other times it was just ugliness and abuse and it's a real shame that that's what people are capable of equating sex with. I'm sorry that I didn't have the temple goddess strength to bring those people round.

But how can anyone, really?

I don't know. It's so deeply ingrained. All the ugliness is so deeply ingrained in us and so much of it is connected to not having a way to talk in a healthy way about it.

Do you think there was more ugliness because at that time you were in the bracket of sex worker in their heads? And therefore on the slut side of the slut/virgin dichotomy? All of this feels deeply related to porn.

Absolutely. The commodification bit, right? If money is what I value and I can get it for money then sure, the person doesn't matter. That's gross. Even if I was telling myself that it was just a job, the experience of commodification in sex work was still physical, it was going into my body, and there were unscheduled long, weepy baths on the bad days, soaking that stuff out. And that was without any of the *truly* bad stuff having happened. So, yes. I don't know how we fix porn, but it feels important.

It's not just porn, though, is it? Porn has emerged from and plays into this enormous patriarchal capitalist system. And it's so hard to imagine just fixing one part without fixing the thing in its entirety.

It'd be fine if we could fix everything. Are you having these conversations with co-workers as well as friends? That's a sort of church and state thing, isn't it? Is there a sense of, we talk about work-related professional things and now we're talking about this very personal, intimate thing?

I feel as if the real church and state divide in my life with porn has been the gender divide, at least within heterosexual relationships with cis men. I find that conversation tough. Maybe it would be different now because I'm a slightly bigger person and slightly less insecure but I felt so threatened by the secrecy of it all. Then also, because it was secret and therefore wouldn't come up naturally, I also felt some compulsion to be a kind of spy or undercover policeman, which was not a role I enjoyed, to say the least.

133

Finding out someone's porn is somehow more scary and more intimate than having actual physical sex with this person. What is that? There's the part where you're looking at it, and looking at them, and saying, 'Wait, *this* is what you're attracted to?' And there's the part where there is something itchy about it and you don't want to be in the room. And then – oh my God, maybe this is something I'm not allowed to say – I'm going back to the piercing porn person, umm, who actually is an amazing person, and that's it: people with 'dodgy' porn can be amazing people. What made it worse for me with him was his take on it, that it's good porn if it gets you off. He just wanted to watch the boring cis het porn until he came and then turn it off really quickly. Does everyone do that? Is that normal?

I think so. It's this Jekyll and Hyde thing dictated by whether or not you've got a boner, metaphorical or not.

And I'm sitting there wanting to know what happens next! Is she going to go off with the plumber now? I was all about narrative, because nothing else about it interested me. But he'd be like, Turn it off, turn it off. It was suddenly distasteful. So yeah, shame comes in, right. If you have a desire and then shame comes in once you've satisfied it, does that need to be looked at?

When I was young and wanking to sex scenes in Rose Tremain or whatever it was I was reading, I would still have this sense of a definite split between before and after the fact. Not finding it gross, necessarily, but just failing to see what was sexy about it. It's a weird split that feels physiological even if it's not. I understand that when you're turned on, things become charged, and they quickly lose that charge after

134

the orgasm. But there are definitely levels, and one level is wanting it immediately out of sight, to compartmentalize very rigidly, and my sense is that comes from shame. Have you had to deal with shame in the past or has it always felt quite easy?

Sure, I have plenty of shame. It ebbs and flows, doesn't it? But sometimes an emotional response teaches you something, right? The first time I came with a john, I felt like, Whoa, you're actually in there. Your body is involved in this, let's talk about that. That wasn't shame so much as surprise. You don't actually know what the body's going through. And sometimes it says, No, actually I do like this, about things that you didn't realize it was going to say that about – at least in my experience.

I've definitely come during sex that I didn't want to be having. And you know, the way that some people can orgasm while being raped, and then that becomes a stick they use to beat themselves with. The fear that they secretly wanted it or people would see it that way.

Or my body betrayed me – that's another way people have it. In terms of shame and lustful feeling, I try things I don't think I'm going to be into, and I think, Oh yeah, that's all right, or that worked that time. Another time, the same thing just doesn't. I'm sure the physiologists or the sex biology people would be able to explain it, why something that felt really good a minute ago doesn't feel good anymore. It's constantly changing. Just like your experience of the porn text itself. Like with Rose Tremain. *Clan of the Cave Bear*, mine was.

135

SEVEN

Seven is a woman in her mid-thirties and is in a long-term relationship with a man.

POLLY BARTON — *You said in the run up to this chat that you weren't sure I should talk to you, because you don't think anything about porn. Can you say a bit more what you mean about that? It doesn't bring on any emotions for you, is that it?*

SEVEN — It's one of those subjects which is seriously uncool. Something really boring to discuss. And that's quite surprising to me, because I am quite political, whatever that means, and surely this topic is ripe for discussion and investigation and interrogation. I think the feeling is a fallout from the seventies. I once went to this feminist reading group, and we read some Andrea Dworkin – I really can't remember what book it was now...

On Pornography, *maybe? Where she talks about how pornography dehumanizes women.*[6]

Maybe. We also watched this clip of her. She was a radical feminist in the seventies, but she found a kinship with the right on this subject, and we watched these marches she went on – it was horrifying. And then when we were reading the book, that was horrifying to me too, because you could tell that not just the content but even

6 *On Pornography: Men Hating Women* is a 1979 book by Andrea Dworkin that argues that the power, sadism and dehumanization found in pornography work 'to establish the sexual and social subordination of women to men'.

the form of the speech was so full of hate and right-wing sentiment. It's the same form and motifs that are used by the far right now. That really shocked and horrified me, and I think unfortunately that rhetoric probably had a big impact on feminism and feminists. Feminism went through this dead zone in the nineties, when it was vehemently hated and demonized, and this criticism of pornography was one of the things that led to that treatment of it. Possibly my relationship to pornography, or to discussing it as a subject, is overshadowed by the sense of the dubiousness of that Dworkinian position, of not wanting to fall into that trap. The contemporary equivalent would be a kind of TERFyness – radical feminism once again touching on a fascist position. My response is to think, quite lazily, Just don't engage, don't think about it. That's just a proposal of what might be going on, to justify that blankness I have. It's probably an active thing that I'm doing.

I really get that. For me there's a big thing of wanting, from a political point of view, to be really pro-porn, and recognizing that it's not all abusive stuff, and there's interesting porn, and so on. At the same time, when I was growing up, porn and everything that it represented was so tied in with that micro-level misogyny that it seemed like the same thing, almost. Such a clear representation of everything that I hated about the culture.

Pornography has gone through a massive change with the internet: there's been a democratization of who distributes it, what you can see and what you can get. Also, the other thing that I was going to say that would explain the blankness and hesitancy with dealing with the subject in my head for a long time: misogyny relies

137

heavily on power dynamics. And of course we all know that power dynamics within sexuality and desire and pleasure are a complex and valuable thing, and obviously in kink communities, queer communities, the presence of these power dynamics isn't a bad thing in itself. Then you have to try to separate misogyny from the power dynamic thing. Which is really bizarre. If you think about domestic abuse, it's all about the power dynamic – and there it *is* a bad thing. It's really difficult to square the positive and the negative aspects of power dynamics in your head, to remember that sometimes they're a positive thing which it's important for people to explore, that they're part of an activity which is vital and should be protected and understood. It feels as if they're more under attack within the kink communities and the queer communities than within heteronormative society.

Under attack?

I imagine there's a lot of discrimination and hate towards kink because people say it's sadomasochistic, it's harmful, it's weird, and so on. But then the very same thing has been happening unchecked and normalized within regular porn forever – the hate, the power dynamic, the abuse, the violence, the assumption of inferiority – yet it's not even questioned.

The other day, I was looking at the Women's Aid website, and there was an article about debunking myths about domestic abuse. Most of them seemed pretty uncontroversial, and then one of the myths was something along the lines of 'Pornography Doesn't Have a Part to Play in Promoting Violence Towards Women', and the writer went on to explain

138

that hardcore pornography normalizes violence towards women and entrenches this power dynamic. Stated as if it were a proven fact. It was amazing to see it written in such bald terms, because that feels quite straight-up Andrea Dworkin, right? And I have problems with that, intellectually, though on some level, there's one part of me which says, Yes, that's true, I believe that somewhere, actually. How do these two parts coexist?

So what did it say again? Hardcore...pornography... increases...violence...

Shall I look it up? Okay, here we go:

> *Myth #7: Pornography is not linked to violence against women. Reality: Most consumers of pornography are male, and pornographic material is becoming increasingly explicit, violent, and focused on male pleasure. It's also freely available to anyone online, and studies indicate it is how many young people find out about sex. Pornography contributes to a culture of misogyny, in which women and girls are abused by men for male pleasure. Women are harmed by pornography in two ways: directly, when they are used for the production of pornographic material; and indirectly, through the effects of mainstream availability and consumption of violent pornography.[7]*

This is a problem with a lot of abuse organizations. Their attitudes towards sex work and sex workers are unfortunate. I understand that in some places, there's a movement among employees who are saying the organizations need to shift their perception, so it is

7   https://www.womensaid.org.uk/information-support/what-is-domestic-abuse/myths/

happening but it's obviously not happening across the board, and not very fast.

What is your view on this myth thing? That it's more complex than that suggests?

In a way, it's totally true. But I think you need to caveat it, to make clear that it's not, actually, about the porn itself, but the forces that drive it. It makes me think about the argument about rape and sexual violence, which says: sexual violence is not about sex, it's about power and control. For that reason, I don't know if I necessarily agree with establishing this direct link between pornography and violence.

As in, this suggestion that we could just get rid of porn and then everything would be fine...?

Exactly, exactly! You need to acknowledge every single time you bring that up that we live in a patriarchy, and in every single part of society we have reinforcements of misogyny. I don't think it's helpful to say, Oh pornography, they fucked up with that! I was thinking about this the other day, actually. I listen to a lot of pop music, and then suddenly it came to me, this is basically the audio version of heteronormative misogynistic porn. And it's the same with films, telly, banter... A product made to serve people's sexual desire doesn't necessarily hold all of the responsibility for patriarchy and misogyny. People find it so much easier to link those things, probably because of the conservative way of thinking that sex is damaging anyway. I relate it to how there are still loads of people who say that we shouldn't have sex education in school, we shouldn't be talking to young people about sex. It's the same thing going on with pornography, and I think it's really misguided. Those kinds of people don't give a shit about misogyny, they don't give a shit about anything. They're just scared, ignorant people, and unfortunately they're harming their children by being scared and ignorant.

Is this the nub of why it feels boring to you to talk about porn, because it's too obvious in a way? It's like, what about all the other stuff?

Yeah, maybe. Talking about porn is not talking about the thing that's the problem, which is patriarchy and misogyny. Yes, porn is the sex section of that, and that is important because people's sexualities and how sex plays a role in people's lives is obviously massive, and I think it's an absolute atrocity that women have been denied pleasure and been demonized for it and have such a fucked-up relationship to their own sexual desire. I'm not massively sexual, sex is not especially important to me, so I think that's feeding into my attitude that this is not *that* interesting. There's a whole lot of pain there from my past, though, for sure. From being a young person growing up with that very damaging perception of women's sexuality. Now I'm agreeing with them a little bit, aren't I?

A lot of pain around sex, or porn, specifically, or the pornification of sex?

The pornification of it. And it's all connected, isn't it? All the bad stuff. The objectification, the body shaming culture, fat shaming, beauty standards, the emphasis on being used and not having an active part to play in that

141

whole section of existence, and then obviously there's all the sexual violence, and yeah, fucking hell. So maybe there is a little bit of the feeling that that is too much. Where do you start? That's before even mentioning the thing I'm actually interested in, and I feel like the only person that commented on this or that I've read commenting on this is Maggie Nelson. She was actually referring to child abuse, so I'm kind of co-opting what she's saying and using it for my own particular purpose. In *The Argonauts*, she talks about children witnessing descriptions of child sexual abuse within literature and film, saying, in very few words, Who knows what effect that's had on children's development of their sexuality and their view of themselves, because there's no control group. And she says something like, I don't want to talk about what female sexuality is until there's a control group. That spoke to me so much, and it really surprised me actually.

We are all – not just men, but women too – a product of this and I don't know where I begin and end in a way, or where my sexuality begins and ends, or what is going on there, which bits to celebrate, which bits to feel shameful about. It's almost an attack when Andrea Dworkin and whoever come in with the critique that all pornography is violence, because although I'm sometimes drawn to the simplicity of that, for me to fully go down there there's some element of self-annihilation that I would have to experience, because I do think it's part of my sexuality – and who am I to say, 'not in a positive way'. If I have to say, Well that degradation of women is a part of me and I don't really like it, what's that going to do to my relationship with myself or my relationship to sex? There's an avoidance there.

Is it akin to the question of, What does gender look like in a post-patriarchal society, it's very hard to say? Or different?

What does gender look like in a post-patriarchal society...? That's interesting. The question of how to own this stuff, to face it and do the sieving out so you can separate the power dynamic from the harmful stuff, is probably something the queer community and the kink community have worked through and dealt with. I feel as though everyone needs to go through that kind of thing. But I find it very hard to do that work, as a woman.

Do you think it makes it harder being in a heterosexual relationship? Do you think it'd be easier to do that work if you were with a woman?

Yeah, totally.

Yeah, right. I feel that too.

Totally. I first started having thoughts about this when I was in a relationship with a woman, because you just can't avoid it, and there's a kind of equality there that would never exist with a man. I found sex with her really difficult because of that, though, and this is when I started to get an inkling that, ahh, I am reliant on the non-equality in a way.

Being led, or something else? What was difficult about it?

She was getting a lot just from the activity – without all the baggage. She seemed to easily be able to get a lot from what I would describe as this wholesome thing. As if sex were like, Oh, let's climb a tree. A completely neutral activity. For me the landscape wasn't neutral. The landscape was maybe a battlefield, maybe a political discussion, maybe a weird contortion act, but it definitely wasn't, We're doing this nice thing and we're getting pleasure from it. That's not how I get pleasure. Watching her made me think, That's probably better, I probably should be like that, not having all of this stuff going on, but it just doesn't do it for me.

In my mind, that worry has been phrased as, Maybe I'm just secretly straight, I'm not sexually attracted to women. Yet I am. It's what you describe, though: it's not being able to do that wholesomeness.

I've never thought, Maybe I'm not bi. Actually, no, I did, after we broke up. I thought, Maybe that's a bit of a red flag. Maybe I don't want to have sex with women.

Did you feel romantically attracted to her?

What does that mean?

I don't know.

Yeah, I think I did. The thing is – and this wasn't to do with her – I don't have this sexual attraction thing. I'm not sexually attracted to people. I don't know whether that's because I've got a low sex drive, or whether it's just not how I work. I don't have the desire before the act.

So does porn – not porn as a concept, but porn as a thing – feel quite far from your life?

Yeah.

144

You don't watch it?

No.

You would never think to, really?

I have done in the past, but more out of interest.

Than to be turned on?

Exactly. Maybe I would if I was on my own? I don't know. This is also what's contributing to being just blank on things, because it's so out of sight for me that I think, Who cares? Is that very different for you?

I don't really watch much porn, deliberately, certainly not of the generic kind. But sometimes, if I happen to see a bit of the generic stuff on TV or on the internet, I feel a glimmer of being turned on by it, and then I'm confused by that feeling. As if, intellectually I don't want to be turned on by it, but on some animal level –

Why don't you want to be turned on by it intellectually?

Because it feels so aesthetically horrible to me a lot of the time.

Is that just shame around sex?

No. I don't think I feel embarrassed about being turned on by a – it sounds really ridiculous, but – a sex scene in an arty film, where it's sensitively done...

You *don't* feel embarrassed about that?

145

I don't feel embarrassed about that, no. But if it's schlocky and badly done, then...

That's just because you've got taste, and that's coming out in your preferences...

But I imagine that a lot of people that we think of as having 'taste' go home and jerk off to super tacky stuff.

I don't know anyone who does that, though. But then I wouldn't.

Exactly. None of us know what people do, because it's all done in secrecy.

Is there a useful or valuable, important distinction to be made between the schlocky, untasteful stuff and the rest? Does it matter if it's cartoonish?

No, it doesn't.

It only matters in the sense of the hetero-misogynistic aspect of it, but other than that...

Have you talked to your partner about it?

We had a bit of a conversation this morning about it, actually.

In preparation?

No, just because he was asking, but then I said, Dude, don't wear me out. So we didn't go into it too much.

So where you're coming from, there's really no point in talking about porn at all, then? In terms of the general understanding of it, my view feels quite similar to yours, but it sounds like maybe I'm different in that, in every relationship I've had with a man, the issue of porn has come up and I feel worried about whether or not they're watching it.

Why does it bother you?

The idea of going out with a secret misogynist is scary. I know that's a really silly way of putting it, but it makes me angry to think about men pretending to be all woke and then actually behind closed doors getting off to 'Blonde Slut Gets Pummelled by my Monster Cock'...

Do you not think that the power dynamic and the misogyny have to be separate? Power dynamic plays a really important role in sexualities and desire, so how do you separate that? You're worried about them being misogynists, but what's to say they're not just enjoying that aspect of desire?

What aspect of desire?

Dominant and submissive roles. How do you separate that?

It's very hard to.

Because there's so much different porn, right? I don't think it's the case that all women outside of the kink community are naturally submissive or get off from being submissive, or that more men enjoy being dominant and that's what turns them on about porn. There is potential for both in everyone, and in a way I feel quite sorry for men because of the influence of porn – potentially the same thing is happening to them as is happening to women, in that they play this role and women play the other role, but they're less flexible and adaptable. When I have sex, I switch between the two roles in my head. I can do that seven times, and I don't think my partner does that, or can do that. He would be quite surprised.

Does the switch manifest in doing something different, or is it just a perception thing?

Exactly, it's just safe within my brain. That's why I don't think he knows.

But it's quite binary? It's one or the other.

No, sometimes it gets really fucked up, where I think, Hang on a minute, what *am I* right now? It can be a really strange combination. Though I see it as a really valuable, positive thing.

And a sign of the equality of your relationship?

No, because it's not really – no, no. Because all of that is within me, and I could do that with whoever I'm sleeping with. My partner could be doing whatever he wants, and I'm having my own play, my own thing. I like that about it, it's completely self-sufficient.

Is that what sex feels like in general for you?

No. Obviously the interaction is very important, and I

get a lot from that. To go back to what you were saying about the secret misogynist thing, though, I do worry a little bit about that. I do see him doing things that aren't necessarily coming from misogyny, but from the pornification of sex.

Doing things in bed? Or in life?

In bed, not in life. Interestingly, clearly, not in life. This is the thing, isn't it: sex and desire is seen to be a safe, sacred space where people should be able to do whatever they want, and that probably makes everyone safer and more healthy in having that place of fantasy. I get that, but I wonder sometimes if it's in part a smokescreen, allowing people to get away with stuff. How much of the sacredness of the space is actually valuable and useful and should be respected, and how much is just a cover-up for not having to deal with things? Sometimes I think that the call to be sex positive actually dilutes the will or force of calling out hate and harm. It's a little bit like confidence feminism[8] in that regard: you get the sense of a sticking plaster being placed over a massive wound, in a desperate attempt not to look at it.

Do you have a handle on whether your partner watches porn, and is that something that worries you? Or are you more concerned about general pornification?

I think he does because, years ago, he mentioned something about watching porn in his workspace. But

8 A school of thought where women and girls are exhorted to work on themselves in order to feel more confident and therefore happier. It has been criticized for encouraging people to turn a blind eye towards the sources of their lack of confidence i.e. the various forms of oppression of women in the outside world.

now I'm questioning that, because what kind of context did that come up in? Did I make that up? No, I'm pretty sure that did happen. What was my reaction to that? I thought, is that a bit gross? I think I thought, Maybe, maybe not? I was just a bit non-plussed, I guess.

When you say that you feel things he does in bed are influenced by porn, do you think that is actually because of the porn that he watches?

Ahh, I don't know. When I say the stuff in bed is influenced by porn, I mean just in a hugely general, vague way, and how do we know? Maybe that's just sex, I don't know.

Right. Our concept of sex is shaped by all of these forces and a big one of them is porn.

Going back to Maggie Nelson, we don't have a control group. What would sex look like if porn didn't exist, and we didn't have this projection or representation of sex? If it was just guided purely by our bodies and blank minds? Can you even imagine that?

No, but there's a spectrum, right? I was talking to someone who'd been with someone who could only finish in a certain way, doggie style and quite porny, and tried to come on her face. Then there're more general power dynamics.

It's hard to isolate certain positions and say, That's more porn than another position, though.

Sure. I don't think I meant just positions, but quite an aggressive way of coming?

It's still hard to say. What came first, the desire or the porn?

My sense is, and this is all just from articles, but anecdotally there are more and more men who can't get it up with anything other than porn. The only thing that turns them on is porn because it's so —

So potent?

So purified, yeah. There is a chicken-and-egg mechanism to it, but my sense is that porn does influence real-world sex. That causal vector exists.

Okay, but let's take the things you described: say coming on someone's face, or the aggression, reflected in doing it doggie style. There's nothing to say that belongs to porn more than it belongs to desire.

Do you think men would want to come on people's faces without having watched porn? I agree with you about the positions, but with something like facials, that feels so totally porn.

Is that not about the power dynamic of submissive/ dominant? It's a motif which is in line with the extremity of those things. And the story goes, that's not necessarily porn or misogyny, that's people exploring something which is somehow linked to desire. Who knows why, but it is. It's not so easy to code stuff as coming from porn. That's one of the mind-blowing things about being human — that it's so difficult to figure out what is affecting what. I could be wrong there.

My sense is that, if you watch porn frequently, and in eighty per cent of the videos you watch the man comes on the woman's face, more and more that starts to become not just something that you want to try, but something that is normal. Maybe before you watched porn, it was something that might have occurred to you to try, but you would never think to ask for it because it seems so out there. I don't know. I think if someone asked to come on my face I would freak out.

If they asked?

Hah. If they asked, or if they did.

I'd be like, Oh, that's very polite.

Maybe I'm a huge prude. Is that something that feels normal to you?

I don't know, let me think about what I would do. Or let me think if it's ever happened. I think it's happened. I don't think I enjoy it, but I don't think it bothers me.

Is the reason you don't talk to your partner about porn because you're not interested, or you feel it's not your place, that's his stuff and you shouldn't be asking? Or that it's too awkward to have that conversation?

It's too awkward to have that conversation.

Would you like to have that conversation if it wasn't awkward?

I can't imagine what it'd be like if it wasn't awkward though. The answer is yes, in so much as I'd like to have

152

any conversation that wasn't painful. I love conversation, and I love knowing about stuff, and when you spend twenty-four/seven of your life with somebody you're always on the lookout for different things to explore that you haven't already explored, so yes. But with the awkwardness, it's just not worth it, you know?

There're some conversations that are really awkward to have, but urgent enough that you have to surmount that somehow, no?

Like the whether or not to have children conversation.

For example.

But with porn there's no particular impetus to have the conversation, no pressing reason we need to.

I think I'm driven to have the conversations that feel awkward because of their very awkwardness. Whereas I think you tend to avoid them more. You seem genuinely unbothered by the porn thing with your partner. You'd like to have a conversation because you're curious, but it doesn't seem to really bother you. If you found out that he was watching rape porn in his workspace, would that affect you?

This is quite painful to admit, because it makes me feel really disappointed with myself, but I think I'm scared to find out something that fundamentally changes my perception of him. I should have faith in my partner, because he can handle it. He'd be totally game for talking about the ins and outs. He is very good with that, and honest. But maybe the problem is more with me than with him. I don't know, something weird's going on.

153

That's exactly what I feel! That feeling is why I want to do this project. But I don't think the problem is with us: it's with the patriarchy. It's with this crazy imbalance. There's some dreadful secret at the heart of everything, and I know what that secret is, and yet it still remains there. Having each time to go about uncovering this –

Insidious misogyny... is painful. That's a good way to put it. *There's a dreadful secret at the heart of everything, and I know what it is, but it remains there.* Yeah. I know. For a very long time I felt that way about misogyny, through the nineties, through the noughties, and it was ripping me apart, and the anger I used to have in conversations with friends where I would freak out and break down because of the gaslighting. It was very nuanced, insidious gaslighting, and semi-silent, but it was definitely there. People taking an out-of-sight out-of-mind attitude to misogyny, feminism, all these things that are so fucking starkly, glaringly obvious.

Then I started working in a field where I had to listen to people talk about misogyny and support them in dealing with that, and work alongside other people doing the same, and the anger started to dissipate because there were people talking about that and acknowledging it. Finally I felt: Okay I don't need to worry anymore. And then we had this explosion of feminism in popular parlance, and society, and books, and movements, and it's sorted itself out and I'm totally at peace with it now, because it's not that secret. I think it still exists within porn, and it still exists within the whole having children thing, it still exists —

It still exists everywhere.

Yeah, there's lots and lots of these painful scenarios. But I'm so happy that there's been this magic shift, and I'm not in so much pain anymore, and I do think I have a sense of laziness. In that I've done so much work and I'm over it, and now I'm in the years of my life of relaxing... or denial.

Not a care in the world.

Yeah, and that's maybe feeding into why I feel I can leave the porn thing, let other people deal with that shit. But no one is. That's the problem, no one else is dealing with it.

After having this conversation, does porn still feel like a boring topic?

I don't think that chat was about porn, though. If someone says porn to me, I go, You're boring. If someone starts to talk about interesting things – and yes that can still be under the banner of porn – I can still think it's a fascinating, important, interesting, endlessly complex thing, that for some reason doesn't come under the umbrella of porn.

So as soon as it gets interesting then it's no longer porn?

As soon as you start talking about politics, as soon as you start talking about how it affects women, and has affected women, and how it shapes and validates misogyny and patriarchy in these ways, and what it does to sexuality – I am really interested in all that stuff. My reaction is a combination of what I said at the beginning, about feeling you have to be really careful when discussing it, and also not being a massively sexual person. Sex is not really that much of a thing. Although I did go through a stage of feeling: This is such an exciting thing that I'm missing out on, I really want it to be a really important part of my life, blah blah blah.

EIGHT

Eight is a queer woman in her late twenties, who has been in relationships with both men and women. She is currently single.

POLLY BARTON —— *Do you remember when we met up for the first time in ages after lockdown? That was the first time that I mooted the idea of doing this book to anyone. I remember we were both talking very audibly and screeching with excitement about porn at 8 a.m., and everyone in the café was looking at us like we were from another planet. Up until that point, I couldn't concretely imagine what the conversations would be like, but then I imagined talking to you about it in more depth, and I thought, I bet Eight would have a million interesting things to say.*

EIGHT —— Even here now I wonder whether we're sitting somewhere private enough to have this conversation, because the implication is that porn is not okay to talk about, or someone might be uncomfortable if we're talking about it, like in the café. Earlier today, I went for a bluebell walk with my housemate, and I asked him, What do you think about porn? It was funny because, as we would pass people, we'd start talking in code. He would start talking about it again a couple of steps away from people, whereas I would carry on in code until we were out of earshot.

Do you think that would have been the same if you were talking about sex, or do you think there's a different set of rules and worries with porn about whether people are okay or not in terms of overheard conversations?

My initial reaction is that it's the sex aspect of porn that produces that self-conscious reaction – that a pure sex conversation would be worse, because it's usually personal. Whereas porn is a bit othered, abstract, over there – you could be having some abstract philosophical conversation about it. Sex conversations are likely going to sound more like 'and then this guy did this and it was weird'.

The lack of conversation around porn is what bothers me the most. My assumption is that you talk about it a lot more than I do...?

I talk about it quite a lot, but more as a political thing than a personal thing, which is funny, because the feminist project is to meld them. I guess it's about comfort levels, and people don't like feeling embarrassed.

Do you think it is easier to talk about it in the abstract?

Yes, definitely. With my housemates, we've become so close that we don't talk about things now that we would have talked about in the first year we were living together, because it's like we're sisters, and it would cross a new weirdness line. We'll talk about sex, but you wouldn't ask, 'Do you like this thing or that thing?' 'What do you normally do in this situation?' We'd only talk about very specific things, or for specific reasons: either there's a problem, or you've learned something new, or it ties in with a wider political conversation.

Did you grow up talking to people around you about sex or wanking?

158

Not at all. I was super late to the conversation – although saying that, I don't actually know what is 'normal' or what is late. I didn't start talking about it until my second or third year of uni, which is when I developed a close group of girlfriends. That's really late, isn't it? Given most people at that age are 'sexually active'. I always think of that line in the film *Juno*, where she says she hates how adults use the term 'sexually active'. And even now, I have those conversations looking back on my wanking journey, but that's with women. I don't really know the situation with a lot of my guy friends. My housemate was talking yesterday about how he used to have wet dreams and I was a bit taken aback. I was interested to hear about it, I thought it was cool to hear him talk about it, but I suppose that reaction speaks to the fact that I'm still not totally used to having those nitty-gritty conversations with men.

I've found it easier to talk to male friends about wanking, and sex in general.

Really? About their wanking? Your wanking? Both?

Both. When I was growing up there was this blanket of silence among my female friends that felt oppressive. I remember really clearly being – wow, this is so nuts to think about – being sixteen or so, there was a girl that I was friends with and we were talking on the phone. She'd spent the night with this guy, and she was saying how they hadn't had sex but he'd fingered her, blah blah blah, it was so dreamy, etc. I think I was irritated by the way she was talking about it, I was probably jealous because she was hot and popular with all the boys. Anyway, I remember saying to her – and I think at the

159

time I maybe had a sense this was a risqué question – Did you come? So she said, 'Hahahahaha, what do you mean?!' For her, 'come' meant 'ejaculate'. It was something men did. I had this real sense of shame, and thought: Shit, I shouldn't have said that. For me this ties into the whole thing that it's fine to talk about sex as long as you're talking about the man's pleasure, but anything around a woman feeling anything other than 'it's so dreamy' was super embarrassing. That's kind of how we were raised, I guess.

I don't think I could have asked that question at sixteen. I don't think I knew what that was. It's scary with how many people that's still the conversation, right? Sex equals men's pleasure.

When we talked in the café, you mentioned watching a porn marathon over lockdown with your housemates. What's it called again? Sleazefest?

Smutfest.

What was that like? Were there any points where you felt turned on, or they were turned on, and was that acknowledged?

Most of the time I wasn't turned on, but it was a really exciting experience to watch porn communally. I wasn't turned on to 'I'll just excuse myself I'll be back down in ten' kind of levels. One of my housemates wrote down the names of the directors or the actresses to look up later. There was lots of running commentary, sharing thoughts and analysis. Then there would be times when everyone was really quiet, and that was perhaps when everyone was turned on. In some ways, it's weirder to

160

say, 'This is really hot.' It's way easier to say, 'Oh my gosh, what are they doing!' We've joked since about how fun/funny it was, but it's not like we ever followed up and asked one another, Have you tried that thing, or did you find that director?

We also go to a virtual strip club together. It's really cool, run by a sex workers' union. It feels double-edged – in some ways it feels good to be paying for sexual services, but sometimes I do feel a bit weird about that. We pay for an entry ticket, and they have additional things you can pay for, like a private dance. One time we paid a fiver each for an ice cube for Jessica Risqué, and she was massaging her boobs with it. The other week, we paid for a private dance, so we got put in a breakout room with this one performer. That was interesting, because we had to negotiate between us, and work out how much we would all put in. I attended the night 'virtually' on my own once, because we'd all paid for the ticket and then no one was up for it that night, and that wasn't as enjoyable because it wasn't fun and communal.

Did you say that Smutfest was 'ethical'?

Yes, the whole thing was that it had to be ethical, and there was a range of different kinds of porn. Some of it was very explicitly queer, some was focused on centring fat bodies, some was surreal shit like people dressed in lobster costumes running around Berlin, and then some was back-of-the-taxi-type stuff, which I think is really hot. So a full range, but the common denominator was that it was 'ethical', and there was a discussion on the event page about what ethical porn is.

Do you feel at peace with porn, and how it is in the world?

161

Definitely not. What kind of porn; who's in it; the individual and the structural impacts – I feel different about all of those things in turn. It's such a politically sensitive topic. I'm conscious of trying to be sex-work positive, and pro advocating for sex workers, to the point that I can get myself tied in knots. I worry about the gap between what I say in my politics and what I do in my bedroom. Back with my ex, I was on his computer while he was in the shower, and I went to type in a web address, and it autofilled all the recent suggestions, and it was pornhub.com forward slash eight person gang-rape or something. I didn't say anything at first and then I was like, I'm going to have to because I can't move past it, so I said, 'What the FUCK did I just find on your computer?' I was absolutely livid. There was no way I would have sex with him that night. I couldn't even look at him. It was mortifying. Just so disappointing to know he was sexually turned on by something violent and lacking consent.

I understand that is some people's fantasy – men and women – and I'm hesitant to kink shame, but as someone who has been sexually assaulted various times, I felt it impacted my sense of trust and ability to be vulnerable with him. This happened years ago; I'd like to think I'd be able to have an interesting conversation about it if it happened now. With that ex, he couldn't quite put his explanation of why he watched it into words, and I think he was always conscious of the fact that a big thing within our relationship was how I was struggling with the fact it was a heterosexual dynamic. There was always this benchmark of 'he's never feminist enough'. With another, more recent ex, he was quite good – probably too good – at explaining his choice of weird or violent porn away, by saying that it's very much in the fantasy

162

domain, there's a very clear distinction to reality, so it doesn't matter what he or other men watch. I've heard some porn stars in interviews say the same thing. He said that most of the porn he watches is not stuff he'd want to do in real life. I have an example of that, actually; I know he watches porn on watersports stuff, and I asked if he wanted to do it, so we toyed with the idea for a bit, but ultimately didn't. That's crazy to me. It's so different to how I understand and engage with porn and fantasy. I also can't help but not fully believe that it's entirely in the realm of fantasy. What's also crazy to me is that I then felt somehow rejected or not enough, because he didn't want to do the things with me that he watches happen with porn stars. Part of my problem is in believing that people are competent enough, in a world where no one's allowed to talk about it, that we're suddenly going to have all these tools where we can separate the reality and the fantasy.

So both those exes you mention watch porn on things they allegedly don't want to do in real life. I find myself wondering: Even if that's true in the specifics, there's a separate question about the underlying outlook. Almost all straight porn is heavily weighted towards the man in terms of power dynamics, unless you're specifically searching for things that aren't like that. We have enough of that misogyny in daily life and I wonder if porn drives that more.

Hmm, that's where I don't know. A lot of sex-positive ethical-porn related people, sex workers, are trying to dismantle that narrative. But hearing you saying out loud that porn is geared towards men's satisfaction and power, I can't think of a situation where it's not, and that's scary. But it's very chicken and egg, it's an iterative process. It spurs on that sense of wielding power over another person being a turn-on, and makes a lot of money out of doing so.

It sounds like you had those conversations with that ex about what you were both watching?

No. It would come up when related to specific acts. I discussed it with him after we broke up actually, because when I look back, I see signs in our sex that I think are a result of him watching too much porn, or being too reliant on it. Do you know what's so funny: he even told me that he specifically didn't talk to me about some stuff he watches because I once told him the story about that gang-rape discovery with that other ex, and after telling him, I said, 'If you watch anything, ANYTHING, that isn't feminist, don't ever tell me because I'll never look at you the same,' and so he was hesitant to ever talk about it. When the feminism comes in it messes it. That's what's sad – the conversation gets shut down.

If I'm going to have a proper relationship with this person, if I'm going to be with them for a long time, then I don't want to have this as a taboo subject. I can't not know. At the same time, I also feel like I'm going to react really badly.

Why couldn't you not know? Does a long-term or serious/meaningful relationship mean that at some point you need to know what kind of porn they watch, or how they watch it?

It's more the idea that there's something about this person I supposedly love that I can't know, because it would horrify me too much, and I'm therefore deliberately choosing not to look at it. That feels terrible. That doesn't mean I think that within a relationship you have to talk about and share every tiny detail of your lives, but I hate the idea of things that must remain secret, an unbreachable gulf, which is a thing in a lot of straight relationships. It's weird that we've got to this place.

In my head, you wouldn't be in a relationship if you couldn't communicate that. Say your partner said, Well, we could talk about it but that's something I view as the last bit of my sexuality that's only for me, and therefore I'd like to not have you involved. Would that be an issue?

Is that how you see it working in a 'healthy' relationship?

I would much prefer a dynamic where you could talk about it. But in the past I have had bad boundaries, so it wouldn't surprise me if someone were to turn around and say, No we're not going to talk about this. I think I want to know for a 'healthy' reason, but actually the reason isn't entirely healthy. I'm hiding behind my politics, but actually I just want to know what you're wanking to, probably so I can then beat myself up that I'm not that.

I've had that same worry before, but when I've been in relationships with women, it hasn't worried me at all. I have wondered whether they wank, and what kind of porn they wank to if they use porn.

But it's intrigue, not a threat.

Yeah! I come to the conclusion that, whatever she's watching, it's totally fine, I don't really feel threatened and I don't even really need to know. With men, I feel like: Are you pretending

165

to be nice to me but secretly fantasizing about hurting women?

The threat of gendered and sexual violence. My friend recently told me, following the Sarah Everard media coverage, that she feels more stressed and concerned that she's supposed to find men threatening, because she doesn't on her day to day. I've been thinking about that a lot. I don't have that many men in my life, I surround myself with women and I work mostly with women, and so that threat isn't there that much. But when I start to unpick how I interact in public, how I feel around men, the mitigations I make when having sex with men, I absolutely do feel threatened by them. When you dig around into what porn means, and its consumption, it feels like a microcosm of wider society – like with the threat of violence and the exploitation. It's weird that it's not on the agenda. People know you're supposed to talk about who cooks and who cleans so you can try to work towards your relationship not operating within the patriarchy, but I don't feel like porn is part of those conversations. Where are your red lines around it, you know? Like with my ex: what if someone said to you, 'I watch rape porn, but I wouldn't ever rape you'? That sounds like a crazy question, but it's one I've been faced with.

It's the politics versus the practice... I would like to be totally fine with it.

So for you the end goal IS being totally fine with it?

Oh, I don't know. I know, with rape porn, the whole argument is: Just because you fantasize about this, it doesn't mean that

166

you want it to happen to you or you want to enact it. Yet I in-
stinctively feel better about the thought of a woman watching
rape porn than a man, and that's about the violence aspect.
How much does it tie into the worldview that this is the sexy
dynamic? I think it's really hard to gauge.

Definitely. I have a friend who is into quite heavy BDSM
stuff – I don't know about rape, but I think she would be
pro-rape fantasy – and I struggle with it, but I definitely
feel less responsibility lies with her, because she's a
woman. Sometimes I get myself in such tangles about
the question of where your responsibility lies in terms
of your fantasies. I'd like to feel that everyone's entitled
to their fantasy for whatever reason it exists, whatever
childhood trauma or fantastic childhood experience
it comes out of, but I don't think that. I do think people have responsibility towards their desires, at least
sometimes. The kind of man I go for, even for dating,
not even just for sex, is quite harmful for me, and I have
a responsibility towards myself to not perpetuate that,
even though it's what I naturally go for. I think a similar
thing applies to sexual fantasy.

What's interesting about this iteration of porn is how whatev-
er you want is right there, and nobody has to know. There's
no human interaction or transaction needed, because all you
need is a screen and an internet connection, and so it does
create this new – not exactly permissiveness around it – but
maybe there is less space for the thinking mind to intervene.
Perhaps it's easier for things to escalate?

I'm a TikTok user, and I love it, but what I'm alarmed
by are the number of BDSM TikToks I see from people
much younger than me, eighteen or so. You could say it's

167

my algorithms and it's probably being geared towards me, but when I went home recently, I sat behind my seventeen-year-old sister's shoulder while she was scrolling, and it comes up on hers too. I worry this is a boomer attitude, but I really do fear for a lack of boundaries and regulation. I discovered what porn was because – I don't know if you remember this brand called Bang On The Door? They used to make children's pencil cases. One day I was at a sleepover and we typed in bangonthedoor.com, because we thought that was how the internet worked, we didn't know about Google, and that was how I saw that site, a porn site. Looking back now, it's obvious that bangonthedoor.com could well be a porn site.

How old were you?

I think I was still at primary school. I didn't fully understand what sex was and I found a porn site. We were all crowded round a computer that was shared by her whole family. I can't imagine the context that parents are dealing with now. A huge worry for me when it comes to porn, especially with regard to my sister, is that it leaves nothing to be discovered, and that she's straight in at the deep end. And that, crucially, means lots of expectations placed on her.

There are always pros and cons aren't there? One of the pros to increased access to porn is that the kink and fetish community might not be so marginalized. Although in part they're built from being marginalized: you don't want to make it so mainstream that every other person on TikTok is talking about it. Also, is it a good thing that it's being talked about more? I'm not sold on that, but I do think it could be a good thing. Is TikTok better than whatever I was doing then: watching *Sex and the City* and reading *Cosmo*?

Where you feel you're skirting around the edges and not actually seeing the real thing?

And then you wonder, does easy access to porn mean there's less knowledge sharing and exchange between friends? My friend told me that they used to practise giving head on Mini Rolls. Her and the girls at a sleepover would buy a pack of Mini Rolls and practise together. That probably is not going to happen now.

I realized that when I hear you say porn, my first thought is the not-good stuff. Is that what you mean when you're asking questions about porn?

That's the thing, isn't it? It's so hard to be nuanced when talking about porn so generally. When you watch porn do you watch 'good stuff'?

I haven't watched porn in ages. What's the good stuff? When I say I haven't watched porn I'm talking about videos on streaming sites, but there's a whole range of things that could be interpreted as porn. I'm subscribed to a couple of OnlyFans accounts, for instance. Then there's Instagram, which isn't porn but you can get porny Instagrams, and I follow quite a few ethical sex worker type people on there. I have watched more stereotypical porn in the past, Pornhub and so on, but I've never been worried about my porn consumption. The only thing I've been worried about is the kind of porn I was watching, and I did notice when I was watching it that it would become regular, and I didn't want to wank without it, so I immediately stopped. Sometimes I get worried about that with my sex toys, but I think that's different.

That you can't do without them?

Yes. Then I don't, and it's great, and I think, I'm okay, I'm fine. When I think of my male friends who now have a fifteen-year-long relationship with porn, there's no way they could just rebuild it like that, as I can by turning the porn off and putting the sex toys away. Or at least, the friends I've spoken to can't.

I don't want to be too gender essentialist about this, but from talking to both men and women about porn and wanking, my sense is that, for so many men, porn = wanking, wanking = porn – they are inseparable. Whereas for women, my impression is that, even if women sometimes wank to porn, it's not as straightforward...?

That chimes with my understanding. My ex gave up porn a couple of months ago, because I encouraged a porn break. We were fully broken up by that point but he went along with it out of curiosity, I think. I tried to pick the conversation back up and he wasn't very forthcoming, but he did say that he had a couple of wanks that were really great, but overall he struggled to stay hard. That was interesting to me. I instantly thought, Thank fuck that's not my problem anymore, because if we were going to be in a relationship that would need to be addressed. Also, that's so sad and limiting. I accept that, from what I can tell of my female friends, my wanking is more on the unusual side in that I'll wank when I'm driving and in public places, and if I couldn't do that, that would take away a lot of the fun for me, because I'd need to be on my phone, watching porn at the same time. I feel sad for the men for whom that's the case, and there're probably some severe political implications as well. For their own sakes it's sad, and they are hardening themselves: do anything every day and you become dampened.

I've listened to relatively mainstream podcasts suggesting that men who watch these particular kinds of bodies and this particular kind of sex for too long are then physically unable to be aroused by 'imperfect bodies'. I don't see porn bodies as perfect, but if that's what you're used to, perhaps they are? They're hyper-sexualized, at least.

My best friend who's a guy, and who I know watches quite a lot of porn, said that as much as he loves porn, when he's having sex in real life, he wants jiggle. What's really sad is that I remember feeling in school like I wasn't entitled to sex unless I looked like the women in porn. Again, it's that question of the pro-porn people being over-reliant on the understanding that people can separate those things. I listened to this fantastic podcast about an Asian-American woman who starts exclusively dating Asian men[9]. Asian men are considered the bottom of the dating hierarchy, and the podcast host says: I am of this race, this is ridiculous. So she changes what her Instagram feed looks like, and starts only replying to Asian men, only swipes yes to them on apps, and she eventually realizes that what she thought was her type is less her type now. Do you know what would make a good *Black Mirror* episode? If your porn history, your search history, was disclosed before you went on a date with someone. Would people consume porn differently,

9 'A Very Offensive Rom-Com', *Invisibilia*, series 5, episode 5, 5 April 2019.

if they were conscious that people knew what they were consuming?

Shame is still a thing, though. I just sold my old Converses to a foot fetishist, and people kept calling him a pervert. I was saying: Yo, ease up! I'll take his money, he can do whatever he wants with them. If everyone's history was disclosed, we would start having to accept people saying, 'I watched some stuff just to see what it is like.' There would be an understanding that there's some experimenting or some learning going on. Even I don't do that, though; that's what I find funny about people learning from Pornhub. If there's something that I'm not sure about and think I should check out, as soon as I see the thumbnails, I feel like I can't – I actually can't. Part of me understands that your wanking time shouldn't be policed, I understand that you shouldn't be thinking about what so-and-so is going to think if I do this, because I know how detrimental that is. I think it's good to be able to be turned on by what you're turned on by... At the same time, I wish that we didn't live in the patriarchy where people are turned on by women in pain.

Back on the issue of reprogramming or reimagining desire, there is a site I've been obsessed with at various stages called Beautiful Agony, have you heard of it? People of all genders take videos of themselves wanking, but they only show their faces. You would think that wouldn't be sexy, yet it's the hottest thing ever. You have to pay to subscribe, though.

I'm happy to pay. That's one of my biggest issues with porn, that it's created a culture of no paying. Definitely pay for your porn.

I'm increasingly coming around to that way of thinking.

172

Anyway, Beautiful Agony: on a conceptual level, the fact
that it initially sounds quite out there and wild shows up this
preconception that the face alone can't be sexy, or sexy enough.
You need the body for porn. I think we are pushed in certain
directions by what we're told sexuality is without realizing it.

I love how subversive that is. When I'm sending videos
or photos, often I don't include my face, and people say,
Where's your face? I cannot for the life of me do a sexy
face, but also I'm not just going to smile, because that's
weird, almost schoolgirly. I love the subversion of it
being just a face.
    The relationship to money is so interesting, right?
What would happen if there was no free porn?

Well that was how it was until really recently, right?

Nuts. All VHSs!

And magazines.

Would people not push it so far? The person who starts
off being a bit into holding a woman down and who now
ends up wanking to intense rape content: would that
transition not have happened? Or would it have happened but just cost more? Then is the flip side: Would
people experiment less? Maybe you are into some niche
things that are relatively harmless but you wouldn't get
to find out about them?

The analogy I want to reach for here, and maybe this is dubi-
ous, is Amazon Prime. Humanity got on totally fine without
it. Why do you need to have your detergent delivered to you by
9 a.m. the following morning? You don't. Yet if that's offered

173

to you on a plate it's hard to say no. I wonder if it's not the same with porn as well. How many people do you think have developed a porn addiction during the pandemic, suddenly in front of their computers all day?

It must have been really hard for recovering porn addicts. My friend's partner is a recovering porn addict and relapsed during the pandemic. Once the gym reopened, he got addicted to going to the gym instead, because that's what he does instead of wanking. She was very forthcoming about him having the addiction, but not so much on the effects of it. She did say something like, 'It makes me sad because I like more of the making-love style, and having sex outside, and he doesn't like that stuff, he just kind of...' and trailed off. Another friend of mine was dating this guy, and she told me that he could only finish if he was holding her down and pounding her. She didn't enjoy it, but she said other bits of it were nice. It's a mess. It has the capacity to really affect people's relationships, whether we realize that's the case or not.

You mentioned sending nudes before. Are you happy to talk a bit about that?

I was wondering about whether that counts as porn. At the moment, for instance, I'm not having sex with anyone, so when I take a cute nude I'll send it to my friends.

Really?

Yes. I think: It's a good picture, it shouldn't go to waste. I appreciate that's probably not so normal.

174

I can't imagine having that relationship with any of my friends.

It's interesting because it's mostly removing the sexual aspect of the nudity, which I'm all for, so it's just a cute nude. It's not a full frontal of me inserting a toy or anything. But then I don't find that kind of full frontal sexy. If I'm wanking off then I'm enjoying myself, obviously, but with the videos I send guys of that kind of stuff I think: I can't believe you get off on this. They always ask for videos and angles which are close up, which seems so grisly. That's the word I want to use: it's grisly.

NINE

*Nine is a woman in her early twenties and towards the
hetero end of the spectrum. She is currently single and
intends to remain so.*

POLLY BARTON —— *When I mentioned the anonymity
aspect of this conversation you said you weren't particularly
concerned by it. Can you tell me a bit about that?*

NINE —— I think my relationship with porn was one
of the things I worked on early on in my journey of
sexuality, feminism, understanding my relationships
romantically, and all that sort of thing. I've been in the
place I'm in now for a while, and I feel pretty comfortable with it. The other thing is that I feel quite strongly
that the way to change the shame and everything else
that everybody has to work through is to talk about it,
and I feel quite passionate about doing that. I believe that
that's how you change, and it feels good to talk about it.

What was that working through like for you?

I'm twenty-four, so the internet was around when I
was growing up and, like many people my age, my first
interactions with porn were actually my first sexual
experiences. Being twelve, thirteen, feeling horny and
thinking, What can I do about that? My mum's a doctor,
and she was very good at saying, before I needed them,
Here are books, here is this, here is that – especially
compared to what other people's experiences were with
that. I don't think you can really protect your child from
porn, though. I also think it's a difficult thing for girls

176

who are very mature for that age and who don't feel like children, but who absolutely are. Their parents see them as children and these girls see themselves as mature, sexual beings. With my first interaction with porn, there was definitely an element of shame, and that lasted a few years, but that was no longer with me by the age of fifteen, sixteen. Whereas I still have a few friends who don't masturbate. I try to tell them they should, otherwise I don't think they're going to have good sex. But you know, actually, my first interactions with porn were written porn. That remains, to this day, ninety per cent of my porn consumption.

On the internet?

On the internet. A website called Literotica. I stumbled across it at an early age. I read a racy book at one point, and thought, Oh I love that, and then I found this site, and that's been my go-to ever since. I'm thankful for that discovery. Obviously it's got its own world of problems, but still. The other early interactions I found that I liked were with lesbian porn, because it's so much less scary. The men in porn are terrifying. So many of my friends say that they watched lesbian porn to begin with, and they are largely women who identify as straight.

That's me too! Although I don't identify as straight, but I still to this day find heterosexual porn quite a scary territory.

I agree. I want to say hentai was another less scary place, because it's not real. The real-world questions are never triggered in my head. I have always quite liked things that look non-consensual, and that's an impossible thing to explore in real-life porn, because I'm not interested

177

in actual abuse – it's a sexual fantasy, and so real porn is too real in that respect. You can't watch non-consensual porn and not have your brain ask if it's consensual. That's why written stuff and hentai lets you explore that without actually having to consider what that would actually be like in real life. In video porn made with performers, the non-consensual world joins up with the BDSM world, whereas those two things aren't necessarily the same or enjoyed by the same people. There are elements of BDSM I enjoy, but it's not really one of my turn-ons.

For good reason, there isn't convincing non-consensual real-life style porn, and the stuff that is closest to it sends off those alerts in my brain because it's a fantasy and it's not meant to be enacted in real life. I don't want to see the real-life experience. It's meant to be in my head, so I think it's better not looking realistic.

It's a fantasy, which you feel you want to see actualized, but when it's actualized too 'actually' within porn, when it becomes too real, then it's distancing?

And when it's not real enough, it's not doing the job.

Given that, it makes sense that reading would be the ideal thing, because your imagination is supplying all of the turn-on stuff.

Exactly. It's a really big website, based on how many stories are on it, and how current it is, despite having quite an old interface.

Does it work like Pornhub in that you can search for terms?

Yes. I tend to use it by category. You can search by term, but the categories each have top-rated stories, new stories, and that tends to be quite valuable because it's an open platform, there's stuff of all qualities on there. Also, in the last six to eight months, I've found two porn couples I enjoy watching. They're both real-life couples. Their usernames on Pornhub are Jolla PR, and Daddy Long Dong – I don't know why they went for that name, because it doesn't align with what they're selling. The fact that they're real-life couples makes it radically different, and they're quite different from each other, too: Jolla PR is a married couple living in Texas, both from Puerto Rico, Spanish-language. It's more glamorous in a way – not full glamour by any means, especially not by porn standards, but they obviously really like each other. They'll play out scenes, but they don't commit to the scenes at all. It's just two people who love each other. The other couple are a very normal couple who've decided to film themselves and put it online and it's very unglamorous, watching-TV sex. I've quite enjoyed both of these couples.

I can imagine that even if there are performative elements there, the connection would be more believable. This is what I can't get past when I watch most porn: I'm always hoping that it's consensual, but I just can't believe most of the time that they're truly feeling desire. Whereas to see people being genuinely turned on...

... is so sexy. And I think that correlates with a lot of feminist porn. I've tried some of it, but I can't really afford it – quite rightly, they want you to pay more, because they're paying their performers fairly well. But even the stuff I have seen hasn't really worked for me, because it's still fake. It's better – there are more realistic bodies, there's more realistic everything – but there's still a lack of actual desire.

Do you equate masturbation with porn? Is it hard to imagine masturbating without it?

My best masturbation is without porn, generally. However, probably eighty per cent of my masturbation is with some sort of stimulus, maybe even ninety per cent. Of that ninety per cent, seventy per cent will be written, twenty per cent will be video. I think it's a question of whether I'm feeling like I would like to enjoy it and be present, or whether masturbation has been motivated by niggling horniness that is a bit boring. It's very hormone driven. Sometimes I won't masturbate for several weeks, and then other times it becomes much more frequent. Sometimes it is just a need, and my motivation then isn't to have the best orgasm I can possibly have, it's just to get rid of that need. Like: There we are, good, now I can get up.

I'm interested in what you said earlier about saying to friends who don't masturbate, How do you hope to have good sex if you don't? That's something I feel quite strongly too, yet I think if I was asked to justify that I might struggle.

The more communicative I've gotten, the better sex has gotten, full stop. That communication comes from comfortableness and comfortableness comes from confidence, and there's an element of that that comes from knowing what turns you on, knowing how to orgasm yourself. Men don't know what the fuck they're doing, especially when you're a teenager: those boys have

180

never had other sexual partners, so they really, really don't know what they doing, and you have to tell them. Boys rarely have that problem because there's less of a shame around masturbating for many men than there is around women masturbating, so it's more common for boys to be like, This is how you do this thing for me. But women aren't doing the same thing. They expect the men to know. Meanwhile the boys are doing nothing pleasurable.

It's also about having the confidence to say, Actually, penetration really doesn't do very much, that's very uninteresting. For me, good sex comes from telling your sexual partners, No, your concept of sex needs to alter here. With the women I know who don't masturbate, it generally ties in with insecurity and the fact that they tend to have sex when drunk. I don't want to label anyone else's experiences for them, but in my experience, those experiences are essentially non-consensual. They're a very common, socially acceptable form of sexual assault. The more insecure you are, the more likely you are to have those horrible experiences.

If you feel a lot of shame around experiencing pleasure and desire, it stands to reason that you would need to be drunk and kind of forced into it to be able to allow yourself that. That sounds really radical and problematic, but I'm saying it because I was a bit like that when I was younger. Maybe not with masturbating, but with feeling desire for someone else. It was like I needed them to do all the work.

That's what makes the consent situation so difficult because the person is actually experiencing desire, but it's also happening in this non-consensual way. It's been a bit of a thing I have consciously tried to do, for

181

the last eighteen months or two years or so, to come to the understanding that actually every single woman I know has been raped. If we understand that, we also have to understand that every single man is also being a perpetrator. Even though I reached the consciousness at a much earlier age that most people have experienced an act of sexual violence, something non-consensual, an experience that they didn't like, didn't enjoy, I think there's something quite powerful about actually labelling it as rape and understanding it in this way. I've found that quite useful.

I've been thinking about this for a number of reasons, partly because I trained as a volunteer on a domestic and sexual abuse helpline, so I was doing a lot of reading around it, and I've recently had a spate of friends and people I know telling me about their history of being sexually assaulted. On top of what's happening in the media. Which, like you say, gives me this staggering sense of how utterly universal an experience it is. So I'm drawn to that way of thinking. I think back to my own past and I've definitely had things which I think I could say were non-consensual, but I didn't experience them as traumatic. And then there have been other things, not pene-trative sex, but times where people have kind of forced things on me that I definitely did find very difficult, and borderline traumatizing. At the same time, I feel that having a differ-ence in degree is important. I don't want to appropriate that label from people who are the survivors of rape where that is devastating and life-shattering. It feels so tricky.

I agree, when you're talking about something that's happened to most women, non-binary folks and many men, you are talking about a whole variety of experi-ences. Like most women who've been raped, I've never

182

reported rape, it has never been by someone I don't
know, and it doesn't define me. But, it's not as though I
don't remember the bad experiences I have had vividly.
And even though I wasn't traumatized by them in the
way in which rape-induced trauma is popularly portrayed, I can still recall them, and name them. I can still
maybe trace elements that *are* trauma, actually – they're
just not that type of trauma. You know, when rough
periods in your life follow certain incidents, and are
representative of those incidents. I do actually think that
most people have gone through that trauma. They have
either just kept it in or haven't even worked through it
themselves, have just seen it as part of life.

Certainly talking to people of the boomer generation, it's
completely that. A few months ago I had a conversation with
a friend of that generation, I think it was #MeToo related, or
maybe I was talking about helpline stuff, and at some point in
the conversation she was like, I've been raped. Off-handedly,
but also with a kind of hardness in her tone. I was silent. Then
she said, Did that shock you? So I said, Yes, I do feel shocked,
and inside I was thinking: I'm shocked largely because of the
way you presented it. I feel absolutely terrible for you, but I'm
not sure where to go, where to take this conversation. I think
there were a lot of things at play for her there, but maybe one
of them was a slight resentment along the lines of, We all just
had to put up with this and be taught it meant nothing, and
there was no invitation to scrutinize that trauma. And now
suddenly the light of attention is being shone on it.

So was that coming from her? Was she implying, What's
the big fuss about?

I don't think she was saying what's the big fuss about. I think it was more, I came from an age when you didn't have the opportunity to make a big fuss about it, when you did just have to push it down. To then be around people who are not pushing it down, at a time when the not pushing down is being celebrated to a certain extent, that potentially creates a kind of rift.

That ties in with understanding trauma, because maybe what's most uncomfortable is acknowledging what a big impact that had. Especially when it's also tied up with relationships with men, in general. And I do just mean relationships with men – it's not in any other relationships, romantic or sexual. It gets directly to the heart of this question: can women live with men and be in partnership with men? And maybe... not?

Can we talk a bit about non-consensual porn and sex and the nature of the turn-on there?

This is really interesting. I've expressed this in several different ways and every time I disagree with myself later on. Fairly recently, in the last year, I slept with someone and we had a conversation about it, and I said to him, There's an element where women learn that they shouldn't enjoy pleasure, but if it's non-consensual, well, then they can. There's an element of removing those boundaries, removing control from yourself, and if you're not the one in control, well, then you can't be blamed for anything, which then makes it sexual, etc. Then I was thinking about it afterwards, and thought, Actually, I don't think so. You can approach it in different ways too – at other points in my life I've wondered, Is it because I'm the type of person who would never be submissive in any other aspect of my life, and is that

184

what's fantasy about it? Escaping from that, being a different person, relinquishing control. But then I thought, That's just not right. If that was actually a desire I had, I could just be a bit less that way in real life. So I think it is just a pure sexual fantasy, which I can trace to quite a young age.

I thought about this the other day because of a *Jane Eyre* podcast. I hate *Jane Eyre*, I don't like Gothic books in general. I acknowledge that *Jane Eyre* and *Wuthering Heights* are brilliant books, technically incredible, but they're really not my cup of tea. I'm giving this woman a chance, though, because a lot of her podcasts are about de-stigmatizing books by women, something I feel really passionate about. So I was giving this podcast a trial, and she was talking about the first chapter, which I'd forgotten about, and which was the only bit of *Jane Eyre* I liked, where's she punished by her cousin. I read that sexually, I remember it, and I was quite young, almost pre-puberty, pre-sexual desire. I remember enjoying how she was being punished by her cousin, and I was very uninterested in the rest of the book. I also remember that in a childhood queen-king-servant game I always wanted to be the servant, and being really annoyed when the others weren't bossy enough, weren't in character enough.

Gender is learned so young and it's not like I wouldn't at that age have known subconsciously about sexual desire and how people are allowed to express that, so it's not like it couldn't have been a learned thing at those ages, but I feel like there's something more than the learned stuff. It's not that I don't like romantic sex as well, but there are whole worlds of other types of sex, other kinks, that aren't interesting to me. So it does feel like there's something about submissiveness specifically

185

which I like. It's coming from a place gender has interacted with of course, but feels like maybe it's not.

For a lot of people who are attracted to non-consensual sex, or sex with an obvious power dynamic, it does feel quite innate, and yet the power dynamic in the vast majority of cases is in one gendered direction.

Yes, absolutely. I don't like reading submissive men, they don't turn me on at all. If I'm honest, I'm someone who enjoys power play in the world full stop. With close friends, there will always be an element of that... There's a side of a person's personality that can enjoy games in this way, play games that aren't sexual – although what isn't sexual in real life? – but certainly without the intent of sexual action.

That's taking place as a kind of subtext within your interactions as friends? Or is it more demarcated than that?

A subtext. One example is, in a house I used to live in with a large group of friends, we had a basement living room. Quite a few of us studied politics, and are of this personality, and the thing would be to get someone to go upstairs to get us whatever we wanted. It was a question of who is going to play this game the best, who isn't going to have to get up. There were several of us who were much better at it, and you knew who to target – to the extent that there would be somewhat meta conversations about what just happened. There would be a narrative of me and this other guy always winning and getting a couple of others in particular to do what we wanted. That sort of playing, that style of interaction is what's fun to me, and I think that's probably not unconnected to the

186

sexual thing. Enjoying that kind of power play indicates that I don't just enjoy submission because it gives me permission to enjoy sex, but because it's fun.

It's interesting to hear that you are into that kind of thing, tend to come out on the dominant side, and then suddenly in an explicitly sexual content...

I'm the absolute opposite.

Is that because it's bad for men to be submissive in a patriarchy, but it's also bad for women to be dominant sexually?

A place I think it could come from is that I'm attracted to very masculine-performing men. Which has been the source of quite a lot of comedy, given how unlike me that is politically, socially, and so on. It's always been a great source of joy for my friends to watch this happen and laugh at the type of person I go for. Especially because I'm not a very outdoorsy person, and yet my 'perfect' men are very rugged, mountain types. Things like calloused hands have been a turn-on in the past. I love calloused hands! There are certainly some problematic elements with that attraction, in that I think there is an element of society projecting competence onto those men that they don't have. They are probably more likely not to have done their emotional work. Why do I find that attractive? Why do I want that? Why is it that things like that appeal to me sexually? I believe it is a choice, but also there's a bit of it that feels like it's not a choice. I really do believe it is a choice, and you can definitely decide to change that and say, That's not working for me. But the other part of me says: But I really like these kinds of men!

This keeps coming up in conversations and what I read: this question of the malleability of desire, of being torn between two untenable positions. It's problematic to say, for example, I only want to sleep with slim, white blonde people, I know that people's tastes along those lines often just replicate society's hierarchies and systems of discrimination wholesale and I'm OK with that. On the other hand there's the problem associated with making prescriptions about desire, and saying to people, No, you have to find everyone equally desirable. Clearly, neither of those positions are okay, but how do you navigate that huge territory in between? It's hard when it's so unclear how much of what we're feeling comes from social conditioning. The strongest pulls of animal desire I've experienced have been to quite rugged, big, not very emotionally aware but still quite warm in some way, earthy men. Then, afterwards, I think, Where is this coming from? It feels innate, but what is innateness in this context?

Exactly. I'll occasionally also get it with somebody very random. On the spectrum of sexuality, I'm very close to the straightness end, but that doesn't mean that I don't occasionally get that with women and I don't occasionally have those feelings. What is motivating that? Why that woman and not all the others in the world? And actually, when it comes down to it, why not most men? Most people's experience of being on a dating app is, No, no, no, no, no, no, no, hmm, maybe if I have to.

I get the sense you talk to your friends about this stuff a lot.

Yeah.

It's hard for me not to see that as a generational thing. I don't think of myself as a radically different generation to you

188

talking about other things, but this stuff makes me think that I am. When I was at school, no one talked about masturbation, and I've only really talked about it in my thirties, and even then not much. Have you always talked about porn and masturbation with friends?

To different degrees. We've grown into those conversations. I see a difference between me and my sister in that regard, and I'm only four years older than her. I think there was a huge difference between our experiences, and I put it down to whether you had a phone. I had a phone, but I didn't have an iPhone. They came out when I was around thirteen. By the time I was seventeen, everyone had a smartphone. When my sister came to secondary school, when she was eleven, everyone already had smartphones, and online spaces created a dialogue, an education, that allowed her to understand sexuality as fluid much earlier. She and her friends operated with the default understanding that there was just a fluid spectrum, and nothing essential about it – whereas, say, in my friendship group, it was more like you identified as one thing. So even in those four years, there was this shift towards the understanding that I now feel to be the right one. I feel like it was similar with stuff about sex and porn, in that people of my age weren't having these conversations at fifteen. Probably by seventeen, though, everybody understood that everyone masturbated and we were all interested in promoting a lack of shame around that, a narrative of sexual agency.

Does your respective porn consumption come up in relationships?

It has come up. When men bring it up, it's very easy

to recognize how problematic it is. I can think of one partner who clearly was incredibly insecure and had a difficult relationship with porn and sex, and he would want to watch porn whilst having sex. And that's obviously completely fine.

Is it completely fine?

It is, but it wasn't in this instance. I can see how hypothetically in certain situations, it would be. In this instance, I just felt, Oh, you poor child. I knew he was quite interested in me, that we were having a really nice time, and actually watching porn wouldn't do anything for anyone, but his relationship with it was such that he needed it. I felt: Aww, go work through your issues.

A kind of addiction, but also serving a function of giving him confidence and muting the scariness of an actual, other body?

A familiarity, exactly. A male friend of mine believes that when he masturbated less and watched porn less, he had much more impetus to pursue a relationship and to find someone. Men have the ability to discuss with friends earlier on that they're watching porn, and definitely lack that shame around it. If you haven't yet spoken to someone with a penis about Death Grip, that's a good conversation. I would also say that in their desire to not be hyper-masculine, men will shut up about porn with close male friends because they recognize the problematic way in which it's discussed largely between men. So then I'm either the one leading the conversation with my male friends about sex, or it's happening more with my female friends than between men.

The last serious relationship I had was with a man who was really sheepish about porn. I found that problematic. I felt like: Okay, you might not feel proud of it, but don't hide it from me. But I'm not without understanding, now, why that might happen.

This is part of a general problem, isn't it? It goes for other experiences, too: as a white woman, I'm not going to think about race as much as I think about gender, because race is not in my face in the way gender is. Thinking about race is a much harder thing that I have to consciously do. I often think about that in relation to one of my main problems: there are no men of my age with whom I can have the sort of relationship I want. My female friends and I have been thinking about this stuff so long, and they've just started thinking about it. I feel like they've got another ten years before we can have a conversation.

A lot of my best friends are queer men, and I often find myself wondering why I don't meet straight men who have this degree of awareness about this stuff. If you are in a relationship with a man, are you likely to talk to them about porn and feel curious about their consumption?

Yes. I would be likely to talk to them about it. I don't think I would be very curious about it. I wouldn't really care unless it was problematic.

Do you find that most men's relationships to porn are not problematic, then?

No, on the contrary, I do find that most are problematic. In the last year or so, after quite a big heartbreak, I was very angry, and felt like I was being forced by the world to not be with men because they're all inept and incapable. That I was being forced into the position of deciding that I couldn't be in a relationship with a man. And as I got over that pain, it got reframed into a choice. All those things I was thinking all are completely true, but actually this is a choice I'm making, and a really important part of that for me was disassociating my desire to have children with partners. I've always known I wanted children from a very young age, it feels really important and clear to me. So about eight months ago, I decided that they're not the same thing, and they will never be the same thing and I will have children – even if I am in a partnership – completely by myself. I'm not going to do that with a partner. That's been really liberating. There could be something that might last ten years or something, but it's not going to be for life. Right now, I want to maintain my own place. I just cannot see how you don't sacrifice everything otherwise, you know?

So now, the men I see myself having conversations with about porn are friends, not sexual partners. I don't really care unless I'm emotionally invested in the person. I don't think it's impossible for me to be emotionally invested in a sexual partner – it's just not what I imagine happening in the next year or so. When you have a conversation with your friends about porn and everyone unpicks their relationships with it, that's good work, and if they do have a problematic relationship with it, it doesn't affect your sexual relationship. And then with any sexual relationship, if you're not committing to a heteronormative relationship where you are a unit and their problems are your problems, then suddenly that problematic relationship with porn is their own thing to deal with and it's not on you.

I think that's where that answer is coming from: the sense that I'm not going to do that for a man, and that their relationship with porn says nothing and means nothing about my sexual relationship with them.

I can see how just saying, Yeah, if we're just having sex, I don't really need you to be my custodian, would be really liberating.

Me and another friend have reached this place at similar times, and I think it comes from having difficult experiences with our dads in particular ways. I don't think it's a conclusion I wouldn't have reached otherwise, but I think that's basically why it's suddenly come to me. Both of us felt confronted by having to sacrifice something by being with men, even when they are loving, kind, nice, and even across different family setups. In my family, for instance, my mum was the main breadwinner and that was never really a problem. And yet, these things still become a problem because men aren't capable. That big heartbreak was with a very close friend who was the best partner I could possibly imagine. That was what was really hard about it, because I felt, if it's still an impossibility for someone to be in an equal relationship *even with you*, then where's the hope? It's obviously not *these men*, it's all men. There's something you can't do in nuclear arrangements, no matter how liberal you are, how socialist you are, how much you think you've changed.

I imagine that removing that sense of pressure and expectation of finding this miraculous nuclear arrangement that will work suddenly takes a lot of pressure off. You can still potentially be in a long-term partnership when you're not buying into the myth.

That's how I hope it will pan out. Also this understanding that people are different people at different stages in their lives. Why is it ever going to make sense that someone who can be a good partner at one stage in your life is going to be a good partner at another stage?

Also, I know times are changing, but you're twenty-four, and I imagine if you're not looking to date someone who's several decades older than you, it would be virtually impossible to find a man with like a quarter of what you've got going on in the emotional maturity department. Twenty-four-year-old men are...

Babies. Absolute babies emotionally. Completely not in touch with themselves. Even the really good ones: babies. If you're a girl you're more likely to take on emotional responsibilities in the household. I've gone through certain experiences and have grown from them. I don't think that other young women should have to go through those experiences, but it does often happen that young women go through these sexual experiences at quite a young age, and by the time you're out of it, you have all these experiences. Whereas for men, sexual experiences start a bit later, and are a bit less complicated. I think a good example is that some of my friends had their first sexual experiences within a relationship, it might have been only a façade of a relationship but even that façade seems to have made a difference to the experience. For those of my friends who didn't experience the safety of that façade, first sexual experiences are often more violent and scary. I think for a lot of men, sexual experiences might happen in those proto-relationships, where there's this idea that you're exchanging more than just sex. It might be more common for young women

194

to have nastier experiences that are just exchanges of sex. I think that's also the case for gay men. I know my gay friends growing up have had really transactional, horrible experiences. At this age, what do straight men know about those sorts of things? They just haven't had the same experiences. They haven't had to do the same things – of course they're babies. And they are.

TEN

Ten is a gay trans man in his thirties.

TEN — In lots of the movies I watched as a kid or a teenager, there would be coming of age scenes where the boys go through sexual awakenings by finding a magazine. I always wondered: Why never the girls? When the girls do get to do it, it's always a boy doing it to them, whereas boys get to have this adventure with themselves or with each other, conspiratorially finding porn stashes or whatever in the woods. Why is there always porn in the woods? I was always jealous of the boys getting to come of age and have sexual awakenings.

POLLY BARTON — *That's reflected in the discourse around it too. It seemed like boys at school were often talking about this stuff. Even if wasn't in a 'these are my true feelings about pornography' way, it was still a topic of discussion, and it's commonly understood that as a teenage boy you are constantly masturbating.*

And talking about which girls in class you want to bonk.

I imagine it's difficult being part of that as a boy if you're not particularly sexually desirous or you're queer. But growing up as a girl, I couldn't talk about any of that stuff.

The idea that girls have sex drives is still a weird concept to some people. I remember, in high school, when I got my first boyfriend, my thought process was not: He's cute, I want to have sex with him. My thought process was: He's cute, I would let him have sex with me.

196

Sex is a thing that's done to you.

All of my early sexual experiences are tainted by the fact that I had these gender issues. I totally ignored my genitalia for so long, until it started bleeding. I was like, Oh, you're supposed to wash that? I was not engaged at all, so even the idea of trying to masturbate didn't occur to me until guys were telling me, You should masturbate. In college I had friends who'd say, 'You've never gotten off? You should try it.' It was one of my friends in college who told me how one of the girls he knew got off. Eventually, when I was nineteen, I ended up trying her thing and it worked. I was not at all oriented towards any of that for so long.

I watch a lot of videos and get off to them, but they're not necessarily porn. The stuff that I get off to doesn't traditionally have to do with sex at all, actually. Ethically, it's kind of a grey zone, because some of the videos are edited to be porn, but from videos that are not porn at all. So you're consuming people's other videos as porn, which is weird. Porn itself is not that interesting to me, just gross most of the time. It reminds me of how biological and dirty sex is – not morally, but in a physical way. All the juicy stuff is gross. I hate getting stuff on my hands, or anything wet or sticky. Sex is a nightmare because there are body fluids all over the place. Even the lube freaks me out. Oh my God, now there's lube on my hands! What the fuck! Porn reminds me of all the things I don't like about sex.

Can you say more about the videos that aren't but are porn?

I should back up and explain that a bit, shouldn't I? Something happened when I was twenty or twenty-one.

197

I was with my first serious boyfriend at the time, the first I had sex with. We were living together, and one day we were at a party and basically the fetish thing got triggered, and I got turned on at this party. That was the moment I realized that the feeling I've always had around this thing was sexual. All these moments from my past, some going back to childhood, and sketchy stuff I had done in the past, started appearing to me, and I realized they were all sexual. By this point I was freaking out, and started saying, 'We have to go home', and crying. I ended up telling him about it. I was realizing that there were games I played as a kid that were about it, or stuff I watched online or did in chat rooms, and that I was getting turned on without realizing that I was turned on. Or maybe I thought I was turned on, but that turned-on feeling made me think it was bad. The realization that all the stuff I'd done was connected to this thing was so strange.

One time I was babysitting a kid and things got really weird for a moment. I realized I was being weird and I stopped immediately and I think it was fine. The kid probably doesn't remember and nothing bad (or actually sexual) happened, but I feel so guilty about it because now I think about it and go: Wow, that was a fetish thing, and that was a toddler. Then it brings up these things where you think, Okay, so what are the boundaries of this? How do you enforce them to make sure you're not being a paedophile? Luckily I'm not, so I'm safe from that, but I really feel for people who are paedophiles... Not for those who maliciously go and gratify themselves, but I feel for the ones who struggle with it and try to act appropriately because I know how it feels to have a fetish that you hate.

Are you happy to tell me what it is?

I'm not happy to, but I can. I really hate telling people because it's so embarrassing. I know there are lots of weird fetishes, but I wish it was something a little sexier. I'm into burping. Right? The look on your face is how I feel every day.

I don't know what my face looks like, but there's no judgement in my mind. Just surprise.

I judge harshly because it's so stupid. It's interesting, though. Once you get into it, there are lots of different levels and different kinds of content. I was using my account to comment before I started making videos myself, but I wasn't meeting anyone that way. When I started my channel, though, I also started a Snapchat. I said, If you're into this stuff and you want to trade, hit me up. I have friends who I exchange stuff with on Snapchat. No faces, no real names or anything.

I'm finding it hard to imagine what it is when it's not faces. What is it you're sending on Snapchat?

It's audio, or videos of stomachs, or from the neck down. Some people are into faces. Some people are into getting burped on, some people are into smelling it. I'm not in that zone. For me, it's the audio. Also, after watching countless hours of this stuff, I've been primed to find the stomach attractive, to some extent. There's a lot of overlap with the gaining community – people trying to gain weight – or the vore people... I'm not into vore, but I've grown more tolerant of it because sometimes vore people make good burp videos.

199

What's vore?

Vore is the fetish of wanting to be eaten. You'll find a video where someone is super bloated, pretending they just ate a bunch of people and burping a lot or something. It's so absurd, and everyone is getting off on different aspects of it, so the comments are interesting. You start to see the same people commenting on different videos, so you figure out, Oh that's what this guy is into...

Recently I started talking on Snapchat to this girl. I'm not sure if I ever told her I was trans, so I think at first she just thought I was some guy. I did eventually tell her because things got weird. She's adorable, she'll send me all these emojis and stuff saying how much she likes my videos, but saying it in a way that makes me think: You're totally getting off on this, aren't you? We were talking more and more, and she's so happy to be talking to me and to get any content that I send her. We started getting attached to each other and it started to feel weird because I don't think I'm into girls, you know? I ended up having to tell her that, because we were flirting a lot. We still flirt a lot, but I think we're on the same page now.

I just want to make sure that she wasn't thinking we were going to be a thing, because it was getting intense for a while. Now, she sends me stuff too. She's been teaching herself how to burp. She'll say, 'I'm trying really hard, and sometimes I make really weird noises, but I'll just send it and you can tell me what you think, and I hope it's not too weird.' She's really cute, but it's like: God, what is going on? Why are we this way? So bizarre.

You look smitten when you talk about her.

It's nice to get positive attention from someone, even if it's about something stupid. Sometimes she sends me pictures of the sky and talks to me about it. That's one of her hobbies: looking up at the clouds and thinking about what they look like. Or she'll send me her outfit for the day or something. Not recently, actually – we've been toning it down a bit since our talk. It's hard because in terms of the fetish stuff, I'm actually pretty bi.

With the fetish stuff, does gender not really come into it?

No, which is interesting, because lots of people are pretty picky. They say, I only want to see hot guys burp, or, I only want to see girls burp. Whereas, even with people I would normally be frankly repulsed by, if they're doing the content, I can get over it and even find it pretty hot. I'll pretty much watch anybody except kids. I don't watch kids. Although lately there's been this kid who popped up in search, I think he's Russian, but he's not eighteen. Yet he's making fetish vids and wanting feedback and looking for a girl. I look at that and think: You should not be here! Run away!

You talked about that moment of discovery at a party, when you talked about it with your ex. In relationships since that, have you brought it up with people? Or does it feel like two separate worlds?

I've been trying to more, actually. Right before the pandemic, I was seeing this guy – I guess the last time I saw him was April last year. It was a weird relationship because he's married, but he's been cheating for twenty years or so. He realized he was gay but he doesn't hate his wife. He just wants to be gay. I thought, Well, if you've been doing it that long, I guess I'm accepting this lifestyle that you've created and taking advantage of it for my own benefit. So we were essentially friends with benefits and he said he would do it. He said, 'So can I just drink a Coke or something?' Yes, yes he can. So he was going to do it, but then the pandemic happened and I don't like his attitude around Covid. It was stressing me out, so we just fell out of touch. Then there was another guy who also said he'd do it, but he turned out to be an asshole, which made me think, Why did I even have this conversation with this guy? I really am not interested in the whole world knowing about this, you know?

Because it feels vulnerable and scary to talk about it?

Yeah. My experience has been that most people think it's weird, or they'll laugh, but they'll be fine with it and say it doesn't matter. Lots of people have their own weird things. The guy who turned out to be an asshole was into getting peed on and stuff. If you trade weird things it's a little easier, I guess.

What about in long-term relationships?

I was with one guy for a while, but we never talked about it. I can't remember if I told him or not. I don't think I did. If you don't tell someone, you can secretly enjoy it if you happen to catch them, because people burp all the time. It's pretty easy to hear someone, even outside, and certainly if you're living with them, so you can secretly enjoy it if they don't know. But then you wonder, If I tell them, are they going to be self-conscious, or are they going to use it to tease me? Is it going to be awkward and stupid?

202

When you want to get off, is that always the go-to thing?

It is now. Originally, when I first started getting off, I got off in the shower using the water stream. That was what my friend told me his friend did. When I studied abroad, I happened to have a tap in the bath that was the perfect size of jet and strength and everything. The first time I orgasmed, it was an out-of-body experience. It was insane. I was looking down at myself and thinking, What are you doing? It felt really strange, I don't even really know how to describe it. Anyway, I did that and obviously there were no visuals there, there wasn't even any fantasy involved. There was no thinking about anything. It was: Let me see if I can get this thing that's supposed to feel good to feel good. I somehow managed to do it, so for a while it was just that. Let's get the thing to feel good again, okay, cool, it works, I can do this now. Yay.

I almost never come with guys. There are two guys who've ever gotten me off and they were both more than ten years ago. There's probably reasons for that which aren't just that guys are inept. I could be more patient and actually put effort into it, but it's just a pain. I'd rather move on to the fucking than mess around. That's just my opinion. I've never come from vaginal stuff like intercourse. So most of the time I just don't get off. I'm trying to think of when I bought my first vibrator. That's when I started thinking about sexual stuff: fantasies and so on. Once I learned how to make it work, I didn't have to focus so much on what I was doing, so I could think about other stuff. So then I would start to fantasize. At that point, I knew I had the fetish, but I hated it so much that I didn't want to do it. And then I think I must've just gotten curious one day, and tried it out when I was using my vibrator. Once you start leaning on it, you're kind of screwed. It's like that with a vibrator in general. Relying on a vibe and porn is just screwing yourself over, at some point. How are you ever going to have good sex if you're doing that all the time? But then, frankly, how are you going to have good sex if you're single and in a pandemic?

To answer your question more directly: yes, I'm always watching that stuff. I never watch porn because porn doesn't really turn me on that way. Even if it turns me on, it's not going to get me to a point that I can come. The fetish is really good at that.

It's a fast-track to that?

Yeah. Which is bad, probably, but it's also good, because I like getting it over with. It doesn't have to be a whole thing, especially when you're by yourself.

You said that you've been speaking about the fetish a bit more, trying to be a bit more vocal about it. Does that come out of a feeling that it would be nice to come with a man?

I don't know. Really, I'd like to just do normal sex stuff and not care. I've never done the fetish stuff in real life – I've gotten close those couple of times when people said they would, but I've never done it with somebody else before. That's another bridge that you can't really return from once you've crossed it. Not only with that person, but in general, in your life. Now you've done the thing. Which is funny to say, considering how many other 'things' I've done. But I don't even consider it an essential part of a relationship, honestly. Maybe it would be fun, but I'm already so complicated that the chances of someone who wants to do that and is okay with a trans person and so on... My criteria are pretty difficult and frankly, I don't really care. I can enjoy sex in other ways. At least, I think I can enjoy it without getting off? I mean, it'd be nice to get off. I do find that me not getting off is also putting pressure on the guy, though, because if no one gets off, then it's really depressing.

When you say it's not solely about them being inept, but you find it kind of difficult... Do you do a 'let's just do what you want to do and not focus on me' thing?

Possibly. Sex is easier when I'm just being used. In a nice way, you know? In a respectful way. It's mentally more fun for me that way, too, because I can chill out. I'm also lazy, to some extent.

You alluded earlier to the grey zone, ethically speaking. Can you explain that?

There's a type of massage that's specifically for making people burp – I believe it's from Indonesia. People upload these videos and it's obvious that some people in the comments are watching it as porn, basically. Certainly, that's what I'm doing. I can't really decide what these people are putting the videos up for. Do they know that they're tapping into this weird community, or are they just trying to advertise their massage therapy? Or what? There are lots of people who make compilations. They'll clip every time a cute YouTuber girl burps and make a three-minute video of it. Or someone will do a gamer burp compilation and clip all the burps out of game streams. Those are always really goofy and crazy because gamers are always just drinking their energy drinks and annoying each other over their mics. Frankly, there's too much laughing in those for me... It's a serious business.

That must create an illicit feeling, to be watching something for sexual kicks when you know the person creating the content possibly had no idea. Hearing you talk, I feel amazed by the sense of a community existing around this. You talked about the fetish stuff coming as a moment of revelation, that this was and always had been a thing for you, but what was it like to discover that there were people who felt a similar thing? Did that come soon after?

No, it took a while. I never really thought that I must be the only person in the world who feels this way. It felt nice to find a community, but we're still a bunch of weirdos. It's interesting how specific everyone is too – the specific kind of stuff they make, or the stuff they're into.

I know you have a lot of self-loathing around it, and you wish it wasn't that way, but do you think becoming a part of these communities and finding out what different people like has made you more tolerant of what turns other people on?

I've always been pretty chill about other people's stuff. I'm always harder on myself, no matter what it is. I try to be pretty honest. I did so much stuff with one guy when I was twenty-two. We did everything. He peed on me. We did so much stuff that I never even wanted to do or would think of doing, but having done it, I can kind of understand all these things, now.

I have been thinking about that recently, the peeing. I've never done it, I should say. When I was a teenager, and I found out what a golden shower was, I had a pure reaction of:

why the HELL would anyone ever want to do that? At that time I found peeing and puking and any kind of loss of control of bodily functions in other people quite traumatic. Then, at some point, I don't know when, that shifted to being like, Yeah, I'd be up for giving that a try. I don't know what the mechanism is by which that changes.

When you first hear about it, all you can think is: It's pee! You don't think about the mental aspect of it. I would have done it more if he wanted to, I think he was experimenting and it didn't really do much for him. But if he'd liked it, I would have done it again. It's pretty easy to do: you just sit in the bathtub and get peed on.

When I first heard about it, I assumed it would be in bed, and I was thinking about how messy everything would get.

I'm sure some people are into it that way. There's an infinite number of things that people get off on. So interesting and so stupid. I feel bad for all of us, honestly. When you think about it, sex itself is also really repulsive. There's nothing inherently better about being turned on by a giant cock. Right?

There's something almost nice about the fact that you've had this since childhood. Nothing that turns me on now turned me on then, so in a way I feel almost envious of you having this thing that's just been there, with you.

No, it's a nightmare. Seriously. As a kid, we played this game where we made up a fake illness where you couldn't stop burping. We'd stick pillows up our shirts, and then the nurse would take the pillows out slowly. Back then it was just this weird game that we played. We played tons of other games, too, of course, but —

Was this with your brothers and sisters?

Yeah, and the neighbourhood kids and whoever was down to pretend.

I wonder whether those are all the people in the community watching your videos.

I hope not.

ELEVEN

Eleven is a straight British man in his early eighties, with a partner who lives separately.

POLLY BARTON —— *What do you remember about your first encounter with porn?*

ELEVEN —— If we take porn as it's probably recognized now, I never saw anything like that until I was in my forties. But if you take porn as something which arouses people sexually, either deliberately or by accident, then there was material around long before internet porn, which did sexually arouse – me personally, and other people. Maybe it makes sense to divide up my experiences with porn into different phases, the first of which when I was between fifteen and twenty years old, so roughly 1955 to 1960, which is when I suppose a lot of youngsters today are looking at internet porn. What was available to me as far as literature was concerned was pulp fiction: detective books, such as those written by Hank Janson, where you always had the glamorous heroine and there were descriptions of her bust, and low cut blouse, and tight dress, etc. Very much like Lee Child these days. When he meets the heroine, he usually describes her in a certain way – and that was about the level of description, or titillation, that you had then in the books. The plots were pretty awful, but they were handed around among friends and people thumbed them, so you knew to open them at the parts where the pages were dog-eared. Then you had two publications, one called *Reveille*, one called *Titbits*. The word 'titbits' had got nothing to do with slang for female breasts, by the way: it just means, as it does now, bits and pieces. Those two papers had girly photographs usually on the front, nothing nude, just bikinis and so on, and salacious stories inside with horse racing and sports information. If you wanted to look at a young lady in a bikini, you went and bought a *Reveille*. Then, of course, the pièce de resistance was the naturist magazines. Top shelf. They were full of busty, young ladies holding balls in the air and so on. Below the waist, they were tucked behind bushes and so on. It was purely above the waist.

What was it like buying those top shelf magazines when you were fifteen or eighteen?

There was an element of embarrassment because all of this was regarded socially as a bit salacious and dirty, so you didn't spread it around. If you bought one you'd get your best friends and go and thumb through it, you know? If you wanted to access female nudity relatively readily, that was about the only way you could do it. Obviously there was pornography around, but young lads and the general public couldn't access it very readily. You had to join special clubs and it was all very hush-hush.

Are we talking magazines, or videos?

Magazines and – well, there were no such things as videos then. They were films, eight millimetre films, so you needed a projector to show them. They were noisy old things, which you had to set up and darken the room. Not that I was involved in that. I'm sure there were folks who were, but what I'm saying is it wasn't readily available. You had to work hard if you wanted to find this stuff. You couldn't get it off the shelf or even through the post.

Living where I used to in Essex, my friends and I would go into the West End, and Soho was a big attraction. You had the Windmill Theatre, where the girls posed with fans. I never went there because I wasn't really too interested – I was much more interested in going up to the jazz clubs that were around at the time. But there were kiosks where you could pay to go in and watch some sort of blue film. Neither myself nor any of my friends bothered with that, and I never met anybody that did, because again, it was all sort of dirty mac business. Very much underground.

Back then, that was the level of exposure I had to – well, it could be called feather-light pornography, really. No erect penises, no full-frontal, everything posed. Nevertheless, and this is the interesting thing, there was stuff available which did arouse me in the way that people are probably aroused watching porn videos today. So that I and my friends could get aroused, could get an erection from looking at these by today's standards pretty innocuous pictures, or magazines, or books.

It felt like it was enough for you?

You couldn't say that it was enough because that was just what was available. You knew no different. When my friends and I were reading a page of fairly salacious writing in a pulp fiction book, or seeing a topless young woman in *Health and Efficiency*, that was as good as it got.

You said that there were no erect penises, but were there any men at all in the nudist magazines?

No. Although I am straight and I don't know whether, if I'd have been gay at that age, there may have been material containing men, but that would certainly have been underground, because it wasn't till the Wolfenden Report in '57 that homosexuality became legal. There were some muscle magazines with men posing: you wonder who might have bought those. But there was certainly no frontal nudity. Then the next phase was *Lady Chatterley's Lover*, which was released in 1960. Now we knew beforehand that there was a book written in 1920s which was a bit rude but that was all, but when it was finally released, suddenly words which were taboo like 'cunt' and 'fuck' came to the forefront in their literal meaning. You hardly ever used those words up until that point.

So Lady Chatterley's Lover *really represented a watershed moment?*

Yes. It was the beginning of the so-called permissive age of the sixties. You could now get a book where you could read those two words, along with fairly explicit descriptions of sex. That led to books like the *Kama Sutra*, *My Life and Loves* by Frank Harris and *Fanny Hill* being published. At the same time, I should mention that the theatre was beginning to become a bit more liberal, the rock musical *Hair* featured a song about masturbation and cunnilingus. I don't know if you're aware of that song? 'Masturbation can be fun.' Suddenly these words were out in the open. *Hair* ran in the West End for a long time. It wasn't a sex show – it was an anti-war thing, protesting Vietnam. There was nudity, but you hardly saw much because the actors danced under a sort of net, so you just saw a few vague shapes. So these explicit words ratcheted the description of the sexual act up one more quite big notch. And all of this gradually fed into everyday language. People would say to one another, 'Oh, I read *Fanny Hill* the other day,' and then discuss it. It became much more open, it wasn't seen as dirty to discuss it. What with the whole fashion and music thing, the sixties was an exciting time to be around, and pornography was just in the mix of that: trying to cast off the old taboos about sex and sexual acts.

Do you remember having some of those conversations with friends?

Yes. I got married during that period, and a lot of my friends got married roughly in the same period of time. We'd have discussions about whether you'd tried the various positions in the *Kama Sutra*, 'split the bamboo' and what have you. My friends and I at the time were clearly aware of this exciting new literature, and we used to discuss things like *Lady Chatterley*: did it need to use these words like 'fuck' and 'cunt', was this just sensation-alism? People were questioning that sort of thing even then.

Would you say that those discussions happened in a group with men and women or did those sort of conversations tend to happen in a single-sex group?

I was very much into sport at the time, but I don't remember ever talking to the guys about the *Kama Sutra* or anything. People were a bit embarrassed about talking about it in a group of all men. In my experience, it was very much a mixed discussion. So in a period of two or three years, you moved from the pre-*Lady Chatterley* state when you didn't discuss it with someone unless you knew them very well to discussing all this stuff with members of the opposite sex.

Was that true of your sexual partners at the time? You could talk about this stuff?

Yes. Many people would buy *Lady Chatterley* and read it together with their partner. I did, and I think my married friends did. You could look at the *Kama Sutra* together and have a giggle about it.

In those discussions, was there any acknowledgement that female masturbation also took place or was it still quite male-oriented in that regard?

Female masturbation came along a bit later. The world of masturbation at that point was very much a male world and my recollection is that female masturbation was not recognized, really. Certainly in the fifties, male masturbation still to some extent had this Victorian pall over it. Bad things would happen to you if you masturbated, you'd grow hair on the palms of your hands, you'd lose lots of energy, it was unmanly. The fifties were really closely linked with the thirties, although there was twenty years' gap between them. The Second World War brought things to a bit of a halt, and pushed things on in some ways, because when young men and young women don't know whether they're going to survive the next day then obviously they really had to live for the moment, so there was a lot of sexuality going on then. Nevertheless, in terms of the pornographic material and everything available to them, those were the times they were living in.

I don't know whether women talked about it among themselves, but as far as I was concerned female masturbation only became a topic a lot later. In a mixed group, women would say, 'I suppose you're getting a hard-on watching this' but there was never a reciprocal thing you would say to a woman about her getting excited. It took time for some men to recognize that, when having sex with a woman, he could help her masturbate and get enjoyment out of the encounter. You know this thing about male penetrative dominance.

I imagine there was a lack of general knowledge about the female orgasm at that stage?

There was a growing awareness of the female orgasm through factual and fictional writing to the extent that some men would 'boast' about bringing their partner to climax. But there was certainly not the 'science of the female orgasm' that there is today. No one had heard of the G-spot, for example.

Moving back, I should say that men's mags like *Playboy* became popular around that time. In the late sixties, I worked in a newly independent African country and oddly enough, the magazines were much more freely available there. Perhaps they had a more laissez faire approach to things, less of the Protestant approach. Not that you could get many different books, but *Playboy* was much more available. Even in this country, you didn't admit you bought *Playboy*. I remember, though, we had some very good white South African friends who were actually political refugees – they'd come up against the apartheid regime and the South African Special Branch were after them. Back then, South Africa and Rhodesia were still very much under the influence of apartheid,

Ian Smith and people. If you wanted to be safe, either as a black or white political refugee, you had to go north and cross the Zambesi. I made good friends with a white couple, and he told me that the first thing he did when he got out of South Africa was to buy *Playboy* – not because he wanted to look at the girls, but because *Playboy* to him symbolized freedom. It meant he was free, because in South Africa at the time it was banned.

Moving into the seventies, you had a progression of things – more literature coming out and so on. On the stage in particular, you began to get more nudity. A revue came out by a drama critic called Kenneth Tynan, and he got together with all sorts of wild people like John Lennon and wrote a series of sketches with an erotic theme, which were all put together in a show called *Oh! Calcutta!* It shocked people, less because of the nudity, but because of the content: two guys getting sexually excited and masturbating whilst watching *The Lone Ranger*[10]. Or two women having a relaxed conversation about what it was like to masturbate. Both of the sketches said something about the level of taboo over male and female masturbation at the time.

But of course the big thing that determines the spread of pornography is not so much the social attitudes as it is the technology which is available. Up until that point, the only technology available to the man in the street was eight millimetre films, which no one bothered with, but then VHS cassettes came along. That was when you really began to be able to access pornography as you know it, in the late seventies and into the eighties. The Danes were the first to relax the pornographic laws so they were the first source of tape cassettes – they were

10   An American Western drama TV series whose theme song was the 'William Tell Overture' by Gioachino Rossini.

called Danish blue. Then you had another source in California, which was a spinoff of the hippie culture, especially around San Francisco. Initially they weren't easy to get a hold of. You'd have to go into small shops in Soho to get them. Then, gradually, you could get them by mail order, but you never knew what you were going to get.

Because you were choosing by title or because it was a subscription service?

You had the title, but you never knew quite whether it was going to be hard or soft porn. Much of the stuff then was soft porn. The yardstick between hard and soft porn was an erect penis. In fact, you hardly ever saw a penis at all. A lot of the early stuff was *very* soft porn, a lot of hip wiggling and grinding that passed for having sexual intercourse.

You could tell it was staged?

Yes. That kind of soft porn was quite common around that time. Then you began to get imported videos. You could find contacts fairly easily in the video section of *Exchange and Mart.* But again, that was risky because a lot of these had been copied so often that the visual and sound quality was very variable. I eventually got a bit fed up with the quality, and after a time I never bothered. The first time I saw good-quality hard porn was with a group of guys from work. It was in the early eighties, so I was in my forties by that time. I was invited to come round and have fish and chips on a Friday night, and watch porn.

Tell me about that! Both your impressions of the porn, and what it was like to be watching it with a group of guys eating fish and chips.

Well, it came as a bit of a shock. And because it was a shock, and because I was with the other guys, it wasn't really a turn-on. The women looked good – this is the other thing, of course, that's worth mentioning: gradually through the development of pornography, both the male and the female actors or stars became more attractive. But aside from that, it was really a shock. You couldn't quite believe what you were seeing: did that guy just put his cock into that woman's cunt? Of course by that time I'd done it myself. But to actually stand back and see it happening was something else.

Even as someone who's had sex, seeing it on screen for the first time was still a shock?

It was. We were all married men, so we'd all had sex. And although I'd watched myself while doing it in a mirror, that was still me and my partner, who I felt close to. To see it objectively like that did come as a shock and I didn't find it a turn-on at all. I'm not too sure the other guys did either. They made ribald comments about the size of the penises or the breasts, fairly predictable male chat. But at the same time there was that uncomfortable salaciousness that you can sometimes get when you're watching porn with someone you don't know too well. It was a strange reaction. You just wonder, If even sexually mature people in their forties struggle with it a bit, then what effect could that have on twelve- or thirteen-year-olds?

Did you re-encounter that kind of porn afterwards?

It aroused my interest, for sure. That was the point when I started looking around for good copies of videos. One of the classic porn videos I remember was *Debbie Does Dallas*. That was almost the iconic early porn. The plot, if you could call it that, is a group of high-school girls who want to get to Dallas to watch their football team play there, and Debbie comes up with a scheme whereby they can sell their bodies to raise the money they need to get there. They do it in a very open way: approaching an ordinary looking guy, who's hosing down his car, and Debbie essentially says, Would you like to have sex with me?

For money.

Yes, although it's presented more like bob-a-job week than prostitution. The financial element isn't stressed. It's light-hearted and not salacious, even tasteful, if you can use that word in this context, and so it was something which you could watch with members of the opposite sex: your girlfriend or wife or something. It was a full-length movie – an hour and a half.

Can you say a bit more about that set up where you're watch-ing it with a girlfriend or a partner? Would the idea be that you'd watch it together to put you in the mood, or to have on while you're having sex?

I could never get on with having something in the background while I was having sex. So it was really two things: the first was sheer interest. You might watch it the first time out of interest, and your girlfriend would

219

say, Oh, he's got a nice big one and you make various comments like that. Then you might fancy watching it again, and that would be as a turn-on, and you'd finish up having sex usually. Obviously you've got to have a partner who's receptive to that. There are still certainly women, I suppose, and some men for whom porn would have the opposite effect or they don't want to get into that, you know? It's an unknown, really.

When you were talking about the sixties, you spoke about the general culture of liberation and openness. Would you say that persisted into the eighties and the video age, or do you think things closed up a bit?

The eighties were probably the peak of liberalization and then things closed up a bit. I'm in a different place in my life now – I'm no longer a twenty- or thirty-year-old, and my friends are similar – so maybe I would say that. But there are certain things that used to be on television that they say you could never make now. Of course often that's to do with racial issues and so on, but some of it is to do with sex and pornography. It may be that it's just much more accepted now, when so many people watch pornography, it's more a given and so the idea of watching *The Lone Ranger* and masturbating just seems old hat. But in answer to your question, I personally think things are not quite as liberal as they were in the sixties.

I think you're right about things like The Lone Ranger *sketch being perceived as old hat, but I do sense that behind the accessibility and ubiquity of porn and sex, the real conversations about it aren't really there. We think of ourselves as very liberal and open, but actually, I wonder whether there aren't a lot of secret taboos.*

220

I think you're right. When you watch pornography, you're watching pornography.

Exactly. It's very compartmentalized.

Whereas somehow in the sixties, you had a truly liberal society, because it was happening on all fronts – fashion, music, theatre, arts, literature, everything you could think of was moving forward. Opening up new ideas and trying out new things. It was a good time to be a young person. That feeling has gone now, for all sorts of reasons. Look at the government we have now. The government we had in the sixties was a Labour government, it was introducing new legislation, like the Wolfenden Report, which made homosexuality not a crime. When I went to Central Africa, I was partly funded by the British government, which was spending a lot of money on overseas aid and overseas development. The United Nations meant quite a lot. People bought into what the United Nations were doing across the world. It was a different world, really. So without getting too political I do somehow feel that things have closed up and particularly over the last fifteen years here.

I'm surmising from what you've said that you've seen internet porn. Do you remember your first encounter with porn on the internet?

I can't really, no. It was almost a seamless thing. Because after the cassettes you had the DVDs, and DVDs were a lot better quality, both in terms of the quality of the pornography and of their production. So I bought some DVDs. You could select from a wide range of subcategories, and you could play them on your DVD recorder in your home, which meant you were able to watch it on a fairly big screen. I was quite happy with DVDs. It was actually a girlfriend of mine who asked if I'd been watching any online porn. I said, Well, no. Back then I was probably struggling with a computer anyway. This is the other thing: technology is very important in this to some extent. I didn't know where to go to find it. So she recommended a suitable site, called xHamster. But then I found you were looking at it on a fairly small screen on your laptop, so it wasn't a momentous thing. It was just a continuation of fairly good quality porn that the DVDs offered. Except obviously it was just a click of a mouse away, so you didn't have to go and buy anything or have things delivered in a brown paper envelope or get unsolicited porn DVD brochures.

With DVDs, did having that kind of range and choice feel like a big positive for you?

Yes. Although it didn't have the range of the internet – when you click onto this xHamster thing, it must have 200 subdivisions. But yes. I was only interested in certain areas – at the time I was interested in multiracial sex, threesome sex, and possibly normal twosome sex, if you like, but that was it. I didn't hunt down any S&M at all, or any sort of weird fringes of porn. It was fairly mainstream stuff.

With the DVDs, you did have some sort of story to it, even if it was often pretty thin to say the least. But you could settle down for an hour and a half right now. I'm sure you can find long stuff on the net, but in my experience – as I say, I've only ever used one porn site, this xHamster thing – they just show clips. So the longest could be twenty or forty minutes or something, but it's not full-length and I can only watch it on my laptop screen.

So it's really important to you that a porn film is actually a film, in a way?

I think so. It fulfils a different function to the online stuff. When it's ten or twenty minutes then it serves as a relief, but that's all. Occasionally, though, I watch a DVD with someone else, and we settle down and just enjoy it. It moves from sort of instant masturbation and ejaculation to something a bit more. Because good sex is something you have to work at and build on. If you have something which lasts for an hour and twenty minutes, the development gives you more sexual satisfaction than an instant shot of fellatio or cunnilingus or ejaculation.

This person that you're watching the video with, would that be a sexual partner or just a friend?

Now it would be a sexual partner.

You wouldn't do the fish and chips thing with a porn film now?

No, no. I don't think anyone does, do they?

I don't think so. But I don't know of people who would sit with another person and watch an hour-and-a-half-long porn film. I think that would be unusual among people of my generation. I'm interested in the context for that, because I don't have a frame of reference for it.

Well, you may not get to the end of it. You both

understand why you're putting it on. It leads you gradually into a nice sexual state where you are ready to have sex.

How do you feel when you look at porn as it exists in contemporary society? What are your feelings around the way technology has transformed porn?

I suppose I'm concerned really. You know, until I was forty, I had a very good sex life – love life, married life, call it whatever you want – without seeing any porn proper. Porn in your twenties and earlier can enhance your sex life, it can arouse you and do so very pleasantly, make you very ready to have sex. But I just think about let's say twelve- or thirteen-year-old boys, whose expectations from a woman are that she's there to suck him off basically, that she's available for intercourse, she's willing to take off her clothes. If that's the first and only impression you get, it must be quite troubling. One of the lovely things about sex is that you grow into these things. You find someone and you take a journey, and if that journey is leaping onto the fastest train possible, you wonder what else is left. I think of my innocent introduction into all these things: a shapely young lady in a bikini, some rather vague words about tight buttocks and cleavages and stuff. I didn't know any different, my friends didn't know any different. And it did turn me on: I admit to masturbating to some of these things. You could equate it to drugs, I suppose – that you need something stronger every time. I wonder if access to porn by young people can be counteracted in some way, but it's very difficult to know how to do that. It must be very tricky as a parent to say, 'You know, you don't have to fuck a woman the first time you see her,' or 'You don't have to force her head down on your penis the first time you see her.' Perhaps I'm overstating it.

There's perhaps a worry about whether the world of porn as it exists now is so potent, colourful and absorbing in and of itself that people are less interested in sex and other people and developing intimate relationships.

Yes, because it's all about the orgasm, isn't it? That's one thing I've learned: the older you get, orgasms don't come quite as quickly. For either men or women. So you begin to enjoy the journey more. I'd drive back and forth to the nearest big city in my car and all I'd see is hedges and houses. I always remember when the car was broken down or something and I caught the bus, I went on the top deck and I was able to look over the hedges and see the countryside around. To some extent that's how I enjoy sex now: you're not so worried about the destination i.e. the orgasm. You can appreciate the journey. And you can sometimes never arrive at an orgasm, because the intimacy and the love and sensuousness and everything else are just as enjoyable.

As young people, the orgasm seems to be the be-all and end-all and it's very pleasant, of course. But you feel you haven't had proper sex unless you've had an orgasm. Particularly for a man, he needs to ejaculate. But the physiology slows you down. Sex is just part of one's wellbeing, like everything else. I can't run cross-country like I used to, I can't do lots of physical things, and sex is a part of that. Your physiology slows you down. In the latter years, I've probably had longer sessions of sex than I had when I was a young man. My partners are part of that, so it's not just me, but there isn't that drive to get to an orgasm and feel that's it. Sex these days is just as rewarding.

As you get older, you do have to work at it though. It's a use it or lose it scenario. So I try and keep my mind active, I consciously do crosswords and puzzles, and I'm doing it for a reason. Nowadays if I go for a walk, it's not just because it's a pleasant day for a walk through the countryside – I've got to walk to keep the limbs, the heart and the lungs ticking over. Similarly, when I have sex or when I masturbate, it is partly to make sure that I don't lose it. I know that may not seem right to some. People's sex drives get less, and some people will just let it go, and they may not miss it. For me, though, part of my maleness is that I can still enjoy the feeling of having sex with someone or masturbating and ejaculation. I'm sure that when I was your age, I couldn't imagine people of my age even having sex.

Well now we have porn that paints every scenario, so we don't need to imagine.

Oh yes, one of the categories is grannies, isn't it? Pretty young grandmas, mind you, but still. There's all sorts of categories. To some extent that's a healthy thing. If people want to watch two sixty-year-olds having sex, then that must be a liberation to see two sixty-year-olds having good fun, under the category of pornography. People even older than that, too.

TWELVE

Twelve is a pansexual woman in her thirties.
She has been with her male partner for years.

POLLY BARTON —— *Is porn something that you have*
conversations about?

TWELVE —— No, never, actually. That's surprising.

Surprising because you haven't noticed?

Yeah, exactly. Growing up, porn was for boys. I'm certain that boys talked about it. This is primary school I'm talking about. I went to a girl's school after that, and then porn wasn't a thing. No one talked about it. Unless they were in it, accidentally, filmed having sex without their permission, for example – then it might be something that might get seen by a few girls in the year. But I don't think girls talked about it like it was a thing for them.

Do you feel as if that classification has remained, in your
head? Porn is still a thing for boys?

No, not completely. I'm aware that the conversation's changed, but porn is definitely a bigger part of my male friends' lives.

How do you know that?

I guess I have talked about it! Although only to one or two friends.

Men and women?

Women, but really briefly. But then men just bring it up, do you know what I mean? As if it's just —

Something that everyone does.

Yes.

When it's brought up in that 'well everyone watches it, right' way – is that assumption a gendered one? Are men assuming all men watch it?

Yes.

You think that?

Yes, from experience...slash prejudice.

Men watch it and women don't?

That's what men think.

There's also this boys' club mentality thing that exists, right, that men all think slash know that other men watch it, but they all pretend to 'their women' that they don't. It's furtive, so then there's the question of to what extent 'their women' actually know, but everyone keeps up the pretence and so it becomes secretive.

On TV, there are so many scenes where a man is watching porn and gets caught or a boy is watching porn and gets caught. The only equivalent for women I can think of is *Fleabag*.

I was just thinking about that. I love that scene where she's wanking in bed watching Obama give a speech on her laptop, while her boyfriend's asleep next to her.

Yes. And there what she's masturbating to is Obama, and at another point it's the Bible: it's not porn, but it's porn. But is that still porn? Especially the Bible. One thing to say about porn is that it feels really hard to find something that isn't just for straight men. Supposedly everything exists out there, but all you see is really for straight men.

The classic example of that is 'lesbian porn', which is a hundred per cent made for masturbating men.

Porn with two women is almost always for men. They're usually white women as well. In the lesbian porn I have seen, they don't seem like they're actually gay. I can't tell completely, but it seems very much like acting.

It doesn't do it for me if it feels fake. What I find sexy is watching people being turned on, and if it feels like acting, then it's just not.

That baffles me too. Maybe for a lot of men it doesn't matter if the people they're watching are turned on, though? In the porn I've seen, I find a complete dearth of anything that actually turns me on at all. It doesn't look real, especially when it's two women, and it looks like it's not for women.

Going back to Phoebe Waller-Bridge – when did I start talking about her so much? – there's a scene in *Killing Eve* where Villanelle buys clothes for Eve. Villanelle isn't even there when Eve opens them, but

229

it's so hot, because she knows her body. She's changed the way that Eve is looking at her body as well, without being there. I can't quite pinpoint what it is about that scene that's amazing.

It's brilliant. When I encounter it in films, the gaze of another person specifically focused on a woman's body is very rarely sexy to me. It feels uncomfortable or objectifying or degrading. That scene feels like the opposite of that, though – it's actively sexy. Imagine living in a world where the act of looking at someone's body was not weighted down by this power imbalance and tied up with all kinds of unpleasant experiences. What would that feel like?

On TV and in films you see a lot of men buying clothes for women. The man will know her size exactly, and it always feels objectifying, that he wants to consume the woman. Whereas when it's two women – in that scene, it wasn't even on my mind that she wanted to consume Eve. It felt really equal, and intimate.

You mentioned that in lesbian porn it's quite difficult to find people who aren't white.

Saying that, I haven't seen much, because I just give up. But also 'Asians in porn' is not a good thing to google. Even looking up 'Japanese woman' outside of the context of porn will lead to porn.

What's your experience of that as someone who is part Japanese?

I don't know what came first: my understanding that Asian women were fetishized, or being aware of porn.

It's always been in my brain. I don't know when I learned about it, but I think I've always known that they're tied together. For me, one of the main things going on was being compared to a geisha. That, in combination with the misguided belief that geishas are prostitutes. Comparing me to a geisha in their head meant comparing me to a prostitute.

In what kind of context were people doing that?

Probably in the playground at primary school. Then on the street with random men, which started while I was at primary school too and carried on. They'd randomly call me a geisha or China doll on the street, always in an extremely sexual way. One guy – I can't remember whether he called me a geisha or a China doll but it was one of the two – he then told me to come and sit on his cock.

He called that out in the street?

Yes, it's happened quite a lot. That's the main way that the sexualization of Asian women has appeared in my life. There have been other things too. When my partner worked in an office, and was first meeting his colleagues, he told one of them I was Japanese. It just came up in conversation. I can't remember exactly what the guy said, but he implied that my partner liked Asian women, as opposed to me just being a human that he liked, and then asked what my name was because, 'He'd had sex with most of the half-Japanese women in London.'

Although I can't link it directly, I get the sense his feeling that it's okay to say that to someone comes from the way that Asian women are objectified, and that for a long time that objectification wasn't questioned by

231

anyone. The fetishization of Asian women is completely normalized by decades of films and books. It goes all the way back to the American occupation of Japan, when Japanese geishas were forced to be sex slaves for the American army; and to Korean and Chinese 'comfort women' (and people from other occupied countries) that the Japanese Army 'used' and allowed the American Army to 'use'; then further back to Chinese women being trafficked to America during the gold rush to work as prostitutes; and before that, to Japanese women being trafficked to British India, Australia, etc. That long history, on top of the fact that society doesn't call it out as wrong to fetishize Asian women, makes it seem like you can objectify Asian women without any consequences. My partner has had to deal with stuff like that occasionally. Other people have said things like, 'You just like the rice,' that kind of thing. To which he says, No, I just like Twelve. It's weird that people who haven't met me have already dehumanized me and put me in this bracket of consumable – I don't even know what to call it. A consumable ethnicity of woman? It's similar to saying, Oh, so you like blondes, but it's worse, somehow.

And more overtly sexual? Although that's there with blondes too.

One of my friends from uni was very conventionally attractive. She had blonde hair and was beautiful in a 'Golden Age of Cinema' way. There was so much she had to deal with. Since she was blonde, people assumed that she wasn't intelligent and that she was a certain type of woman. She left university with the top marks in the year and surprised everyone, because they had low expectations. That's similar.

232

Having big boobs is another thing that gets instantly sexualized.

As if it means something about you, rather than just a fact about your body.

When it's not just an attribute but an ethnicity, it's far more inescapable and damaging, I imagine.

I can talk about how this affects me, being the one that's part-Japanese in the relationship. My partner, though, can't really talk about the way it makes him feel. People just assume that he fetishizes Asian women, and that he's with me because I'm part-Japanese, as if he wants that, as if that's what he consumes. When people say to him, Oh, so you like the rice, or anything generalizing in that way, it's as if they think those are his porn habits. Whereas it's just a relationship like any other human relationship.

You prefaced talking about this by saying that it's hard to tell whether it was the awareness of porn or the awareness that Asian women were fetishized which came first, which ties into a more holistic difficulty with separating out cause and effect with those two things. Clearly, the fetishization of Asian women predates internet porn, but pornography itself goes back to the beginning of humanity. Now, those two things feel impossible to separate. It would be ridiculous to blame it all on porn, because porn is a reflection of other things, but I suspect porn ups the stakes and perpetuates these ways of seeing.

Also I think because Asian women are fetishized in the West, it serves as a route for the sexism that exists for instance in Japan to feed into the West. When you go to

Japan, you see how women are treated, and how much gender inequality there is. Obviously there are really great Japanese guys who aren't the traditional 'do all my laundry, do all my cleaning etc.' type men, but there are men there that expect women to be 1950s housewives, essentially, and that's just accepted, and not questioned in any way. There's still so much inequality in marriage in Japan. And that becomes a part of the fetishization of Asian women in the West – the gender inequality in Japan becomes a part of what is sexualized in the West, as if all Japanese women want to be in these 1950s marriages, all of them are submissive and serve their husbands.

A hundred per cent. I mean, it's analogous with the going-to-Thailand-to-find-a-Thai-bride phenomenon, right? It's not just the externals that you're after but that whole dominant-submissive package. Relatedly, my sense is that when we're talking about porn, the portrayal of Asian women – or people, I guess mostly women – is markedly different from how certainly the default blonde white women, but also other fetishized ethnic categories are portrayed, like Black or Latina women.

Asian women are portrayed in two ways. One way is as very submissive, quiet and easy to dominate. You see that playing out in real life, not just in porn. Do you remember that white, Swiss pick-up artist in Japan a while ago who was giving people advice, saying that if you're white, you can go to Japan and just grab women's heads and kiss them, and they'll giggle and like it? I don't know whether that narrative comes from porn, but it's there in porn as well. The other way Asian women are portrayed is as hypersexual crazy women, all the 'they'll do things that you can't even imagine' type narratives.

When they're articulated like that, they seem to be oppo-site ends of the spectrum, but in a way, they're very close. Ultimately both come from a culture of mysticizing and othering, and not actually engaging with Japanese women as people.

People can consume porn easily – to clarify, I'm not against porn and it's going to start to sound like I am – that presents those narratives and doesn't contradict them. There aren't many other narratives about Japanese women that contradict that for people. Then there's that crazy, 'weird Japan' side of things, all the fetishes and so on. If a Japanese person is cast in porn, it's probably to represent one of those strands.

Those strands are different to the stereotypical portrayal of other ethnicized groups in porn like, say, Black women. Maybe the sex-crazed bit is there, without the submissive element.

Black women are portrayed as sex-crazed, like you say, but also more aggressive. That has been a stereotype for Black women for centuries, going all the way back to when people would say they were savages. With Japanese women, it's as though people think they're refined on the outside. They'll do your laundry, and then have wild crazy sex.

Seeing any group as 'hypersexual' is a way of disowning and projecting your desires onto them. You could say the same thing about women full stop, throughout the patriar-chy, right? Within that broad category of women, certain

235

subcategories of women are singled out, often the most
disenfranchised groups in society.

The portrayal of Japanese and other Asian women as submissive goes wider than porn. They're seen as liking to submit. That's why a lot of men think they can talk to Asian women in a way that they wouldn't talk to other women. They expect you to submit, to be quiet and not defend yourself because you're Asian and you're polite. I was talking about this recently with a Korean friend. She's very small and she gets a lot of abuse on the street about being a geisha, all sorts of things. She was talking about how she feels that the men don't expect her to say anything back, and when she does, they look really, really shocked. Genuinely shocked, not just offended. It's almost as if they were expecting to be able to talk to her like that, that she would accept it because of her culture. But she does talk back. Some men also expect Asian women to automatically be attracted to them because they're white. The white man has such high status in a lot of East Asian countries. There's a superiority thing: Asian women, and by default Asian people, are below them.

That shock just speaks to how much they're infantilizing those people – they see them as mute children. I say that but then I think, but actually, people don't *shout at children on the street, because they're seen as vulnerable. Yet that dispensation isn't given to those women of Asian heritage, despite perceiving them as vulnerable.*

In Japan, there is a culture of women not doing anything, not speaking up, and that's been interpreted by some people as meaning that they're fine with it, but actually that's not the case. There's so much that has been put in place by Japanese governments that makes it difficult to organize in Japan, so there isn't a culture of protesting, of fighting for your rights – many women just aren't empowered.

I went to a hot spring resort once with my mum. We were in a lift with two Japanese girls and a drunk older Japanese man comes in. The man was leaning in to kiss the girls, and touch their hair, and they were giggling. You could tell they were uncomfortable, but they were giggling. Before I could do anything – I don't know that I would have done anything because my Japanese was not great, and it was a bit scary, being in this enclosed space – the lift stopped at our floor, and we got out. The man looked at me and followed us out, and started staggering down the corridor the way we were going. There weren't many rooms down there, and I had a feeling that his room wasn't there. I could tell from my mum's face that she was aware this man was following us, but she didn't say anything. So I turned around. I can't remember what I said now, it was a mix of English and Japanese. It was something like, 'Damé'[11], and then, 'Fuck off', and he looked so shocked and so confused. I think he could tell that I was English, and he looked scared and left. The two Japanese girls, maybe nineteen or twenty, didn't do anything – and I don't mean they should have but they clearly didn't have the tools to show even their displeasure. My mum didn't do anything, either, but everyone was uncomfortable.

Within porn, and in lots of ways that Japanese women are represented in the West, there is a sense that Japanese women accept the ways they're being talked to or treated, that they actually enjoy it, that they're just shy

11 'Damé' is Japanese for 'No' or 'Don't do that'.

237

or submissive. But really it's that they aren't empowered.
There isn't really a significant feminist movement in
Japan; #MeToo didn't properly take off there, women
who speak out are villainized in extreme ways. There
aren't structures in place to support women.

*That exploitation of a lack of assertion plays a big role within
the Japanese porn I've seen, which often features someone
saying 'damé' as standard. It's a bit like how things were in
Britain – though it's still true to an extent – in my mum's
generation. It wasn't okay for women to take any kind of
ownership of their sexual desires, and batting the man away
and the man persisting was seen as part of the whole game.
Within that context, where all sexual contact is hard won or
a matter of persuasion, and that element of coercion becomes
synonymous with the sexiness of sex, consent is a minefield.*

Japanese society doesn't place importance on consent.
In the legal definition of rape in Japan, consent isn't
even mentioned. It's defined by the level of physical
violence and injury. When you consider that, consent
– whether you give it or not – has no power in Japan. In
that context, maybe it's safer just to be nice, to try to not
anger the person and just get away quickly. With what
happened at the hot spring, you also have to consider
that the man in the lift was older and a businessman,
so the two young girls are automatically his inferiors,
socially speaking. It's similar to what Shiori Itō says in
her book *Black Box* about her experience of rape: there
isn't the language to tell someone who's your senior to
stop, in full seriousness, in Japanese. If you're saying
damé, it sounds as if you're telling off a child. That's why
I switched to English, because I realized I don't know
how to defend myself in Japanese. That's not because

my Japanese isn't good – it's because the right language doesn't exist.

Damé also seems so feeble that it almost serves as a come on. It has these unwanted porny connotations, a 'you're so naughty!' ring to it. When I think about that, it makes me feel that the world of standard heterosexual porn is so wrought through with aggression and coercion and misogyny, in the visuals and the language in which the videos are described, that it feels like the whole thing is poisoned, and I want nothing to do with it. At the same time, I don't want to condemn porn because I think people should watch things they want to watch. How do you navigate that?

I had an ex, who was lovely and very sensitive, and really upset by people being hurt in any way. He was generally very perceptive of people's pain, and the only thing that turned him on was women masturbating.

Turned him on porn-wise, or even in real sexual encounters?

In real life, but also in porn. He really liked paintings of women touching themselves. He was an interesting man, unusual in many ways. A lot of things upset him, and they're things that should upset all humans, but usually don't. Like the news, for instance. I think he likes paintings because he didn't have to worry about the fact that the woman felt like she was being watched. I'd hate to be him, though, because everything becomes a problem, and he gets frozen. But yes, I find the fact that so much porn is violent so strange. That's why TV and film is so refreshing, because there's room for people actually enjoying sex. There is room for that in porn as well, but it's hard to find.

Why is it different? If TV and film are being made to be erotic rather than pornographic, why is it with pornographic stuff that the violence and the misogyny comes in? Is it just convention?

In the West, when you talk about porn, it's mostly video. Whereas, in Japan, there's all this manga. Here in the UK we have this big underground network of child porn, and that exists in Japan as well, but there's also child porn manga. That's a big topic of debate – whether it's okay. No children get harmed, and you're always going to have people with those urges – and so the question is, is a paedophile harmful to society if they are just con-suming manga? It's really complicated, obviously.

There was an awful Stacy Dooley BBC documentary about Japan[12] where she interviews a man who clearly has complex issues. He identifies as a paedophile, but only consumes manga. That documentary had an agenda to present Japan as weird, controversial and sex-crazed in a weird and creepy way, so they refused to include interviews with people who were level-headed, who had intelligent things to say about porn in Japan, or were opposed to child porn manga. I went down a big rabbit hole after watching it, trying to find other people who were angry about it, and found articles suggesting that those people *were* in fact interviewed, but what they said wasn't convenient for the narrative the BBC wanted to present about sex and porn in Japan. These narratives don't help with the way Asians are portrayed – particu-larly the stereotype of sex-crazed women.

Porn in Japan is interesting because of the existence of manga, and the fact that there are manga for adults.

12 *Stacey Dooley Investigates: Young Sex for Sale in Japan*, BBC, first broadcast in September 2017.

Then you've got manga porn with two guys that's for women – Boys Love, or BL – and anime porn, too, which gets called 'hentai' in the West. It's interesting that the market is spread across different mediums, whereas we only have it in one, which means that we have to see actors, or in some cases, exploited people.

I found some child porn in Japan once, in quite strange circumstances. I was making a lot of collages back then, and I used to go down to the communal recycling room in my block of flats to collect material. People used to tie their magazines together and dump them. I used to check every day on my way out for new finds. One day I went down and found this big stack and the magazine on top had a naked woman on the cover. I took the whole thing upstairs, then went out for a walk, and forgot about it.

Hours later I got back to this stack of magazines, untied it and found that underneath this top magazine there were lots of child porn mags. It was the strangest sensation. They weren't home produced or anything – they were officially published glossy magazines from the eighties with all these young girls. Some of them were eight years old and naked, or almost naked, dressed in these horrible costumes – a cave girl is the one I remember. There were confessional pages from people who used to grope schoolgirls on the train. I was think-ing: Wow, these are now in my room. I had a real quandary about whether to take them back down to the recycling room, but the collages I was making were all about mirroring the misogyny and other forms of hypocrisy in society, so in the end I kept them. I ended up sending some of them back by sea mail to the UK in big cardboard boxes, so I had a period of time where I was praying I wouldn't be called up by customs and arrested for smuggling child pornography.

God, the thought of finding that stuff... I'd find that so upsetting. I understand how weird it must have been having them in your room. It's like letting something you don't want to acknowledge exists into your world.

The different ways different countries deal with paedophilia is fascinating. In Germany, there's more acceptance – or not acceptance, but there're channels people who are paedophiles but haven't offended can go down to get help, like a kind of rehab. If a paedophile isn't offending, are they harmful to society? That rehab centre says, 'No, they're not, and they need help.' In England, I think we really villainize anyone with those urges. Unless they're Prince Andrew. Even if they haven't acted on them, we treat them as if they have and as if they are harming children just by existing. As a result, the consumption of child porn, all the conversations about it, about it being produced, etc., gets buried really deep, away from the eyes of society. It's all there, but it's hidden, because it's so demonized. It's so underground here, and I wonder if that makes it more dangerous, and puts more children at risk? In England, if someone is a paedophile not acting on their urges, and people know, they'll be at risk of violence. People will be angry, aggressive, and the person will be seen as inhuman and be treated that way. In Japan, the attitude is different. One of the main pillars of society is: keep to yourself, don't get involved in other people's business – which is actually something I struggle to accept about Japan, but that's I suppose because I'm Western. If you see something that makes you uncomfortable, you don't engage with it, you step away, push it away, don't get involved. That's why all these alternative fetishes exist and also why, by extension, paedophilia can exist fairly close to the surface of society. That's why you can stumble across what in England would be hidden in the depths of the dark web in a random bin on the street. And perhaps, separately, because of that difference of attitude, there's more space in Japan for unusual fetishes to be serviced. Even if there's weird stuff in a shop, Japanese people will generally accept that it's not for them and they won't engage or look. Here, though, you'd risk being beaten up for admitting anything weird sexually in public. I wonder whether that difference in Japan is why there's space for something like child porn manga to exist. Does the existence of that manga reduce the demand of real child porn? Or does it have the opposite effect? Does turning a blind eye to everything that doesn't concern you result not only in the manga being produced without being questioned, but also actual live porn in which vulnerable people are being harmed and exploited being produced without being questioned? If the BBC's coverage was fairer or more nuanced, we might have the beginnings of an answer.

THIRTEEN

Thirteen is a straight man in his late thirties who lives in the United States. He works in a public library, and has been in a relationship for several years.

POLLY BARTON — *Does porn ever come up with friends?*

THIRTEEN — Never, no. Maybe very occasionally, in reference to some news article about it or something. There's been some very light acknowledgement that it exists amongst my friends, but never a proper conversation. You don't want to be the one to bring it up. Despite everybody doing it. I end up thinking, Will they think I'm a pervert or something?

Is that not something that's changed with time? It feels the same as when you were eighteen or similar?

Yes. I have a religious past, so it was a super-shameful thing when I was younger. I would probably have denied it to my eighteen-year-old friends.

And they would have done the same to you?

Almost certainly, unless it was a friend of mine who was also religious and we were confiding in one another: This is my sin, this is my shame, and I'm baring that to you. We're going to both try to help each other stop looking at it, or something. That would have probably been the only context porn came up in when I was much younger, which was also probably when

I was consuming more, because I wasn't in sexual relationships.

Can you tell me what that was like, and where porn fits in specifically within that religious outlook? I know there's a lot of shame around sex before marriage within that context, but is porn something specific and unique?

While I was growing up, I listened to many sermon-type speeches in various settings where porn would be addressed as a really bad and hurtful thing. To varying degrees of intensity, too: some saying porn is bad, some saying all masturbation is bad, trying to pull Bible verses that support these views. Because the Bible, as far as I know, really doesn't address masturbation, but the verses they use to justify it are very funny. There's one specific verse that's something like, Any man who looks at a woman with a fire in his heart, or with an ignited passion – there's some kind of fire metaphor – has created a sin. I sat through sermons saying, You cannot look lustfully at women. If you do, it's a sin. There's this really in-tense verse that says, If your eye causes you to sin you should gouge it out. So as a sixteen-year-old boy, I had adult male preachers saying, You should gouge your eye out, because that's what the Bible says. Obviously they weren't telling us to actually gouge our eyes out, but they were saying, This is how clear-cut it is. Now I think about that and I think, Wait, that's a metaphor. The people that wrote that didn't actually want a bunch of literally blind followers. To take such a rough interpre-tation of that was pretty crazy. Also, the idea of looking at a woman lustfully being a sin places porn in a very funny sphere, because one argument for porn might be: I'm just looking at this video or picture, I'm not hurting anybody. It's not a woman in my life that I interact with, who I'm having these lustful thoughts over that might impact our relationship in some way.

Let's say you have a friend who you're enamoured with and you're constantly fantasizing about her – that's going to affect your friendship, and the way you treat her, especially if you're trying to get to that next level, and she has already specified that you're just friends. I think that's a bad way to have a friendship. So that kind of lustful looking at a woman is a sin, and the same goes for porn. But how do you differentiate? Is there any hierarchy? Looking at a video and thinking about somebody versus just thinking about them? Or thinking about a past sexual encounter while you masturbate? Where are these lines drawn?

This question about drawing boundaries is something that comes up occasionally at my job at the library, too. We had a really extreme encounter with this just a couple of weeks ago. The back-story is, there're no filters on the internet in the library system I work in, so people are allowed to look at porn and they do all the time, especially in the downtown branch. We don't filter, and it's totally legal for them to do that. The one thing we can do, if people complain, is to say: Hey, excuse me, Sir, Madam, this is causing a disturbance, people have complained, could you put on something else, or could you switch computers to the one that's not so visible or something? And they can say, No, go away, and we have to leave them to it.

Most of the time when I do this – because I have to do it with regularity, more so downtown than at the other branches – just me saying something is enough to make them so embarrassed that they'll either shut it off or move computers or something, or just leave. But sometimes people will say, No, go away, I can do this. And they can, and they know it. Anyway, just the other day we had an incident. I should also say we just got new computers, so our monitors are huge, they used to all have a screen blocker where if you're standing to the side, it makes it look blank, but a lot of them have just been ripped off, because they can make it hard to see. So this family came upstairs to print something out, and they had all their little kids there, and there was this guy watching porn. I could see it from a hundred feet away. It was a really graphic scene, and the father flew into a rage and wanted to attack the man. We had to talk him down and say, The kids aren't really supposed to be on this floor, and they're allowed to do this. It was really crazy.

The reason I brought this up is that part of the reason we don't filter is because it gets really hard to say what's porn and what isn't. Certain things are obviously pornographic – this sex scene this guy was watching, for instance – but at the same time, if we start to filter, suddenly we are the arbiters of what is sexual and what's not, which can be so hard, right? What if it's somebody with a foot fetish looking at pictures of bare feet? Do we filter that? Can we filter red carpet shots where the women are in body-hugging dresses? Or bikinis? Then we have to make every decision about what is allowed and what isn't. It gets grey so quickly, right? I guess we could block a few major sites, but that's the other thing with the nature of the internet, too: it's really hard to totally squash something out, because even if you hit one of the big distributors of whatever it is, like free music or porn, then it just kind of fragments out. If there's a demand for it online, people will find it, and a new site will rise up, you know?

Pornography is often categorized as something that you watch for the purpose of arousal, but then how do you say about a third party whether they're watching it to be aroused or not? Presumably, they're not touching themselves as they're watching.

It happens. They're not allowed to do that. We're bound by the law, and public masturbation is a law that they're breaking. Or, we don't filter for it, but if somebody is watching child pornography, then we're allowed to say, That's illegal, and call the police.

Has that happened?

I've never had it. You know, it's weirdly sad when you see people watching porn in the library. Lately I've seen these guys who just do a general search, 'boobs' or something, probably. So all the thumbnails for their search are coming up, and then they're holding up a flip phone on top of that, to take a picture of a thumbnail. I imagine what they end up with is about six pixels, that's the image quality of that exchange for them. I assume they're going to use that flip phone image to masturbate, later, but for me it feels so sad trying to flip-phone capture a thumbnail of a pornographic image. There's one guy who's doing it every day, you know? I think part of it is something I heard in one of my trainings recently about homelessness. The guy was saying, The thing you have to realize is it's just a complete shattering of your self-esteem. Which makes me think that these guys, whether or not they're touching themselves, are probably at a point with society where they feel so despised and feel such a lack of anything mattering. When you try to confront them and say, Hey, this is kind of inappropriate, the idea that they'd say, I don't care, really speaks to how they can't feel the shame of that moment, because they don't have any self-esteem. Their situation has destroyed it.

One of the things that fascinates me about porn is the machinations we go through to maintain respectability around it as 'functioning members of society'. There's a lot of public condemnation of it, or being disgusted, or not wanting to affiliate yourself with porn stars in any way, or not talking about it in any detail with any reference to personal experience. Everyone knows that really everyone is consuming it. Or do we? I don't know. But at least we pretend that we don't. It all feels like this strange Victorian game. And no one wants to come out and say, Yes, I watch porn, or No, I don't watch porn.

Yeah. Just the sheer numbers, the amount of money spent on it. It makes up such a huge proportion of the traffic online, right? I've read that it's around thirty per cent.

When we briefly spoke about this last time we talked, you mentioned OnlyFans. I was thinking about that and how so many people who either were sex workers before, or had other jobs that they then lost during the pandemic, found a living during the pandemic through OnlyFans. Just the numbers behind that tells you a lot about consumption.

I think about the way people are connecting digitally these days in the sexual arena. I read something about the girls who accidentally fell into doing ASMR stuff, who then stopped accepting donations. They were suddenly making millions of dollars from people donating to them, so they said, I'll keep doing this, but please donate to charity. They're overwhelmed with the amount of money that comes in from it.

The fact that they're inundated by donations speaks to this idea that for the people who are getting something from it, it's not just about getting off, right? It feels integral to their sense of self or building a community, like you were saying.

Yeah. Connection to a human being, and intimacy.

I'm going to change the subject, and bring up something I wanted to raise with you, which I know I mentioned briefly last time. That, basically, I remember having a conversation with you over ten years ago about porn, and that was partly why I asked you to take part in this project. But when I brought it up last time, you said you had no memory of it.

It's interesting, for sure.

Especially because we started this conversation with you saying that you didn't speak to people about porn because it felt too exposing. Whereas this conversation we had back then was essentially you exposing yourself entirely. I'll tell you what the exact context was, as I remember it. We'd gone out to a restaurant and then come back to my apartment, and I remember we weren't getting on very well, there was some kind of tension. I started talking about philosophy, and we got into a silly argument, and after that had gone on for a while, you suddenly said, 'Let's stop this. Let's talk about something that matters.' Of course, from that angry place, in my head I was thinking, 'Hey, what are you saying, philosophy matters!' And then you said, 'I used to be addicted to pornography.' I remember it feeling like: whooooosh. It felt like this shift of worlds, as if we'd moved into a different place.

250

That's wild, huh.

At that stage I was in my early twenties, and hadn't really grown up on the internet, and I'd never heard the word pornography used in conjunction with addiction, ever.

I've thought about it a lot since we brought this up before too, and I think part of it is that, in that moment, the use of the word 'addiction' and probably even wanting to talk about it had a lot to do with that kind of history. We were still quite young, and I think part of it was me still processing it, all that shame and my understanding of porn and the place I thought it held in the world. It's always a little funny to me to use the word 'addiction' when it comes to certain sexual things. I'm thinking of when celebrities come out and say, I'm a sex addict. I mean, sex is one of the most pleasurable things you can do on the planet. What does it mean to say you're addicted to it? You have the opportunity to do it all the time because you're famous, and so you do? I certainly think there's a level where you can classify something as an addiction because it starts to hurt other aspects of your life, or you put off other things. That could be the classification. As a teenager, there was such a stifling of those real sexual experiences, I couldn't have them easily because of a lack of privacy and my religion making me feel bad about it, and other girls I knew at the time often being religious...

That said, it's hard to really put myself back in the place of us having that conversation. I don't know if you've had this experience getting older, but because of the way the internet preserves things, I've been able to see certain things I used to say or do. Did I tell you the thing with finding my old work emails? Basically, I needed my start date with the library for something, so I went back and dug up the first email I sent, and in my introductory email to my new boss, I'd written 'Greetings to my new library Overlord.' I looked at that, and I thought, That was fucking stupid. I think at the time I thought it was a bit edgy, or silly, in a way that I was into being at the time. Looking at it now, I couldn't imagine a world where I thought that was a good idea, but obviously I did. I feel that way a lot with certain things I've been able to dig up, and I feel like that a little bit with this conversation, too. It makes me think, Huh, I guess I thought I was addicted. Which is not to say that I wasn't – maybe I'm not remembering how I spent my time or how I felt about that kind of thing. I know it did involve feeling bad about it or feeling as though the actors and actresses in porn were in terrible situations. A lot of that conversation was me trying to process it, though, and feel better about where I was at, even if I wasn't there yet. Because I was still watching porn around that time. So I think I wanted to put it behind me. By phrasing it like that I was trying to say, I'm better.

It feels a strange thing to be recounting this conversation we had over ten years ago to you in such detail, but I have a very vivid memory of it. I remember you were talking about doing stuff with your ex-girlfriend – this was in the context of you discussing the feeling you were addicted – and I remember you said that the two of you would do stuff in bed and then she would go to the bathroom, and you would want to watch porn immediately afterwards. I think what you were speaking to was a sense that porn was the real deal, and that what you did with your girlfriend wasn't as fulfilling in some way.

Let's say I was in high school or even university, and maybe I saw my girlfriend twice a week, but I was watching porn, say, four days a week. I do think it can cross your wires a bit. This is all a bit theoretical, because I have no idea how the brain works, but I think you could come to associate a sexual encounter more with pornography than with being with a person, you know?

Well, this is the current discourse around the prevalence of internet porn for young people, right? One of the real worries about it, that more and more young men are having huge problems with impotence, that they just can't become aroused having real sex. It's not a turn-on.

It seems like it would be even harder to be a young person now, because you get so much access to it too. I was around when internet porn was birthed, essentially, and actually, I have a very vivid memory of the first time I saw boobs on the internet. I was at a friend's house, there were a few of us there, and we were using the AOL chat room. And at that time, you had to trade images with somebody. So we finally got a person who said, All right, let's trade, and we were saying, Okay, you send a picture first, because of course we didn't have any pictures. And I remember, very slowly, an image of a woman standing topless in front of a waterfall being revealed. It was so dramatic: there's the face, there's the neck – and then it kept going, loading, line by line, and I'm there thinking, I'm about to see up close this thing that's always covered up. That makes for a pretty memorable thing, but it was also a funny kind of let-down, because they're just like you. I mean, it's similar to what a male has, just a slightly different shape. But as a teenage boy, you think about it so much: What do they look like, these things I don't get to see? So then it comes on screen and it looks like a body. In some ways it's exciting, but it's also just the human body, you know?

I remember when Napster was around like putting in 'female orgasm' or something, and listening to the audio of that, and thinking, Yo this is pretty crazy that I can just hear this! It seemed pretty illicit. Whereas I feel like these days, you can enter 'pirate ship foursome' or whatever and find something. It's called Rule 34: if you can think of it, then there's porn of it. I think being a young person and being able to find very specific stuff, filtering down to get to what excites you, is very compelling. Then you have a relationship with a real person who might not fit those same criteria... When I was younger, my real-life encounters were always more exciting than whatever you could find on the internet. Whereas I can imagine certain teenage boys nowadays seeing some crazy shit, and real life not matching up.

If you're a teenager – well, in fact, if you're any person – having a sexual encounter with someone, especially for the first time, that can be scary and make you feel insecure about yourself in all kinds of ways. Whereas with porn you don't have to deal with that. You can pretend you are the bodiless penis on the screen.

Yeah. It's almost like the ego is removed again. It's funny because when you're in the privacy of your own home and not sharing intimacy with another person, that's all removed.

You're in a relationship now. Is porn something you talk to your partner about?

This is the first relationship I've been in where we've acknowledged casually that we consume it, and that it's part of our lives. That never happened to me before. Usually it was just completely unspoken, completely disregarded. There was one time when I was dating somebody and she came over and my pants were sitting next to my computer desk. I had obviously been at my desk and taken off my pants, and my girlfriend said, 'Why are your pants there?' I just looked at her, as if to say, 'What do you want me to say? You know why they're there.' She was upset about it, but we didn't talk about it. I just looked at her, and then the moment passed. I was younger, and I think it was harder to talk about certain things. Now I would probably joke about it. There's just a lot more healthy acknowledgement in my current relationship, though. This is the first relationship I've been in where, sometimes when we're walking around and somebody with a crazy body walks by, we'll casually acknowledge it to each other. I think it's about having little ways to ease that tension a bit: we're humans, we're sexual beings. So we'll just be like, That was a tight bod. And that says to the other person, it's okay if you were glancing at it or you noticed it and you were like, Whoa, because it happens. Just because we're committed to each other in a relationship doesn't mean that we won't find another human body attractive. That's insane to think that, right? But that's the weird expectation in society and maybe especially in the past when in America at least there was more of that Protestant purity. Even if you weren't religious, there's that weird sense that you've got to remain pure and committed in a way that's almost otherworldly. Nobody has the ability to ignore a beautiful body in front of them.

I sense that these days the 'weird expectation' is felt more among heterosexual couples. I suppose that makes sense in that queer couples are for the most part explicitly outside of the Protestant context, but it feels as though in general there's still more permissivity there than among straight couples who have no religious affiliation, say.

A lot of the time, the power dynamic within a heterosexual male-female relationship and that male insecurity that comes of it has involved the male ownership of the female in a way. I felt that, growing up in that religious environment, it was always up to the women to be the gatekeepers of sexuality and for the men to take as much as they could, try to get as much as they could out of the encounter before the woman said stop. In terms of looking at other people, it's a similar kind of power structure where, if a woman is looking at other men, it makes the man more upset than if he looks at other women. And even the level to which women have been allowed to enjoy sexuality, right? There's this aspect where the guy doesn't see his transgressions as equal. It's his right to look, but she shouldn't get to do it, or something.

This is interesting to think about in terms of the assumptions about who is watching porn, right? Among most men, there is the assumption that other men are watching porn, and I think most women probably assume the men are but...

I think a lot of men don't want to think about their girlfriend masturbating. I've heard people say, It makes me feel like I'm not enough. But it's like, *You* do it. Something that just occurred to me is that, in a way, the porn I watched and some of that religious upbringing I had, I think in a weird way it almost circled back around to give me a healthy view of this stuff. In the religious context I grew up in, women were supposed to be pure, and not desire sex, and one of the things originally I was really drawn to and still am, in pornography, was women who wanted to have sex. Women who are just really into it. That was really exciting to me, because I thought they weren't supposed to, it was almost a taboo. She's not supposed to do that. For me, that's the background for a healthy desire for the girl to be really into it. I never really liked the rapey aspect of a lot of porn. I found it much more exciting for people to be excited to be involved in it. Because that was taboo, even though it's the way it should be, but then that loops back around to a 'healthy' attitude to consent. That's kind of weird. It's operating on – I don't want to use the word 'slut', but you know what I'm saying? When I was younger, that's definitely how it was framed, that kind of slut-shaming was always in the background.

Yeah, the virgin-slut dichotomy, right?

Right. Even though it could just be healthy. 'She enjoys it, just like you do.' Instead it was, 'She enjoys it, but she's not supposed to.' The excitement that came from the idea that that was kind of wrong. All this stuff is so strange. I've never talked about that until this moment with anybody. I don't know how you're going to put this in a book.

It's interesting to hear that this is the first time you've spoken about all this stuff, because you seem comfortable talking about it. Is it often ticking away in the back of your head?

I think people think about sexuality a lot. Maybe there's no pressure to come to an answer or conclusion or realization, though, on your own. If I'm trying to

257

figure out a murky, hazy grey area, such as the ethics of certain things, I'm like, Well nobody's ever really going to question me on that, so I don't have to come up with a fixed answer. I'm never going to have to talk about it with anybody, because both people involved would be uncomfortable. So then I wind up thinking, Well, it doesn't matter.

How is your relationship to watching porn these days in terms of guilt?

There're times where I wonder a little bit about the industry. There's a conversation around sex work now – that wasn't even a term that people used before – and how healthy the conditions are for workers. In general, I think I feel less guilt because I'm not attracted to a lot of super-produced porn, or that kind of porn star look in general. I like porn to feel like real people. Amateur stuff is what's most interesting to me, because it just gives you more texture to grab onto. As if you could imagine yourself in that situation or something. With some of the other types of porn – the body types and the scenarios and the lighting – it all just looks so surreal that it's not exciting to me. So in certain ways, I feel less guilty in light of those preferences. But I do wonder – is even the amateur stuff toxic for the people involved in it?

It's easy and comforting to make that assumption that, because it looks like it's home produced then it must be, and therefore it's made between people who really want to be doing it, and are having fun.

There're probably a number of problems, especially the issue of consent around those videos being online.

That's something which I don't know whether to feel guilty about. It's tough because there are also a lot of them that are produced and made for consumption, and those people are making money off of it. But there's definitely some that you'll stumble upon where you think, Oh, this was probably this couple's video and either the guy put it online, or somebody got hacked and it got leaked. There are ethical concerns about that, I think.

FOURTEEN

Fourteen is a gay man in his early thirties.
He lives in the States, and is currently single.

POLLY BARTON —— *Can you talk me through your*
relationship with porn as it stands at the moment?

FOURTEEN —— I'm probably watching less porn
than ever. I'm not really thinking that much about porn.
I assumed I'd be watching more porn when me and
my partner broke up, that I would replace 'regular sex'
with my partner with porn, but I haven't. I'm a little bit
worried about it. Maybe I'm becoming less sexual?

Does getting older have something to do with it?

I don't think so. I think the porn is just bad. I would
watch more porn if it was good. If there was porn I could
actually enjoy. Or maybe I don't know where good porn
is anymore.

What is good porn for you?

Good porn is no longer than twenty minutes long. Not
to be overly virtuous, but I think that a lot of the porn
I've watched in the past, and probably the porn a lot of
people consume, is pretty crappy and unethical. I was
interested in the idea of finding more ethical porn, less
problematic porn. There's more ethical stuff for straight
people: a few sites. I've found a lot fewer for queer stuff,
weirdly.

What would ethical porn look like?

Porn that's less about cum, more about intimacy. Less about these 'sexual scripts' that seem to be a really tried-and-tested formula for what sex looks like when visualized. There's a real lack of alternatives. I'm less comfortable watching some of the stuff I used to watch because I feel like it's programming me or it has programmed me and will continue to programme me if I continue to consume it.

Reinforcing scripts about what sex should be like?

Absolutely, and about what bodies are attractive. The only way for me to really move beyond some of that generic shit that a lot of us assume is normal is to stop consuming it on a daily basis. Anything that I'm engaging with on a daily basis is going to mark me in some way. I'm not sure watching problematic porn, even with a critical lens, is the answer for me.

The aspect you've just described of not being all about the orgasm at the end, about intimacy and the wider implications, seems a good way to think about ethics.

Yeah, I guess it's a self-interested ethics. I'm thinking about what the impact is on me as an individual, and my impact on other people, by consuming a certain type of porn. That shit rots your brain.

Have you observed that in yourself with the scripts?

Definitely. The annoying thing is I'm aware of the script but there's still something that draws me to certain formulas, because I've watched thousands of porn videos where you can guess what's going to happen, step by step by step. You can guess who's going to be in it, the types of bodies that they have. I was going to say, That's definitely changing, but I don't even know if it is. Go on Pornhub and it just still seems to be the same stuff. If anything, there's a bit more aggressive stuff on mainstream sites than ever.

Do you know what the part of you that's drawn to the scripts wants?

Familiarity. The predictable is comfortable. It gives people a blueprint. It gives me a blueprint. It's useful knowing how other people see the world, what other people expect in sex, what other people enjoy in sex. I think a lot of my ideas about what my hypothetical partner might enjoy used to come from seeing how people in porn react to people doing certain things. Like, Oh, that person in the video seems to really enjoy a finger up their arse. Then it becomes, Do I even like fingering or do I just think my partner might enjoy it?

And then, Do I know that they are actually enjoying it or are they performing this enjoyment because they also watch porn and think they should be enjoying it?

Are we just acting out porn every time we have sex? Are we just watching porn and then recreating it? Where's the enjoyment? Where's the actual pleasure? It's so easy to go into autopilot and forget how fun sex can and should be.

Do you feel like the stage at which you start watching porn and the way in which you watch it is important in this? Does it matter whether your first encounters with sex are irl or through porn?

Is anyone having sex before they've watched porn!? I've got this really vivid memory of being a young teenager: me and my friends at this particular train station with a news kiosk on the platform. You'd wait for a train to pull up to the station, and you'd time it right so you could grab the porn magazines from the kiosk and run for the train. Some weeks we might do it more than once. That was where my consumption of sex began, because that was my first interaction with porn. It was theft and it was on a train platform and it was part of this heist.

Would you then take the magazines home?

I would and I'd be confused by all of these boobs. So many boobs. Being a gay boy but still thinking to myself: I'm meant to like this, all of my friends like this, why don't I like this? Then, one day, that big stack of magazines I'd stashed under my bed next to the box of old barely dressed Action Man dolls disappeared and I never got an explanation. I wasn't too upset.

As a gay boy looking at those straight porn magazines, was there enough male presence in there to be stimulating or was it all women?

It was basically all women. On some level, I was always searching through the pages to see stuff where women were interacting with men, and I don't think I often found what I was looking for. Most of the people reading them don't really want to be confronted by a dick. I preferred the images where there were men and women, but I never got into straight porn, it never made much sense to me. So many boobs. So I had a big period in my teens where I just didn't watch porn. When I realized what homosexuality was, I didn't switch to gay porn. That felt too scary. I just had no porn.

It felt too scary?

Being unsure about who I was then, consuming gay porn at that point might have tipped me over the edge. A gateway drug. Catholic schooling, through and through.

So what was it like when you eventually started watching gay porn?

It felt right and wrong at the same time. It felt right because I could tell I was more excited about what was going on, but it felt wrong in that it was so tied up with feeling uncomfortable in that identity and in my skin at the time. Once I started watching it I couldn't stop. It'd be daily consumption, in secret, with headphones on, blinds closed, when nobody else was home. It was a real shame cycle. Instant feelings of real aversion after I'd finished. Clear browsing data. Clear cookies. Clear cache, whatever that even is. And my relationship with porn was really marked by that almost immediate feeling of discomfort after. I don't know what motivated me to continue to watch porn, but I wouldn't say it was pleasant.

At that time, all of the bodies seemed identical: masculine-appearing men, having sex with what looked like their siblings. They were mainly white, everyone had abs, and all the bedrooms were the same. It was as if every studio had one bedroom and they just went in and used that one space.

Did you have a clear sense of what was missing or was it a sense of, This is what porn is?

I went as far as saying, This is what sex is. Sex is inter-course between models. I didn't even start to think about what other people who didn't look like that would be doing. Maybe reading, or watching TV, but not having sex. Sex was for skinny, attractive, masculine men, at least in my consumption of gay stuff. That was partly because I probably wasn't doing that much looking round. I went to the mainstream sites for gay porn because I didn't really want to be online, searching through lots of different stuff. I had it in my head that if I got too exploratory, that would be how I got caught, and I couldn't get caught.

Was this when you were still living at home?

Through into university. I had this thing once where I was watching porn and I was in my halls of residence and I got a pop-up saying something like: You can't watch this, we're going to punish you, we've noted your IP address and you now can't go on this website. I was certain that the other people in my halls would get a pinged notification and be sent a link to what I was watching and that would be what would out me. It was horrible. I heard them coming down the hallway and I had my jeans down and my bedroom door for whatever reason wasn't locked. Oh god, I can visualize it now... I thought porn would be what outed me. Another time I was living with a guy who studied computer sciences and I was sure he was able to see, through our wifi, what websites I was using to watch porn. I was really paranoid, because I was trying to consider all the angles. I thought porn would be the end of me.

The more shame there is, the more paranoia can take hold. What you were describing sounds like a very powerful script to be going into sex with. Did it make your first real sexual encounters quite difficult?

It didn't, because it made me very selective about who I would have sex with. I went on to perpetuate those ideals in my sexual partners. The first few guys I slept with were all tall, built and more masculine. It took a while to unlearn all of that. I'm still unlearning it.

Would you say that unlearning process was conscious?

More recently, it's been conscious, to do away with the ends of that. I still have to regularly remind myself of basic shit that I've got to learn. I realized that being with someone conventionally attractive doesn't have anything to do with their personality. It doesn't mean they'll be nice. It doesn't mean they'll be funny. I was dating people because I thought they were 'hot' and realizing, Hold on a second, we have nothing in common. I don't even think I realized I was unlearning it. I was just connecting dots and realizing that whatever gauge I was using to pick people who I thought I was interested in just wasn't working. It's not easy looking back on my behaviour. When I started learning how to date in my twenties, I'd gravitate towards masculinity.

I appreciate the scare quotes around 'hot'. I don't think there's anything wrong with wanting to find your partner attractive, and potentially that is something that you have to weigh up against them being a nice person. But I'm fascinated by 'hotness' as received message, as social capital: how much do you think they're hot because you think they're hot, and how much do you think they're hot because society has told you to think they're hot? It's easy to stand on your high horse and say, No, no, no, this is my personal taste, it's nothing to do with social pressures, but it's only once you start that process of unlearning, intentional or not, that you kind of realize, Okay, no, I'm much more affected by these standards than I thought I was. Even if it's hard to subsequently alter them.

If the porn I was watching when I first found gay porn featured people with size thirty-eight jeans, then the people I would've been drawn to when I first started dating would've looked different. Obviously, it's not just porn: a lot of industries are to blame for how skinniness is so prioritized across genders. But fuck me, there aren't many things that teenage boys consume on such a regular basis during that critical period of identity formation. It's like learning a language. That's what I was doing: I was learning a language of sex. I do want to watch more porn, I've realized. I just don't know where to find it anymore. Of course this is not practical at all, but sometimes I think that the type of porn that I want to watch, I have to make or direct myself! I don't think I could do that alongside the work I do. I don't even know that I want to be working in porn. There's loads of red tape, in my life anyway.

Generally speaking, though, I feel like there's less red tape, as compared to twenty years ago. If you could imagine what that porn would be, you could get it out there in the world more easily. Right?

More easily, for sure. With porn, though, you might stumble upon the perfect video, but then once you've watched it, you're done. I don't know anyone that re-watches porn. Which means it just takes so much work.

I guess it could be about creating a space where people who feel like-mindedly would be posting stuff. A porn community, in a way.

That feels like a lot of energy to be pouring into the consumption of porn, though. I barely have the energy to read the books I want to read. I don't necessarily want to watch more porn. I just still feel like I need it.

I get that sense of not wanting to spend time finding it, let alone making it, it's just ten minutes or forty minutes out of my week and I just want to do it and then be over with it. At the same time, I wonder how much of that is tied up with shame and de-eroticization. The culture is to have it as an objectified, disposable zone that's very separate from our creative faculties.

What if it wasn't disposable? There's a lot of work that could be done around sex shows. Going to watch a performance with a narrative and some character development. I don't know whether everyone would need to be in their own booths or what, but you could do what you want in that space, and you get a whole story with sex that is played out. There's also a discussion of consent, within spaces like that. I think that way, there'd be space for all forms of fun, but maybe it'd be —

Messy? Or maybe not, necessarily. When you're watching bad porn, do you feel like you've seen it all already?

It's harder for me to box it up and compartmentalize as I used to. Maybe you're right, maybe I am desensitized to some of the classic tropes and some of the repeated devices that crop up in porn. I'd be more interested in porn that looked a bit different. Traditional porn is no longer representative of the sex I'm having. So then it becomes the visceral disjunct between porn that's super, super formulaic and heteronormative and my sex, which doesn't always look like that. It's harder to marry up with my experiences.

The classic narrative is that desensitization pushes men to seek porn that's more and more violent or more extreme in some way. Whereas you were just talking about it in the context of wanting something new, not necessarily more hardcore.

Or they're desensitized to the point of wanting none of it. The amount of porn out there and available enables people to explore their more specific kinks, rather than necessarily extreme stuff. If you imagine that the majority of porn is super generic, whatever that means, then you've got stuff that really taps into specific kinks and fetishes. For someone who's super vanilla, some kinks might seem extreme, but I view it as more specific to an interest.

I wonder if it's easier to have that discussion within a queer context. When you are having that discussion against the backdrop of the misogynistic vein of mainstream porn, then men are consuming stuff that looks very much like kink in terms of power dynamics, but they don't acknowledge that.

What do you think they're seeing it as?

269

Hardcore porn? I don't think it goes much beyond that, you know? The choking and slapping are part of what porn is.

I think choking's great. I'm glad that's on record. But sometimes, you can be so specific beforehand about the type of stuff you're into that it can feel like going into sex with a playbook. Almost like a tick sheet. Sex should be able to extend beyond what's discussed beforehand, because sometimes the fun is just following what spontaneously feels good in the moment. Sometimes people's sexual playbooks are the things they're searching for in porn. They're acting out different elements of it. They'll have twenty tabs loaded up, each one focusing on a different thing that they only want to consume for about three seconds before moving onto the next tab. I'm probably speaking from personal experience. I open loads of tabs.

And move between them?

Yeah. A whole playlist.

And would you only want to see three seconds of each?

It may be that hovering over a thumbnail there's been one scene that I thought was really hot, but I've got seventeen tabs to get through.

Are you saying you'd open up the tabs before, so it would all be ready?

I might start wanking while putting it together. I don't wank very often, so I make a whole big deal of it. I've not watched much porn in the last four weeks partly because

I've been so much more engaged in other stuff. If I was watching porn on a daily basis, I'd do less curating.

Do you ever wank without watching porn?

I would rarely ever wank just with my imagination. My imagination is probably more conceptual than visual, and I need the visuals. I've wanked to audio porn, though. Before I came out, I used to do a lot of cam stuff, and I wonder where that factors into it. I'd angle the camera below so you couldn't see my face, and then I'd enjoy the big wide world of the internet. I haven't told many people that.

It's interesting that you led into that with 'before I came out'. Was there a reason the cam stuff happened at that stage?

I think I was able to not come out earlier because I was – depending on how you define it – having sex with people online. In my head, it was as close as I could get. I don't think I thought of it as making porn for people to consume, but I really got off on people watching. I thought it was great. It was really liberating, but there was also a discomfort in the many reactions you and your body might get within a reasonably short space of time. I don't think that element of it is particularly healthy without some real critique or analysis. But I got very accustomed to being consumed by a reasonably large amount of people in a short amount of time.

Can you explain a little bit what the cam stuff looked like?

It would be a website that you logged into and there'd be a bunch of people who were on camera, and you could

271

just go in the rooms if you wanted. I would be in one room, mostly in my bedroom. And could engage or not.

Engage meaning chat?

Well, watch and chat. There were also private rooms if you wanted to chat with one person individually.

Was it very anonymous? Would you have regulars?

I still can't believe how this happened – bear in mind, this is the whole internet, the whole world – but once there was this guy I got talking to, and it came up that he was in England. And then it came up – I don't know why he thought it was a good idea to disclose his workplace – that he taught at the uni I was studying in. Here I am with my dick out on camera, and there's this guy showing me his staff card, in a private room. So we arranged to meet.

This was my second ever sexual encounter, facilitated by the internet, which at the time for me was really, really scary. I had to wait until it was Christmas, and everyone had left my halls of residence. I had this backstory for who he was in case anyone was there, and I had to sneak him upstairs into my room when we had sex. All facilitated through a camsite. I didn't meet anyone else from that website. Not much could top that experience.

Have you ever felt that prospective sexual partners' expectations of you are shaped by the porn that they're watching? Are there special expectations that attach to you as a Black man?

Yeah, absolutely. Before I came out, whenever I interacted with women, there was an expectation that I'd be very masculine, very dominant and aggressive, and in fact, that's pretty similar with men. That's been my experience navigating the world through heterosexuality and navigating the world through homosexuality. A lot of people expect what they see in porn to be recreated in person, though that's rarely explicitly verbalized. I think they'd get defensive. Then the conversation easily becomes all about them. Even in relationships, I think the ideas people have got from porn have shaped people. Not expecting me to have an emotional – anything, really. I can't see a better candidate for what has shaped this other than porn.

That's heart-breaking. It's also illuminating, if not surprising, to think that what lies on the flip side of the 'aggressive' stereotype is a total denial of someone's emotional reality.

It's not that I don't want to be dominant sometimes. It's just that that's not how I always want to have sex. The expectation is that that's where my preference has to begin and end whereas I'm like, Well, sometimes I want to be thrown around too. Being boxed in like that pretty much ended one of my earlier relationships. I'd initially accepted how fixed his views of me were, and it transferred outside of the bedroom, where he didn't expect me to have feelings. It made me feel like a piece of meat. I'm a whole person! He wasn't a bad person, it was just a bad fit.

Have you felt in the past like you're being fetishized?

Definitely. There have been times where I've been talking to a white guy on an app and they've used the n-word. People have asked me if I'm into race play.

273

There've been times where I've felt ignored. Obviously it'd be problematic to demand I get a response from everybody, but my experience and the experience of other friends of colour who have navigated apps is one of being second-class citizens in that context.

For dating, or for sex as well?

This is it. I hope this doesn't come across as egotistical, but I find there are more people who want to have sex with me than want to date me. For some people it can be fulfilling a sexual fantasy, whether they say so or not, but it's not meeting a potential partner. People are allowed not to be looking for anything serious, of course, but I've had the thing where someone's not looking for something serious, so we just have sex, and then maybe a week or so later they're in a committed, exclusive relationship with someone who looks like their sibling. I'm like, Okay, cool.

Are people ever vocal about the fact that you're their sexual fantasy?

Oh they're not just vocal, they expect you to be grateful. I chatted with a guy on Tinder about it once. It was a debate more than a conversation. It went on for hours until I realized it wasn't my job to shift his understanding. Pouring energy into those debates is a trap for sure. If I'm just a thumbnail for someone, that person isn't necessarily going to care about my comfort and safety during sex. So not having certain conversations has implications for my welfare and health. I also have to remember that I've been watching porn for a really, really long time as well. What am I doing to people?

274

You're not always aware that you are trying to live out a fantasy, right? That's the scary part. It's safer if you can own it.

If I'm swiping on some guy who's six foot four with loads of gym pics, am I thinking about whether he's got a sense of humour or whether he's got a good relationship with his mum? Even with sex, you've still got to be a person. A whole person. I'm not saying I need his life story and star sign, but we can afford to care about more than someone's sexual role and what we want from them in the bedroom, right?

It's hard to imagine a six foot four guy with abs feeling really upset after sex. Your mind doesn't go there in the same way as it does with other people.

Because we don't see enough of those stories. If we slowed down a bit we'd see everyone has feelings, regardless of their height or shoe size. We all have feelings.

FIFTEEN

Fifteen is a straight woman in her early thirties.
She is married with children.

POLLY BARTON — *When I emailed you, you said you'd*
just been having a conversation with someone about porn.
Can I ask what it was about?

FIFTEEN — Something I sense is that the way that
straight women and straight men consume porn is
completely different – that they're two different universes, and they seem to not overlap. By now it's mainstream
knowledge that young men, especially, watch lots of
porn and get wrong expectations of sex and stuff – it's
almost a cliché at this point. But I've found there's also
something even beneath that, on a foundational level,
where the very conception of pleasure seems different.
That kind of surprised me. That was what I was talking
about. The idea that the mainstream porn straight men
consume every day is often premised on quite violent
acts. There's often lots of pain involved and as a straight
woman watching it, I just think about how the porn actress is in pain. You can't unsee it. Yet from a male point
of view, they don't see it as pain. They're interpreting it
constantly as pleasure, or as sexual stimulation, while I
think it's actually the opposite of that. That tension isn't
just something superficial – it's actually quite fundamental. There's a mismatch that's deeply problematic,
isn't there? And that translates into all sorts of social
problems.

Where do you think it comes from?

276

It's all very phallocentric. If that's your base transaction, then you end up with these violent metaphors and scenes – or, from a women's perspective they're violent, but from a man's, they're not, they're forms of pleasure. If you're going from that idea that the penis is essentially the centre of pleasure, it'd make sense that the thing would be banging it into various orifices. You can see how the pornographic culture we have might evolve from that, as a starting premise.

Men's bodies aren't really shown, and it's all about the women's body, so that even when it's not a point-of-view camera, it's still the male gaze replicated by that third eye. Is seeing the actress in pain incompatible with feeling turned on?

Oh, yes, it's impossible. But I understand that for other people those boundaries are blurred. That takes you into the whole arena of fetish and that's something else. I don't think the majority of people are into that. It's interesting though: in fetish stuff, the boundaries of pain and pleasure are blurred, whereas in the mainstream pornography I've seen, that pain is constantly there, and that's interpreted as pleasure. It's not seen as painful. Do you know what I mean? It's not really identifiably S and M, is it? It's just part of the accepted sexual practice.

Totally. I'm unclear to what extent that is the product of a misogynist patriarchal society, and to what extent it's its own thing. If a man brought up in this world who had somehow not watched porn was suddenly shown it at the age of thirty, would they see that pain? And what would it make them feel?

Are they connecting the two, I wonder? You know, I was teaching on a module this term called 'Romantic

Eroticisms', and one bit about that was the evolution of pornography. In the eighteenth century, you can't really talk about pornography per se – it didn't exist in and of itself, so erotic elements were woven into different cultural artefacts. You could have erotic prints, erotic poems, but it wasn't its own thing. Yet even then the phallocentrism is really clear. Also, this sense of sex as a violent act against women that they would find pleasurable is already there, in the very beginning of conceptions of eroticism. That has developed, I suppose, and porn has followed that trajectory. Some historians suggest that there was a shift in sexual practices that came with industrialization: pre-seventeenth century, there was a sense that sex was not just intercourse, it was lots of different acts. As industrialization slowly got going, though, the mills and mines and other industries created a need for more children and more labour to ensure economic survival. The economy needed people to procreate to generate enough children to work. That's when the shift happened: sex, which was formerly a multiplicity of different acts, became streamlined to-wards penetration and penises, basically – to ensure the conception of more children. So there was an economic reason for it.

At the beginning you said that the porn straight men and women watch are separate universes.

I'm aware that's a generalization. I'm sure everyone has very different sexual tastes in the end. It's hard to gener-alize because sexuality is so personal.

Sure. Do you assume that most straight women watch porn? And do you assume that most straight men watch porn?

278

Definitely the latter. I assume that all straight women have had some contact with porn or watched some, but I wouldn't assume that that's something that they would necessarily do lots of, or choose to do. Those are my assumptions. I wouldn't assume that they don't have any contact with pornographic materials at all; it'd just be slightly different to men. For instance, I prefer reading sexual things than I would watching them on screen. I think that might be kind of a stereotypical male versus female thing – I know lots of women read Mills & Boon and all that sort of stuff, and find that more pleasurable or attractive than watching it on the screen. Maybe it's something to do with imagination and feeling in control, being able to personalize situations, so you're more emotionally connected. If you just see random strangers on the screen, it can feel disconnecting.

I've not thought about it in terms of being in control. I imagine men don't have to worry about being in control so much because —

Because it's for them.

So they're unlikely to have to encounter anything that is suddenly alienating or pushing them away.

That's it, isn't it? I haven't watched all that much porn, but I have watched some porn that's for straight men. And sometimes, it's fine, but sometimes I do feel almost queasy watching it. Because you know what it feels like. Some shots feel like watching a torture scene or something. If my partner is watching at the same time, I think: You're getting off on this, while for me it's actually slightly disturbing, and I need to stop watching.

Does that feel upsetting, the idea that your male partner gets off on that?

No, I don't really feel upset by that. I suppose I recognize it's something bigger than him. It's a whole... What would you even call it? An ideology? It's a whole way of seeing the world. It's not really about his particular tastes. It's just what he's grown up with. The one thing that does upset me is the idea of him watching it as a teenager. Part of me feels very conservative, implying that men shouldn't watch porn, but you watch that sort of thing and you think, well it is harmful, isn't it? You think, Oh God, it's a long process for men to unlearn that stuff that they were watching when they were growing up, and realize that actually it's not how it works, and that can only happen if they're on the right path, or have got supportive partners.

If the thing was just porn teaching men wrong things about sex, I would feel happier about it, but what upsets me is the way that I tie it in with this sexualization and objectification of women in all scenarios. Rightly or wrongly.

That's what I mean about the watching it when you're young – part of it is that kids that age don't know how sex really works, because it doesn't show that really. And the second part of it is that you absorb this other way of seeing the world, which is – yes, an expression of violence against women. That's there, isn't it? Objectification of women, the sense that women have to look a certain way, obviously, or be used in a certain way. Also the whole idea that the whole world of sex serves straight men. There's no sense of there being another person at play. The whole world of sexuality is not

280

represented, and it's almost as if it doesn't exist at all. You only have very fringe books or films that might counter the mainstream narrative.

You said that you don't feel upset if your male partner is getting off on that because it's not about them as a person. I recognize that, but in the past, I have felt a quite over-powering sense of an unbridgeable gap. Which makes me think, If this is how straight men are then I can't be with a straight man. That's not my calm, settled position, but sometimes that feeling flares up.

I know where you're coming from, absolutely. The thing about having a long-lasting relationship with a man is that you have an understanding that you share this private, intimate sexual world. You have a language together that you don't share with other people. And if you're not speaking to each other in the same language, then of course you could just be friends, because you're not giving each other what you need. And also, you never really know... I had something with a partner in the past where I found out about his tastes in those things – he never told me, but I found out. I think it must've been one of those moments where I opened up his laptop or something silly like that. Anyway, I saw that he'd been looking up – it's quite funny to think about now, but he'd been looking up loads of really, really muscly women. Bodybuilding women. That was his thing. It was more sexualized images than videos: photos of them wearing skimpy outfits or topless. I realized after that he also watched porn with those kinds of very muscular women. It was so strange to me that I didn't know this about him, and yet I'd been with him for years, you know? That was a real moment of: ...what? I felt in that moment, exactly, like: We can't be together. This is a secret world of pornography, a fetish that you have – is it a fetish? I don't know. Anyway, I had no point of access to it and I didn't understand it.

Did you have a conversation about it afterwards?

No, never. We never had a conversation about it. I think I made a passing comment about it, and he sort of laughed it off and I thought, All right. I also thought at the time that if he didn't want to tell me that was his choice. Everyone's entitled to their privacy. But I did at that time think that if that was how things were going to be, there was something not quite right... It was in the relationship as well, you know. The sex we had felt as though he had his own sexual life that was just about him, and he wasn't able to connect. Maybe that was a porn thing, now that I think about it. It was all about him and his consumption of those videos and images. He wasn't able to connect with real-life women.

When you found that out, did stuff about your sex life up until sink into place?

Yeah, because he was the kind of person who would retreat a lot. He would retreat back into his own kind of sexual world that was excluding me, for sure. I think porn makes that easier. It's there for you as an individual, and it's easier to do that than to make an effort to relate sexually with your partner. There's a lot more work involved because you have to think about where things are coming from. You've got to change what you're used to, change your practices, you know?

I liked what you said before, that when you're with someone for a long time, sex is like a language between you, it's your own world that you've built up, and I guess the same is true for your own private sexual world. I'm really interested in the relationship between those two. I imagine there are some people who feel that when you're in a relationship with someone, that private sexual world should of course disappear, so all you have is your world with your partner. And then others who clearly don't feel like that. I don't have a fixed position on it, but I suppose again here I'm interested in the unquestioned assumptions we make. Around, say, whether people continue to masturbate when they are in a healthy sexual relationship, whatever that means.

There's a whole range of difference. I think people should have both. It's like life, isn't it? You're entitled to your own time alone or hobbies, and the same goes with sex when it comes to fantasies or masturbation. But then you also have to make the effort to have the relationship with the person, or it's not going to work.

Are porn and masturbation things you can talk to your partner about?

Yeah, I suppose that's one big difference between him and my ex-partners. With them I was never able to talk about it. It was a real taboo subject.

Where do you think that taboo came from?

It's only my side of it really, because we never really talked about it so I never got to the bottom of it, but I think there were a lot of different things at play. You know, this particular person was a good example of someone who had his own world. Before we met, he'd been single for a long time, and he'd got used to just being on his own, watching a lot of porn.

To be honest, now I think about it, a lot of the things that happened were to do with porn. I remember him being really surprised when we first slept together, because I don't shave my hair or anything, so I was just normal, and he was just really surprised. I remember thinking, Do I have to get rid of it? Having a huge debate with myself. Maybe I'm just being too pernickety and uptight and I should just get rid of it, it's just hair. And then another part of me was saying, It's just hair, so what? It goes both ways. I was saying, Why should I? And he was saying, Well, why shouldn't you? And you end up in stalemate.

So it wasn't just that he was surprised – he was actively saying, Please shave?

Yes. Eventually he had to get used to it, though. So now I think about it, porn probably did have a lot to do with things. He had intimacy issues, whatever that means – I mean, he had a hard time opening up to another person. I think porn made it much easier not to do that. If you've got something there that serves you perfectly well, and is a lot more accessible, it means you end up closing off to reality.

It's easy to think of porn as emotionless, functional, which it is in one way, but the story of your ex is a perfect example of how it can occupy an emotionally rich place in someone's life, or gives them some feeling of connection to something. I don't quite know how to articulate what that is.

284

It must have given him something, mustn't it? More than just something to masturbate to, it must have given him some other kind of satisfaction. I couldn't tell you what that is. You'd probably have to talk to a straight man if you want to know. I can only speculate.

I read an article about how the amount of fan fiction that people read in the pandemic has surged, and the author was putting this down to the fact that, because we've all lost our routines, we're craving familiarity more than anything. I've found that in myself: I've binge-watched some really bad TV shows and been unable to stop because I've felt that seeing the same person's face over and over is crucial for me. Which makes me wonder: obviously porn is mostly not the same people again and again, but I wonder whether the tropes become familiar and reassuring in a similar way.

I imagine most straight men are quite young when they start watching porn, and it does become a habit you build up over years and years, so there must be something reassuring about it, like returning to something you did in your youth. Maybe it's a form of escapism, and locking yourself away from other people and your troubles.

That, in combination with the way that many women feel about it, really does give that sense of two worlds, doesn't it? Personally, I find the aesthetic really gross a lot of the time.

There's something so unsexy about it.

It does make me think, How could this be reassuring or escapist? But I suppose it is.

So men see these pornographic images from an early age, and they're very sexually charged and appealing to them. But what about women's sexuality? What do women want to watch? What would a woman-centred pornography look like and would it even exist? Fan fiction is probably the closest you'd get.

I've seen bits of 'porn for women', images that women are supposed to find sexy, and I find them unbearably cheesy. I saw this one book which had pictures of hunky, very straight-looking men with speech bubbles superimposed saying, 'I'll do the dishes tonight, darling.' That's not what turns me on either. Then I'm aware, as we're having this conversation, that the world of porn is hugely diverse. But I'm like you in that, when the word pops into my head, I think of the really artificial hetero dominant stuff...

In scenes from films, or when it's written, it's a bit more sexually appealing to me. I wonder why? Maybe because in a film it's part of the story, so the people seem more real. And then in writing, obviously, you're filling in the story yourself, so it's your images. It's more about the people who are involved.

Yes, I feel the same. I feel as if I'm in a funny position now, where basically all of my female friends are progressive, sex-positive people who I know don't think that talking about sex is bad, or talking about masturbating is bad, or that masturbating is bad. But the conversations still don't happen – it's just not part of the repertoire. I don't know if that's —

Politeness?

Politeness, prudishness, this sense that it's just not something
that we do and therefore it's hard to break that barrier, and
it's embarrassing as a result.

I often think about this. Even with really close friends,
I don't know anything about that part of their lives. I'm
not being nosy, but wouldn't it just be nice to have a
conversation about it? As you would do any other aspect
of your life. But you can't because there's a block.

I know how important it is to initiate conversations. You
think it's only you that feels X about Y, and then you talk
to someone who feels like that as well, or they've had that
experience too, and that interaction can be genuinely
transformative. Yet, I really don't feel that I want to be the
kind of person who posts on Instagram about their vibrator or
whatever. That makes me feel extremely uncomfortable.

The Instagram world is a different one again, isn't it? It's
lots of performing and posing and writing scripts rather
than having ordinary conversations.

With female sexuality in general, I feel uncomfortable about
the sense that, if we talk about it, we have to do it in an Ann
Summers way. If you're talking about masturbation, you have
to talk about vibrators or sexy lingerie, it becomes deeply
commodified, and also creates this real distance between you
and your body in a way. As though you need the tools and the
gear to deal with it, which feels weirdly porny to me in a way
that I don't like. But then I feel like a prude for not liking it.

Yeah, there's a whole – I don't know what to call it – discourse around it. Female empowerment and so on. It all
becomes very weighted down by lots of things. As you

287

said, commodification for sure, a certain kind of Ann Summers branding on all of it. Then also this narrative that a good orgasm is going to change your way of being, you're going to get the job you've always wanted. That used to really annoy me, actually. It's not *that* good.

SIXTEEN

Sixteen is a woman in her late thirties.
She is currently single.

POLLY BARTON — *Going by what you emailed me*
when I asked you to take part in this project, you seem to have
thought about porn a lot.

SIXTEEN — I do watch porn to some degree, and so
I've probably thought about it to the extent that you have
to, in terms of whether I feel good about it. Is it okay to
watch porn?

Ethically?

Definitely ethically. Both the macro-level ethical
question of whether pornography should exist, and the
slightly more micro-level questions (that are still pretty
macro) such as: Should I be using Pornhub? Is that
ethically defensible? Is there an ethical way to consume porn? Is there a way to find ethical porn that isn't
terrible? I don't have answers to any of those questions.
They're just questions that crop up when you engage
with porn on any level.

Have you explored ethical porn?

No, not really. Before I discovered Pornhub – I don't
actually know when Pornhub started or was widely
available, but I think I came to it late – there were times
when I was looking for porn without any idea where
to look, and only finding professional porn, more

traditional porn made by the porn industry, as opposed to amateur or quasi-amateur porn. If porn is being made by a studio or something, there's at least some sense of accountability, standards, some kind of regulatory framework somewhere. I've also been to sites which advertise themselves as ethical porn, or porn for women, which is not at all the same thing. I've been generally really disappointed with what I've found.

Can you dig a bit into that disappointment?

Part of the reason that websites like Pornhub are appealing is because they showcase a range of experiences and existences, which you don't find in traditional porn. I've been to sites that advertise themselves as porn made for women, which seems to mean 'not openly, blatantly dehumanizing in some way', but it's still always able-bodied people who conform to a very specific set of beauty ideals. It's overwhelmingly white people, with non-white people there only because they're not white, and fetishized in some ways. The focus, in so much porn, even that which advertises itself as made for women, seems to be on penetration and finding penetration pleasurable in a way that I don't think many people do. It's supposed to be porn for women, but to me it still looks like porn for men – or the porn that men think women want, which is still just porn for men – and that's disappointing.

Sex on TV or in films is, again, incredibly limited in the range of bodies that it shows, but on Pornhub, for example, you can find porn that features different bodies. Until discovering Pornhub a few years ago, I had genuinely not seen any images of fat people having sex. I've barely seen any images of fat people naked in my life, for obvious reasons. As a fat person, it's revelatory to see porn which features people with bodies that don't conform to this narrow range of beauty standards, for one thing.

There are two or three lesbian couples I follow on Pornhub, who are more on the ethical aside, in that they seem like real people who are doing this to make money, but in a consensual way.

They're couples in real life?

Yes, it's very much about them – I don't know if there's a less awful way to say this – sharing some of what they do. I've never thought about this before, but the fact that they are couples in real life feels like some guarantee that this is consensual, although now I'm wondering why I am assuming that lesbian couples can't be abusive or coercive in some way. One of the couples did a video a while ago where they guest-featured a trans woman and a gender non-conforming person. I'd never seen that done in that way before. I'm sure that there's plenty of trans porn, that it's a genre in the same way that 'Asian porn' is supposedly a genre, but I had never seen people with the sort of bodies you don't conventionally get to see in porn presented at home, within a sexual setting.

Free from fetishization, essentially.

Exactly. The only place you can find that is somewhere like Pornhub, because it's so open and unregulated, but then the fact that it's open and unregulated is also problematic. Part of the whole experience of watching or trying to access any porn is having to scroll past or shut your eyes to stuff that you think is abhorrent or troubling. It's difficult to feel good about watching porn or consuming porn when that's the case.

I find it hard to put into words or frame where the difference lies between fetishizing certain body types or ethnicities, and representing them. Do you have any clarity around that?

I have absolutely no clarity, because I wonder whether it's still fetishization, but presented as more palatable. It's like with diversity in TV, how some moron on Twitter can make the argument that TV isn't racist because there's a Black family on EastEnders, you know? You see that and think, I don't even know how to explain how wrong you are. That statement is kind of correct, but only if you exist in a position of total ignorance of the conditions of TV production and the world around you, and structural and endemic racism. Sometimes I wonder whether me saying, 'and they had trans guest stars in one of their videos!' comes from a similar position of total ignorance of the conditions of production. Is it still fetishization, but in a way that I find palatable because it's framed as 'these are our friends that we're inviting to star with us', as opposed to some version of freak-show framing? Is it the same thing, but within a framework of what I take to be authentic relationships and friendships?

Separating out the aesthetic and the ethical objections in porn is so difficult. I dislike a lot of the porn on Pornhub because of the sheer aesthetics of it, and yet I could watch what is essentially the same scene, shot with better lighting, in black and white, in an arthouse film, and feel more aroused by it, and much better about it, even though nothing different is going on. Sometimes I feel turned on by things I find aesthetically abhorrent and that creates a disconnect. The tension between

292

those two layers of difficulty, the ethical and the aesthetic, is
oddly discombobulating.

In order to engage with or seek out ethical porn, I
would have to ask myself some real questions about
what it is I am looking for, and that's partly what stops
me. Do certain things that turn me on do so because
they are abhorrent in some way? Do they turn me on
because they are in some sense forbidden and therefore
shameful? Can you have that same experience within a
framework of ethical consumption? Maybe I just don't
know enough about it.

Do you know Girl on the Net? I don't know what
you'd call her: a porn creator? She has a sex blog, where
she writes erotic fiction, and has lots of guest writers and
performers who come to her site either to write or to
do erotic audio, but she's a real person who also writes
about her own sex life and her sexual fantasies, in a
genuine way. The clearest example that comes to mind
is that she had an affiliate partnership with a particular
sex toy manufacturer, and in order to fulfil her com-
mercial responsibilities to them, she had to review this
vibrator, but she had just broken up with her partner
of many years. She'd been writing about him and their
relationship for years, they owned a house together, their
lives were very intertwined, they'd broken up a few days
before and she was obviously devastated, and she wrote
this piece that was simultaneously a review of this vibrator and a confession to all the people that follow and read
her that she had just broken up with her partner and was
totally broken-hearted. She framed it as, Is this vibrator
good enough to make me orgasm when I'm crying all the
time? It was incredibly moving. So she is both an erotica
creator and a real person who insists on her existence as

such outside of the world of erotica. She has a Patreon and there's a whole community of fans around her. That's what ethical porn looks like, for me: a real person who is transparent about the way what they're doing is produced. It helps that she's not filming anything, that she's just writing, though she does still use or need people to appear in her writing or act out certain scenarios with her. Even then, I don't feel entirely good about engaging with her, I'm embarrassed that people might see that I follow her on social media. It's embarrassing to admit that I am embarrassed to admit to consuming porn. Written porn is still porn, right?

I think so.

I think of it in the same bracket.

Is it embarrassment at consuming porn, or is it embarrassment at being turned on full stop?

I hadn't made the distinction, that's an interesting question. The implication is that, if you are consuming porn, there's a utilitarian aspect to it, there's a purpose. The assumption tends to be that you're looking for content you can consume to get aroused and therefore almost certainly masturbate, have an orgasm and move on.

That's my assumption as well but I sometimes have experiences that lead me to think maybe that's overly black and white, and I don't know the truth of it.

I'm sure it is overly black and white, but that probably also has to do with my feeling of embarrassment. Maybe if I had a more nuanced view of what consuming porn was, I wouldn't be so embarrassed about somebody knowing that I do. It's fascinating that it's so little discussed, and yet it is something that so many people must be doing – many people I know and am quite close to, with whom I talk about a lot of things. Yet we would very, very rarely discuss this.

Even into my thirties, female masturbation still feels like something that is not easy to talk to people about and admit to. There's this enormous vapour trail of shame that follows the subject around.

Did you watch *Bridgerton*?

No.

I watched it with my mum – that's my defence for having watched it. I'm roughly as embarrassed about having watched *Bridgerton* as I am about watching porn. There was a scene in it which absolutely infuriated me. The heroine is supposed to be around seventeen or eighteen– but in Regency terms, seventeen or eighteen is closer to our twenty-five. One of the plot lines is that nobody has communicated to her what sex is, and she was talking to the hero, with whom she was having this intense, ambiguous flirtation. I can't remember exactly how it was phrased, but she asks something along the lines of, What is it that happens between two people that is so overwhelming? And he basically tells her to masturbate – he asks, Do you ever touch yourself? To which she says, I don't understand what you mean – she is ignorant of it entirely. So, he says, When you go to bed tonight, touch yourself like this, and then there's the scene of her doing it. I was furious when I saw that.

It shouldn't make it worse that this was written by a woman, but it made me even angrier. I hate the idea that women are entirely ignorant of their own bodies and their own sexuality until introduced to it by a man. I remember ranting about it to my mum at the time, who just sat there with a long-suffering expression. Even if the heroine had never independently discovered masturbation, she's got sisters, she's got friends, surely they would have talked about it? Yet I have to admit that there is a tremendous conspiracy of silence about it, and I really don't remember talking to any of my friends about it. I have one friend who's very open about this stuff, but also tends to discuss it in a self-consciously titillating, 'look how shocking I'm being' way, which to me is very unappealing. Masturbation is not something I would really talk to my friends about, even though I talk to them about so many other things.

When I was teenager, it felt possible that I was the only person doing it. I remember a couple of times trying to hint at it and being met with apparent incomprehension.

A part of me wants to believe that it's not possible for girls or young women growing up these days to have that same experience, because they've got the internet, which we didn't have, or, had only in its weird infancy. But even on the internet, are people talking about masturbation and orgasms, in any way that teenage girls can access?

Or is it all still geared towards the male gaze? That's my fear about it. I feel your rage about the fact that it has to be a man who teaches the girl to touch herself too. Sometimes I have these little flare-ups of rage about the way that society alienates women from their bodies...

296

...and from each other.

And from each other. But the fixation with sex toys and porn is sort of often presented as though that's the only way into touching yourself.

I haven't thought about it in those specific terms, although I completely agree.

Did you read Katherine Angel's *Tomorrow Sex Will Be Good Again*? I liked it, partly because it talked about acknowledging the difficulty and sometimes impossibility of knowing what you want. It's entirely possible to be in your thirties and to have had sex and various sexual experiences and masturbate with some regularity and still not really know what you want or what you like. It is about alienation, but it's more about compartmentalization, which structures the way I think about porn and masturbation. It's utilitarian, it's a need you take care of in a little compartmentalized corner of your life where you do things like consuming porn or using a vibrator in the attempt to speed the whole thing up, to get from A to B as fast as possible, and then not think about it anymore.

Of course there is every possibility that for some people using a vibrator might ultimately bring them the most pleasure, but I don't think it's about that for a lot of people, and I don't think watching porn is about that either. The fact that it's entirely possible to masturbate and orgasm without engaging with yourself in any meaningful way or being kind to yourself or trying to bring yourself pleasure on any other level than a strictly utilitarian one is bizarre. Again, it's this very compartmentalized sexual experience which almost has nothing to do with the rest of your body or life or surroundings.

This might not be true of anybody else, but I do have the sense that I don't really want to engage with this, to open this can of worms. I would probably be a better person, and more in touch with myself, pun not intended, if I did, but these things feel quite dangerous and unsettling to explore. What if I really engage with my own sexuality and it turns out it's something different to what I always assumed it was? What would it take to be open with another person? It's a lot. There are so many facets of experience bound up with this that I don't really know how to begin to unpack it.

Do you think the formulaicness of porn enables you to be distracted from the troubling stuff? Does it provide a structure and a channel for experience that prevents you from going near the can of worms?

Oh, definitely. The aesthetic plays a big role in that. I look at the rooms that some of these things are filmed in and think this is completely outside of my experience. I look at certain things and I categorize them: this is a place I would never be, this is a person I would never be with. I would never do these things in this cheesy formulaic, porn way. If I was ever to engage in a version of that act it would *have* to be consensual and discussed and done in a much nicer place and a less tacky way. The packaging, which in theory is selling a fantasy, but to me is selling almost the opposite of a fantasy, means I file it safely as something I would never want or be interested in, which frees me up to engage in it without thinking properly about whether it's something I would ever want.

To clarify: I think the only way to consume porn ethically – to consume anything ethically, let's face it – is to pay for it. There's a series of conversations you have to have with yourself in order to pay for something. Do I need this? Is it okay that I'm spending this money on it? Is this a thing I want enough to pay for it when I could be spending money on so many other things? None of those are conversations I want to have with myself in this area. It's sad that it's such a measure of worth to say: Do I care about this enough to pay for it?

When I've spoken to people who have paid for porn, it tends to stem from an awareness of the needs of the people who are making it. Delving deep and asking yourself how much it matters to you is difficult, especially since socially porn is afforded such a low status.

I know I should be engaging more with it from that point of view, but I have a massive unwillingness to do that. This would all be so much easier if there wasn't a huge burden of shame associated with it. When you were asking earlier whether I talked to people I knew about this, my instinctive first thought was, Well, most of my really good friends are in relationships. Once I'd vocalized that to myself, I thought, Huh, it's interesting that I think that people in relationships don't watch porn or don't masturbate, or don't engage with any of that. It's an acknowledged assumption that I had never voiced and therefore never actually examined. Part of the shame for me is that I am what you might call a perennially single woman. I haven't been in a relationship for at least a decade and part of the burden of shame this carries is that I can't be open about doing this or needing this or wanting this because it'll be in some way connected to my failure to be in a relationship or having sex. The idea that porn is something you consume or that masturbation is something that you do if you can't find a partner is such a reductive, retrograde idea that I didn't even realize I was holding onto until we had this conversation.

That assumption that friends of yours who are in relationships don't masturbate or watch porn – does that come from a sense that it's because it's just not what you do *in a relationship, or because they're genuinely sexually fulfilled?*

I know for a fact that some of them aren't sexually fulfilled, so they must be masturbating. Yet we never discuss it, and it's not part of the way that I think about their experience, which is bizarre. Now I'm thinking about how difficult it must be to be in a relationship and not feel fulfilled, and the additional shame you must then feel about what you're 'supposed' to feel.

All the different kinds of shames.

Yeah. There's just no way out of experiencing it, is there?

Do you feel that watching porn shapes your feelings about the prospect of having real-life sex? Does it make you more or less nervous about it?

Both, but in different ways. I'm not really sure what my sexuality is at this point, or what it's ever been. I've been wondering over the last few years whether in fact I am gay, and have just never really known that about myself, or whether I think that because I find women so much easier to talk with than men. Seeing people with bodies that look like mine engaging in sexual activity, being desired, and also seeing the range of sexual things you can do that don't focus on penetration – both those things have made me feel less nervous about having sex and like it's theoretically possible that I could meet someone whose needs and desires coincide with mine, in a way that we can communicate to each other. Then there is also a dimension of nervousness because the mainstream normative ideas of what is sexy and titillating and shocking are so prevalent and ingrained. The idea of running the risk of engaging with someone who's going to try to fit you into those categories brings a lot of potential for humiliation.

There's humiliation if you conform, if you fit within those categories, and also if you don't, and they're different kinds of humiliation, but both horrible in different ways. It's probably less immediately and viscerally horrible if you conform, but there's more a creeping sense of being objectified. The sense of being outside of it is unpleasant, too, obviously. This also leads to the question of how much crossover there is between porn and real sex – how much does that categorized way of looking at things transfer over? Is a person who watches very objectifying porn necessarily going to be a bad feminist? That feels like a crucial and yet impossible question to answer.

I do think that what a person enjoys in terms of porn consumption or masturbation-specific fantasy is a very different question to what they enjoy doing with a person. One of my English tutors at university once made this distinction about the Gothic novel, where he was talking about the difference between a gothic novel like Ann Radcliffe's *The Mysteries of Udolpho* and something like Henry James' *The Turn of the Screw*, and he said, It's like the difference between masturbation and sex. On reflection I think maybe he shouldn't have said that to me, but I did find it illuminating and it stuck with me. With something like *The Mysteries of Udolpho,* it's about a safe, containable, repeatable, reproducible, and therefore predictable thrill, whereas with *The Turn of the Screw* there's an encounter with something legitimately strange and other.

I do think there's something to that. Maybe in part this is because so much of the world's porn is not sexy. If I can find a video which has a few seconds that I genuinely enjoy, I will go back to that video or to those few seconds just for that purpose, because I have finally found something that isn't awful. It's looking for that dependable, repeatable, containable thrill, which is the opposite of how I think about encountering another person, where there's an inherent unpredictability and weirdness to it. Being sexually aroused with another person is a much more holistic experience than masturbation, in the utilitarian way it's often done. That said, you can try to think of these things as separate and distinct, but is there also a crossover, a bleed-through? Is there a possibility that when someone was with you, they were thinking about one of these safe repeatable thrills they go to? My main concern coming into those conversations would be: Do you understand the potential for humiliation in this conversation for me? Which is weird: why do I assume that men will be less complicated about sex than women are? I know why, it's because culturally everything tells me that that's supposed to be the case. But in reality, are men as complicated about sex as women?

I think men are – or at least the men in my life do have complicated thoughts about these things. Hearing you say that, I'm reminded of how my ex used to call masturbating without porn 'having an ethical wank'.

I've never heard that before.

It was probably his invention. It used to make me feel itchy in a way I couldn't identify, but now I think it was the glibness of it all, a way of doing lip service to the issue without actually doing any work in addressing or dealing with it. What about the eighty per cent of wanks that are unethical, then: what are you doing about those? And do you really believe that or are you just using that word to seem aware and enlightened? I suppose it smacked to me of the kind of privilege to not take things seriously – a privilege which of course doesn't just apply to gender, but also to ethnicity and sexuality and able-bodiedness: that if you belong to a group who isn't widely objectified and discriminated against then...

You don't have skin in the game.

If you see a woman in pain and you're turned on by it, then I imagine something in your brain, if you are a relatively deep-thinking sort of man, says, This is not good, and maybe you feel something –

But you are able to compartmentalize it.

Whereas I think many women see that and think: What the fuck? When you stand back from that, you think, They're people, how can you do that, you're a monster. As white people, we do that all the time in all kinds of contexts – we compart-mentalize. That's what you learn to do as a member of the socially dominant group. That's hard to come to terms with.

There's a danger of being reduced to being a woman when you are in front of a man, which is always a humil-iating experience.

When you talk about the potential of having these con-
versations and being humiliated – what, for you, are the
cornerstones on which the humiliation hinges?

I don't know if I've looked at the face of it enough to
have a good answer. A big aspect of it is a fear of having
a body that potentially doesn't operate as it should. Did
you ever watch *30 Rock*, the sit-com with Tina Fey?
That's the only time I've ever seen any discussion on TV
of female sexual performance, not in the sense of being
good in bed, but literally being too tense, for whatever
reason, to be able to allow or enjoy penetrative sex. It's a
well-known issue that lots of people struggle with.

Vaginismus, or is that the extreme example of it?

I think it's a scale. Vaginismus is when it's a lasting
condition, but it can be something that happens to you
either a lot or just once, presumably a bit like erectile
dysfunction. Anyway, there was one episode of *30 Rock*
where that was a plot point, and that was revelatory
because it was the first and only time I've seen it discussed. That's an example of something where there's a
feeling that if my body doesn't do what it's supposed to
do, I'd feel I was failing to be a proper woman, to function properly as a woman. If this thing that every bad
romance novel I ever sneaked off my mum's bookshelf as
a child told me was supposed to be universally enjoyable
is something I don't find enjoyable, *what does that mean*?
Nothing, is the real answer. Yet there is this fear. What if
I'm deficient, or deviant, or defective in some way?

SEVENTEEN

Seventeen is a straight man in his late thirties.
He is currently single.

SEVENTEEN — So this is my basic argument
against porn. There's a novel by James Baldwin called
Another Country, and he's describing this couple in
Harlem begin to touch other. It's beautiful. They're
beginning to explore their bodies, to explore their
possibilities. And then at a certain moment, a certain
crudeness emerges, and with it, a fear, and they fall back
on very standardized forms of male-female physical
interaction. He pushes her over, she enjoys it, or says she
enjoys it, and they lose sight of each other. There's this
moment where they don't know what they're doing when
they touch each other, they are exploring each other,
and then they can't grab it, so to speak. They're grabbing
each other, obviously. For me, that's what happens with
porn. It's a mechanism. I'm saying this polemically,
because it's a bit more complicated than that, but
essentially I think porn is a mechanism for not touching
each other.

   The example I will give, which is a trite example,
but I'll give it nonetheless, is that when I first moved to
America in 2008, which was a great revelation coming
from Europe – I'd only lived in England, France and the
Netherlands up to that point – in terms of people being
very open about wanting to have sexual contact or not
wanting to have sexual contact. And then, once you'd
be beginning sexual contact, I would start to receive
instructions, and it would be like, Okay, now you're
going to do this, and now you're going to do that, and

now you're going to do this, and I'd be there thinking, Wow, I'm doing a ballet show, but I don't really have the moves for a ballet show. It felt empty of content, somehow, formulaic. Where did you get this from? And why am I strangling you? And why is that the sine qua non of what we're doing? Because I don't know what it is to strangle someone. It's not that I'm against it. I'm not against any of it. It just all became really pat, it felt like we were living out these genres, these narratives, and it felt like I was in some bad novel. I would say, Where's this from? and she would say, Well, it's from porn. That's what I watch, and that's what I enjoy. Compared to the repression I had encountered in England, in some ways it felt liberatory. But also, I was thinking, I met you literally two hours ago and you want me to strangle you? It felt forced. Like we were actors inhabiting a script. Maybe I'm just not enough of a man. Maybe there was some weird masculinity anxiety there.

POLLY BARTON — *This was with multiple people, a recurring thing?*

It was a recurring thing. I'd be with American women. They'd say, Okay, now it's doggy style and you are going to strangle me from behind, and that's what I want. I demand that. Compare that sense of openness to my very British mother, who first had an orgasm at forty-five with a woman, when she discovered she was bisexual.

She told you that?

Oh, my mother and sex is a very open, explicit, long book. She was with my father for a relatively long time – I mean, she had me. She lost her virginity in the sixties

306

after a car crash. She had whiplash at the time, and I
think that set her up for her sexual life with men. Then,
she told me, I discovered this woman – who she's still
with – and I had an orgasm. She thought: What was that,
that was amazing. I thought that was fantastic. I was like,
Yes, thank God! Finally! I'm glad it happened for you.
When I was with these American women, though, it felt
like I was repeating what she had with her male friends,
the encounters with men that she had had before,
including with my father, which is: Okay, I'm doing this,
I'm playing this role, I am assuming a certain type of
position. What is that? That sort of role-playing is not
only determined to porn, but it's in relationship to porn
that I have most frequently encountered it.

*Did any of the desire to repeat what happens in porn come
from you?*

From the age of fifteen to the age of thirty-seven or so,
I did not watch porn. I refused to watch it, I absolutely
refused. I'm not saying that to make myself seem virtuous, incidentally – I can tell you billions of embarrassing
things about me. I just found it so banal and objectifying
and I couldn't inhabit any of those positions – I didn't
want to be the headless horseman. Then I think there
was a point later – which I don't think came from a good
position in my life, I think it came from a position of
frustration – where I was in a long-term relationship and
porn became one of the avenues of fantasy, maybe the
only avenue. But it was always marked by failure. It was
marked by the sense that I wasn't in a good relationship,
so there was this other possibility. It was never: Do I
want to do that? The possibility was: Here, I can have
an exploration of fantasy, which was not happening in

the relationship. And I still felt it was – as anyone who watches porn knows – banal, terrible and yet somehow compelling. What is that? What does that do? In a way I think that's just a cipher of how crap people are – I was going to say Western people, but I've experienced people from other spheres being crap about it too, so that's not right – at talking about sexuality. So I guess I still see it as a negative. I still see it as a failure, I still see it as something that emerges because we can't talk about our own desires: we fail to connect with each other as human beings. I can't see porn as positive, subjectively, as open as I am to the possibility that that is theoretically possible.

When you came to porn, after all that time, was the porn that you watched quite mainstream?

The first time I watched porn, which I wrote an essay about that I never published, I watched it for twenty-four hours. And I watched everything. I went through all the algorithms, just to write about it, just to see it. The essay turned out very impersonal. I had no real substantive reactions. I was like: Okay, so mothers is a thing, apparently, and daughters is also a thing, and mothers and daughters is a whole other thing. Then let's talk about fathers and sons. I decided to chart it, as ridiculous as it seems, because ultimately it's just contours of fleshy cuts, right? Which make you wonder: this is... sex? It feels like an almost abstract geometry. You go through being hard and being soft and then being hard again, and you end up with a moment where you're not sure you feel anything.

A good friend of mine, an Italian guy, has directed porn most of his life. If you are ever in New York, and you want to meet someone who does porn, he's a terrible human being. And I was explaining this experience to him, and I said, What do you do? How do you still get off on this? He said: Dwarfs. I was like, What? He said: I just like dwarfs. I was like, Man, you're an awful person, this is pure objectification. Then he explained, and his explanation went like this: desire begins – this is a bad historical narrative – by being open, innocent somehow. But then, as desire moves along the contours of the algorithms, as it's exposed to everything under the sun, the only place it can eventually end up in is with a very particular obsession. At least, that's where he ended up.

Before, in this one particular relationship, I had been obsessed with equality in sex: I will not orgasm unless she orgasms. So we'd begin with oral sex for her and that's first, and then, once she had climaxed, everything else became possible... And this was a terrible error on my part, or on our part, because sex just became this very moribund, dutiful, one-two-one-two thing. You orgasm, then I orgasm, then we sleep.

The possibility pornography opened up for me – falsely as it turned out – was an exploration of untrammelled desire, and the idea that untrammelled desire could be reciprocated. So it was domination, but it was a submission – it was various plays on that. It wasn't necessarily male domination, female submission, either; it was a playful shifting of roles. Exploring the question of what sex would be like if it wasn't just a reciprocal exchange of orgasms. What would it be like if it wasn't some version of the banal question posed in women's magazines: Are you getting enough orgasms?

So it was the reverse of that. It was letting go of the orgasm as telos. The dream of pornography, for me, was that there could be reciprocated, asymmetrical desire.

309

Maybe I think that. Again, that's not necessarily about male domination per se, but just that there could be a differential relationship to desire, that wasn't about both partners coming and then going to sleep. That was what brought me to porn for the period that I was really involved in it.

So after the twenty-four-hour marathon you carried on?

The twenty-four-hour marathon was before, that was just pure intellectual stimulation. It was out of the failure of this relationship, the she-orgasms-I-orgasm relationship, that I got into it. There was the classic moment where you say, so what does it mean in reality? What does it mean when people decide to move those fantasies and explorations they experience virtually, as it were, into the relationship itself? That was what that series of conversations with my then partner was about: What do you want? Our sex life isn't working. It's obviously not working. What would you like? Tell me! Tell me something, tell me anything. I didn't say I'd been watching porn, but probably that was evident, sadly, and it totally failed.

Why did it fail?

Because she said it was great. Our sex life is great, there's nothing to talk about. Whereas my take was: I don't know if it's great, we only have sex once a week, and we've been together a couple of years. It's not that long. We don't have children. So it didn't work at all. Which brings us to the question, why is pornography *really* interesting? Because having a good sex life is really difficult and really interesting and necessitates being vulnerable. Pornography is a total evasion of that for most men, for sure, but maybe its seductiveness – perhaps I am being too utopian here – is that it can also promise a path into that.

Do you think?

Maybe sometimes? I *think* I have friends who have watched porn together and that has been a conduit to them talking properly. It's not like they're going to model their sex on the pornography, that's not what happens. But it's so crude and it's so banal that in a way it opens things up, and makes people feel that they can talk about what they desire. It doesn't have to be difficult, but for some reason it is very difficult. Maybe porn can do that sometimes – can enable that conversation.

Now I want to interview you. Why even begin this book?

From when I was quite young, I associated porn with everything that I hate about the patriarchy. It feels tied up with everything unpleasant I've experienced as a woman, from teenagehood on. It's not that during school I rationally thought it was precipitated by porn, but when I first encountered porn, I had a strong feeling that this lies at the heart of everything I'm experiencing in interacting with men, this is why I'm being treated the way I am. Porn encapsulated that, and I felt endangered by it. Now I see, in retrospect, that kind of porn as a manifestation of this much broader thing – misogyny, and the patriarchy. My attitude these days is far more tolerant. I fully accept there's a real range of interesting, ethical porn, etc. But there's still something about the visuals and the language that's used in mainstream porn – the descriptions of what's going on in the videos – that I find objectionable. The second, possibly even bigger thing, is the gulf that I feel it creates, particularly in my experience within heterosexual relationships. At times in the past, I've had big arguments with people I've been in relationships with about porn where I feel like I can't bear it, that it's the sort of visible manifestation of everything that I find —

Because it literally *is* violent as well, right? Let's not forget this about porn. Looking at these images, sometimes, fucking hell.

I remember talking about porn with the guy I was going out with at uni. I was explaining how distressing I found it, and he was saying, We need to change the structure of our society. You can try pinning it all on porn and get rid of it but you're not going to get very far, and then he spoke about some experiment where they'd tried to evaluate the effect of porn, but they couldn't, because there was no control group, they couldn't find any men who hadn't consumed porn. I remember him declaring that triumphantly as if to say, See, your position is unrealistic and untenable. I think about that a lot, and this feeling I couldn't articulate then: I'm totally okay with the idea that lots of people crave visual stimuli. What I'm not okay with is the inbuilt violence.

It's not about sex.

Exactly. It's a basic point, in a way, to the point that I feel naïve even formulating it to you, but I do feel like it's not really spoken about. That's perhaps what this book is about.

There's a horrible, basic question in what you're asking. Which is not to say that male sexuality is entirely violent – but is it somewhat violent? What's striking about porn

312

is that it's all basically images of women being abused. That's what's fucked about it, right? And so then you get to thinking whether that is actually male sexual desire – or is it a desire for power? And are these things different? Men don't want to fuck someone; they want to debase them. Is that part of what their sexuality is? Or is porn an expression of something else entirely? There are so many explanations possible. One is – and this is my Italian friend's explanation – that it is porn itself that corrupts male desire, that it is an expression of the algorithm. You begin looking at nice vanilla sex, and soon you are staring at something wildly fetishistic or exploitative or violent. That's a common account of the dangers of the internet. The more banal but scary explanation is that this is actually what male sexuality looks like.

Then you're approaching the road that a lot of radical feminists in the seventies went down, which was that men like porn because they're men and they are fucked, and then we're back with Dworkin, and all sex is rape, because that's fundamentally the drive of male sexuality and that's what pornography teaches us. I don't think that's basic at all. It's a huge question: what does pornography teach us about sexuality – and it sounds as though what you're saying is, particularly, about male sexuality. That's really uncomfortable. I don't even think it's easy to argue against Dworkin here. I think you have to get some really good interviews with men. (Oh, is this what you're recording this for? Ha.) But you have to get some men really talking honestly about sex and that's hard. Because they won't even talk honestly about it to themselves. So how can you talk about it to anyone else? That's the first step. They'll say, Pornography is great, everyone loves sex, women are sex positive, I'm sex positive. So you have to say: But the porn you're watching is people being strangled until they're blue in the face and then passing out. What is that? That's what's so disturbing about sex.

I began this chat from the assumption that you were writing something that was pornography positive, because I couldn't imagine you writing something pornography negative, which is why I ran into the other extreme of my own thought, which is: maybe I can redeem pornography. Whereas most of me is on the other side. Obviously, I exist in the dichotomy, but anyway, it was interesting just then to hear you say, What the fuck is this?

Most of you is on the other side?

Porn's bad! Porn's bad! I mean, everything I said is true, and I've looked at porn. But porn should be annulled from this world, in the same way I think Instagram should probably be annulled from this world. There's a parallel between the anonymity of these endless images through which one scrolls and the horrors of the headless horsemen that populate porn videos. A friend of mine, my cousin, stopped drinking alcohol, but he didn't tell me that. We went out to a bar in Soho and he ordered a bottle of vodka. I didn't know he was in AA at that time. He made me drink a bottle of vodka in front of him so that he could get a kind of thrill from it.

That sounds like weird behaviour.

He's a pretty weird guy. I asked him why he was doing it and he said, I want to tell my sponsor at AA that I watched my cousin drink a bottle of vodka and I didn't do it. I said, So what do you do now that you don't drink or smoke? How do you get your kicks? To which he replied, I have my white noise. For three hours before I go to bed, I watch the most violent pornography I can find. I don't masturbate. I don't even feel anything. I just watch it, and I don't think about anything. Hearing that, I thought: My God, man. Have a vodka. Which is all to say, there's something numbing about it. It numbs relations. That's what got me about those young women or old women that I slept with in America. I know I sound ridiculous when I say this, but I'll say it anyway: I felt like I was not a person – I was a function. They weren't relating to me as a person. They had their set of tricks that they want performed and then that's it, and it just felt totally anonymous. I've never seen non-anonymous pornography. That's my basic objection. Maybe there is some amazing feminist pornography somewhere.

That's one standard argument against getting rid of porn, right? That there's so much queer and fetish and interesting porn. That the democratization afforded by free internet porn has brought about this huge prevalence of different perspectives, different manifestations of desire. I get that, and I want to believe it, but —

But it occurs in the same algorithm and for that reason, I'm not sure. What's the difference between eroticism and porn? There's a huge difference, but the democratization of the porn industry so that anyone can make it was actually a disaster because it means everyone is making algorithmic porn – determined by likes and views and the internet marketplace – and then their sexual relations become porn and they post them on Pornhub or whatever... That seems pretty bad: we have reduced our lives to the dimensions of the algorithm.

The performativity of it is a difficult subject. I fully accept Judith Butler's lesson that we are continually performing ourselves, our identities. And yet when I have good sex, it doesn't feel performative. It doesn't feel like I'm doing it for an outside eye.

I don't think we are performing. I've read Judith, but I don't think that's true. If I'm at a publishing party, then my God I'm performing, of course. But there are also moments of vulnerability – and I think Judith would agree with this – which are predicated on the performance breaking down. That could be sex, that could be conversation, that could be all sorts of things. I think they would agree that you can't frame that in the same way that one talks about performative sex, on a one-night stand. There are times when you don't know your way about, to quote your favourite philosopher Wittgenstein.

The way people talk about sexism in pornography is normally reductive because it's always a question of a legal framing. It's about banning it, and I think banning is a dumb thing. You can talk about prohibition, but people are just going to carry on. That can't be the crux of the issue: this endless debate about whether it should be banned, in which we acknowledge a ban is not feasible.

The issue has to be: what lies beyond the current relationship our society has with it, and how does one get there? Can pornography be singular – can it escape cliché and script? One of the terrible things about pornography is that it's so anonymous. It's my cousin watching three hours of white noise – as he calls it – of people being tortured. What is that? But take it seriously, he literally doesn't remember shit: pornography becomes not so much an experience of life as an a-experience, a chasm, a place in which life stops happening... I'm used to telling stories and they're about human beings who have experiences, and they change, and the same is true of you and what you write. Yet so much of porn for me feels like it's about – it's not necessarily what it needs to focus on – nullity and boredom and forgetfulness and tiredness. How do you tell a story about that? How does one get at that? It's not even the worst part of human beings. It is evil, but it's not the evil of death or murder or something Dostoyevsky would write about. It's the forgetfulness of someone who can't even get a hard-on masturbating. How do you write about their boredom looking at the scene they used to masturbate to three weeks ago, their compulsive desire for new content, and their nagging realization that they have to go to the office tomorrow? That's a strange scene to write.

What would even happen if we banned it all? It's impossible to imagine right now.

That's the problem, isn't it? You can say, Ban it all, and then you're in the Dworkin position of being on the banning committee, which is fine, and you're probably in the right. On the other hand, that's not going to stop new porn. Then you're left with the question: What is the liberating gesture relative to the porn industry? So then it feels to me, controversially not controversially, that you have to write the book for men. I'm not saying you *should* write the book for men. Let me just explain the thought process, though. If one wants to not just take a Dworkin position, but say, This is really bad, do you understand why it's really bad, then that has to be addressed to the people who consume it. Of course there are loads of

317

women who consume it, as I experienced in America, but the majority of people are men, right? It's made for men. That's why I find the women who love porn deeply problematic, even if they're not as problematic as me, because it's male porn.

When I initially conceived of this book, I thought I was just going to talk to women because porn is conceived of as something 'for men', and I felt like women were being left out of the conversation. But then at some point I realized that talking only to women would only give half of the picture. It came up in early conversations, actually – other women saying they wanted me to talk to men, and the scales falling from my eyes a bit. It's awkward to have these conversations with people, and it's more awkward to have them with men, but in a way, that's the proof that this needs to happen. That there's a gulf that needs to be bridged. It now feels very important to me to include men. Although I still don't know if men will read a book a woman has written about porn.

Then it's like, which men? I guess that's a question of market. I think there is a book to be written addressing men in a popular vein about porn, and I don't think that book has anything to say. It's the book Malcolm Gladwell would write. You know: You like blow-jobs, don't you? Please, please, let's not write that. It's not going to tell us anything. Meanwhile the book you will write will probably only attract men who like to think that they're emancipated. But we all know that men are not emancipated. So maybe that's a good place to begin.

EIGHTEEN

Eighteen is a bisexual woman in her thirties, living in the UK. She is married to a man, and has children.

POLLY BARTON —— *Is there anyone you can talk to about porn, or does it not come up?*

EIGHTEEN —— It's not a subject that comes up much. I can count the times I've talked about it with friends. I remember talking about it once, in my twenties, with friends at university: there was my gay friend and my lesbian friend, and me who's bi in the middle. At that point, I was a bit anti-porn, so I was saying I felt like it reproduces a very patriarchal view of pleasure, and women are victimized, and it's a terrible thing for society, it shouldn't exist. I remember my lesbian friend saying, 'You're only saying that because you haven't seen any good porn. You can only have that opinion of the things that you've seen.' That made me think, Yeah, maybe they're right. So the three of us sat and watched some together. The point wasn't to get aroused – it was more educational in a way. That was quite a fun moment. It hasn't really come up since.

Was the porn you watched then what you'd call good porn?

Well, I didn't continue to watch it, so I clearly wasn't hooked. It did bring about the realization that it's a subject I don't know much about. I don't know the scope of it. Now, like with anything else, I think it makes no sense to even try to forbid it. The more diversity or the more options, the better.

*There is this mainstream type of porn, which is what lots
of people think about when they think of porn, and which
is probably the only porn that a lot of people have seen. It's
very heteronormative, features the same kinds of bodies,
promotes a phallocentric idea of sex, and feels very tied into
the mechanisms of patriarchy —*

And rape culture.

*Then there's a diversity of queer, body-positive, kink, fetish
porn. And everything in between. How do you reckon with all
of that?*

It's hard. My way of thinking changed when a friend who
likes burlesque and Dita von Teese introduced me to her
Instagram account, and then I found Gia Genevieve,
who is a model and a burlesque performer. She's also got
this Dita von Teese burlesque style. I really enjoy her art,
her body, and how beautiful she is. I think this would be
my kind of porn: it's very empowered. She chooses how
to appear, or at least I get the impression that she chooses
how to present herself, and with curves. It's interesting
because she was on the *Playboy* cover. Before, I would
have had a very stereotypical image of *Playboy* girls as
being used as puppets or objects, but when you hear her
talk, it doesn't seem that way. I feel conflicted for liking
her so much. I really think she's hot. But I still have
issues with the Hugh Hefner world. I remember, when
he died, both Gia and Dita posted something really
beautiful about him. I don't know much about him, but
my view is that, even though he advocated for 'sexual
liberation', he grew to be an old man who continuously
exploited young female bodies. It seems like there's more
to it than that, though.

When you say you're conflicted, are you saying that when she says she's not exploited and enjoys it, you can't a hundred per cent believe her?

No, I believe her. The conflict or the tension that I am addressing is this idea that it can be something very empowering for a woman to embrace their body and decide to show it. At the same time, this act of showing the body is part of a larger society that commodifies and sexualizes women's bodies from a very young age, since they're babies basically. I'm the mother of a daughter, and I hate to see bikinis made for babies, for new-borns. Seeing those two triangles bothers me so much, but I see the connection between those two triangles for the baby and the content I'm enjoying. That's the conflict.

Do you feel that it's different for you to be turned on or find pictures of her beautiful, and for a man to be experiencing that?

I don't know. In the private act, there's perhaps not much of a difference between the ways people are turned on. I've seen some videos of her, though, and in one of them, there's a man nearby, screaming as she's doing the striptease act. And the way he shouts at her – I wouldn't shout like that. Howling, very macho, as she's perform-ing. I would never react in that way. In the privacy of our homes, I wouldn't see a difference between me and a man getting turned on, but I think in the context of the spectacle, there may be some reactions that are more masculine. The kinds of things we've all seen on TV, like the image of the man paying and having a lap dance, and whooping and howling. I don't see a woman doing that or playing that role.

321

Those pictures of Gia Genevieve seem quite soft and tasteful, with nice outfits and good lighting. I sometimes feel that mainstream porn, by contrast, can feel quite harsh.

Yes, it's definitely connected to the production and lighting and everything. When I was living in Osaka, my partner and I went to a few love hotels. In one of them, when we'd go into the room, they would have these videos playing which I desperately wanted to turn off, because they had the opposite of the desired effect. They would play videos with very young women, almost children really, who looked about fourteen, fifteen, wearing traditional costumes. Maybe they were of age, but they looked very young, and it was the kind of porn where they would say, 'Oh, it hurts.' I always wanted to switch it off, but I couldn't figure out how. It's complicated though, isn't it? A bit of roughness exists in my fantasies – not super extreme, but there is a little bit of that. I understand the fantasy of being taken forcefully, that will play out in my head, but I can't bear to see it, because then it becomes one of my biggest fears as a woman, which is to be raped.

When you're with men who don't have that same visceral reaction to that type of porn, it can feel quite troubling. Even if it's not necessarily what they would choose to watch. Is that kind of discrepancy something you've experienced?

I don't know. In the love hotel, I was a bit more upset than my partner, but he was also trying to turn it off. I haven't been in this situation with other men where I could judge whether they were less bothered. It makes sense that the woman feels more connected to that victim role and bothered by it. Especially when it's the woman being

322

abused in the video, which is often the case.

Let's say the love hotel was playing nice porn. Is the idea of having sex or being intimate with someone with porn in the background something that you might want to do? For me, porn feels more like a private world.

Yeah, totally. Porn is more tied to masturbation, which is like a solo dance. Some people do masturbate with their partners or in front of their partners, but for me it's also my own thing. I don't need porn to be with someone, but if it's there and it's enjoyable, why not? It could be a special thing, but not something you need every time.

In love hotels, sometimes there's a mirror on the ceiling and whatnot. I'm not going to put one in my house, but if it's there, maybe you can use it somehow. Mirrors emphasize the fact that you're looking, but also being looked at, so they might feel scary, but also quite exciting.

I guess love hotels are great for creating an atmosphere that's different to something you might have at home. In many cases, that's their purpose.

Yeah, it's a fantasy world.

Porn is also a fantasy world, and I think that's one of the reasons I want to affirm its existence, you know? We should have fantasy worlds. That's a form of freedom. I guess what I worry about is that everyone is fed the same fantasy, and it's starting to feel prescriptive and constraining, and anything but free. Are masturbation and porn things that you feel comfortable talking to your partner about?

Yes and no. I think we talked more about it in the beginning. We've been together for years, so we don't talk about masturbation so often anymore. I do feel quite comfortable with him, though. I haven't addressed it lately, but I'm sure I could. He knows I have my vibrators, but I don't use them with him – I think we tried once, at his suggestion, but it just didn't work. When I'm with him, I don't use them as often, but if he goes away on a trip or something I will recharge them. I don't think it's a replacement for sex, though.

It sounds as though you are both comfortable with the idea that the other one masturbates. Does the idea of him watching porn and the kind of porn he watches ever cross your mind or worry you?

At this point, I feel quite trusting. I am sure he masturbates but it doesn't bother me at all. He may be watching some stuff, but it's not a topic we discuss, so I don't actually know. I can see myself being bothered by it if he preferred to do that than talking to me or watching things with me – if he were just locked in his room watching porn. Even then I would be bothered more by the fact he was ignoring me than the fact he was doing that. I don't feel any competition or threat or anything.

What about with previous partners? Has porn ever been something that's worried you?

Not really, but in the past I didn't necessarily have the openness that I have with my current partner.

I get that. At times in the past for me, the whole thing has felt like this big untouchable.

It is a bit of an untouchable. For me it's very connected to sex work and sex trafficking, and those industries. It's very different to consume porn than to pay for sex, but somehow I feel like they co-exist, or inform each other. There's an overlap in my view. Not all the people that do porn are sex workers, obviously, but maybe some are. Especially those people who are sex trafficked or part of human trafficking – they are sometimes exploited through porn, through being forced to be with people. I have these fears about the whole thing, which is one of the reasons I'm hesitant towards the porn industry, and buying things or paying.

That's an important comparison, isn't it? I'm thinking about the way that we treat those women in society. My sense is that almost all men watch porn and probably a lot of women do as well, and yet the way porn actors are viewed by society is terrible, even if it is improving. There's this unclearable cloud of shame around it.

Yeah, exactly. On TV and so on, the worst thing that they can pull out of your drawer is: You did this when you were younger! Now, with the pandemic, and the rise of users of platforms like OnlyFans, a similar thing happened. I read about a medical student in the US who was doing OnlyFans to make a living and was then shamed for it. Seeing that, I think: Fuck you!

Compare that to actors who do films with sex scenes and escape totally unscathed, reputation-wise. What does the difference consist in there? Is it the idea that you actually want to do it? Or the fact that the organ actually enters the orifice? It's so Victorian.

There's a big moral hypocrisy there. It's ridiculous.

I was once with this guy who told me that he paid for sex and I freaked out, in a way that feels bad to me now, like I was being a bad feminist. I think it comes from a similar sense of freaking out about porn. I had this sinking feeling. Oh, you are the objectifier of women, you know? I don't think it's morally bad to pay for sex, but I find the whole ecosystem within which that happens so desperately unequal.

Definitely. It's a complicated topic. Now there's so much tension between abolitionist feminists who think prostitution or sex work should be abolished, and feminists who support sex worker rights. But how can you try to stop something that happens so often and that will continue to happen? I don't believe in trying to stop something that I think is unstoppable, I would rather put my energy into making the world fairer and equal rather than abolishing sex work, while also recognizing how unequal and how oppressive it can be.

Once I was talking with high-school friends in Colombia and I heard that they had a party and hired a stripper. I remember thinking: Aaah what the fuck? But if I were in New York or whatever, I would probably pay to see a burlesque/striptease show. Why am I so hypocritical with these guys who had a stripper come to their house? She's making a living out of it. Still, my feeling or fear is that they're not respecting her, or they are being nasty, or saying nasty things, and I think it's disgusting. Both reactions coexist in me in a complicated way.

It's about the power balance, isn't it? If you paid to see a stripper in New York, you would be seeing her as an equal.

326

Almost the other way around: I'm your follower, your fan.

Do you watch porn if you're wanting to be turned on?

Not usually. Gia's Instagram account is enough for me. That's the level I'm at with it. If I want to be turned on, I can find some images that work for me on a few different Instagram accounts. I've looked for porn in the past, obviously, but I don't do it that often at the moment. Perhaps because of my life situation, if I'm searching and getting onto these websites where things pop up, it makes me feel strange.

When you're on those websites, do you ever feel a twinge of guilt?

Totally. I stopped very quickly. Since I found this Instagram, it's all I need. I don't feel any remorse or guilt. It's been really good.

Do you think of it as porn?

Maybe it's easier for me to show you something like this and say, 'See, it's quite beautiful! It's not just porn.' Maybe there is some looking down on porn involved. It is more than porn: it has a little bit of porn, but it's also pretty...

I know what you mean: it seems more like erotica than porn. Sometimes if I watch sex scenes from films or TV series to be turned on, I wonder if I'm just trying to sidestep the problem I have with porn aesthetically, so that I don't have to think about it ethically.

327

On those sites that I haven't visited in a while, there's a curiosity and some turn-on. If I let my body take it, it felt good to watch. But if I put even the slightest thought into it, I would think: No. Especially if those thoughts were about the possibility of people being exploited, because that's something I'm so radically against.

You mentioned erotica. Embarrassingly enough, I enjoyed *Fifty Shades of Grey*. I don't think I've seen the movie, so I guess I'm not that big of a fan, but I enjoyed reading it. The friend who recommended it to me made a joke about how, after reading it, you won't need to Google any weird stuff anymore. Maybe books feel better because there are no victims.

I'm interested in what you said before about being able to enjoy slightly rapey fantasies, but not being able to cope with seeing it on screen. Is it more tolerable when it's fiction? Actually, that is Fifty Shades of Grey, *isn't it?*

It's terrible, but it works!

Does the fact you're not actually seeing it enable you to get into it more? I know that there are a lot of women who do watch porn with rough sex and enjoy it, and who would say, Just because I'm enjoying it, doesn't mean I want it to happen.

The fantasy is always different.

As far as I know, men don't fantasize about being raped very much. If they do, it gets seen as a kink. I think it's far more common for women to fantasize about being raped, and men to fantasize about raping women. When we're making this porn, which is just endlessly reproducing this fantasy, are we ensuring that it remains the only fantasy that people have?

328

That's why I think BDSM is so powerful. The figure of the dominant woman. That's one of the reasons it's so subversive to have that world where men are receiving orders. A growing world.

Yeah I sense it is too, but don't you think it's still quite niche, men who like to be dominated?

I don't know. There's places where masculinity is so fragile that I'm not sure.

When I've watched porn in the past, I've tended to watch either women alone or women with other women, because as soon as the penis gets involved, this whole dynamic comes in that I don't like.

Yeah, me too. I'm not into penises in porn at all. In real life, I'm okay with them. It's a weird organ, but I'm fine with it.

I know what you mean. I don't think I'm into organs, full stop.

We've seen sex scenes so often, in all kinds of media, all kinds of Hollywood movies and shows, like *Game of Thrones*. So widely accepted, and almost celebrated. Whereas porn is taboo, hidden. It's made dirty or unwatchable – if you're watching it must be in secret. Maybe that's also part of why it is exciting to watch.

Maybe the worse it gets, the more there's that thrill where you think, I'm watching something really illicit.

When I was a kid, in Colombia, we didn't have cable and of course we didn't have the porn channels, but if you waited late enough and you put it on a certain channel, it would be all blurry because we didn't have signal, so it was all this fuzz, and then sometimes you could make out from within the fuzz the outline of a boob or a penis here and there. That was great because I couldn't see them properly, I could only just about make them out, and it was such a turn-on. I had it on silent because it was at night and my parents were in the next room, but it was so exciting.

Now, though, with the internet, children can see anything at the click of a mouse. It's a big change. We live in a different time and porn is way more accessible. It's scarier because if you Google something, then maybe you end up in a place where you have to put your camera on and there's room for online extortion, especially with young people. It brings new dangers.

I wonder about what it does if you're never using your imagination at all. Do you worry about your daughter with that?

Not yet, but eventually I will. I hope I can be open with this and that she grows up a bit grounded and not having weird expectations about what sex is. That in reality, it's short, and it's two bodies...

...that are probably far from perfect.

Yeah, and it's not such a big thing. There's so much more glamour around it on screen, all these scenes where there're roses and candles... You don't need that! Brush your teeth and you're good to go!

Do you have thoughts or feelings on ethnicity and the way it occurs in porn?

It doesn't really occupy my thoughts, but if you are talking about porn, you have to talk about what kinds of bodies are being presented. It really bothered me when I was in Japan to see how Japanese women or Asian women were generally portrayed. I remember going into some sex shops to buy vibrators and seeing again the recurrent video image of a younger Asian person almost crying and saying, 'It hurts, it hurts.' That really breaks me. It bothers me a lot, to this day, the way that Asian women are portrayed as these infantile, weak, suffering, subservient people, when I know that's not the case. Japanese women are very strong and can be very outspoken. It's bothersome. In other places, there's that image of the Latina as a sex symbol, and of course, Black bodies – both female and male – have been sexualized a lot. White bodies aren't in the same way, even though there's the trope of the blonde *Playboy* girl, who has big boobs and is stupid. That's pretty bad as well. I don't think the white male body has any of these exaggerated connotations, though.

Was that Latina fetishization something you encountered when you were living in Osaka? Or do you find it more in Britain?

I think it happens more in the internet sphere. I haven't experienced it myself. There was a time, in the late nineties if I'm not mistaken, when there was a lot of human trafficking of Colombian women to Japan. They would go as mules, with drugs, thinking that was a job, or sometimes even tricked with a job opportunity as entertainers (singers or dancers) but then once there, they were sexually enslaved, had their passports taken away and whatnot, they'd even be given products to whiten

331

their skin, bleach their hair, and so on.

When I went to Japan, I remember a person at the Japanese embassy saying, Be very careful when you're there, don't go to a man's house by yourself or accept any invitations from men, because when you say you're Colombian, they might get the wrong impression, and never, ever dye your hair blonde.Once I was in Japan I never felt that, but later I heard some stories about a Colombian ambassador who was known for asking the male employees at the embassy to go to Kabukichō in Tokyo and other red-light districts to find him Colombian prostitutes. When they'd get them into the bedroom, the employees would say, I'm Colombian, I'm from the embassy, if you don't have a passport please come with me. Apparently he saved twenty women or so like that, or that's the story at least.

Do you think that's true?

At least some of it. One woman, Marcela Loaiza, wrote a memoir retelling her experience, though I haven't read it. That awareness of human trafficking and coercion has made me very critical of prostitution and porn. And when I hear about queer and trans sex workers for whom this is the main way of surviving in this world, especially in countries like Colombia, then of course I don't want to be moralizing and telling them what to do with their bodies. Maybe I am a bit more old school in being critical, because I have that awareness.

If people become sex workers because they want to or they need to and it's in their own power to do that, then I want to respect and protect that choice. There's no part of me that wants to take that away from anyone. But it's also disingenuous to pretend that everyone goes into it out of their own free choice.

The consumer can't know one way or the other, so you end up complicit in the system. That's one of the problems with wanting to do sex work or defending the right to do it, because you may be still supporting the coercive part of it. There's a similar discussion around surrogacy. At this point, I think it's unrealistic to forbid this mode of work. We need to regulate it and make sure that these women are not being imprisoned and treated like womb factories, make sure they have proper healthcare. Some feminists may be very against that, but I'm not, because it's already happening. At some point, the discussion needs to go beyond whether it should exist or not. We have to acknowledge that it exists. Let's start from there. How can we make it fairer for everyone involved? I thought it was quite revolutionary how in *Love Actually*, which was a huge hit everywhere in the world, one of the stories was the porn couple, which is very comedic. A kind of caricature.

A porn couple? I don't remember them.

Yeah, they meet doing porn, and start dating. When they're filming the scene, they're doing this stuff but then it zooms to their faces and they're totally not into it. And then, despite the fact they've just been having sex with one another, they're so cute and awkward by the coffee machine. It's very problematic as a depiction, but it puts the question of porn in a mainstream family movie as a proper job, and with lots of humanity, for these characters. They're very likeable characters.

Huh. I find it bizarre that I just erased that from my memory.

I hate to confess this, but I've watched this movie more than once, so I remember.

NINETEEN

Nineteen is a bisexual man in his mid-thirties.
He is married to a woman, and has a child.

POLLY BARTON — *Can you remember your first*
encounter with porn?

NINETEEN — I can, yeah. It was early internet days,
so I was eleven or twelve I guess? I was round at the
house of one of my friends who got the internet before
other people, and there was a website he had found
called The Hun, and that was my first experience of any
kind of pornography. It was a whole sea of tiny thumbnails on screen, a couple of videos but mostly pictures.
We were looking at them and laughing and saying, Look
at this, watch this, but nothing occurred. We hadn't had
the chance to see it anywhere else.

And that was straight people fucking? Or not that hardcore?

I can't remember specifics, but it was a mix of straight
and lesbian sex. Probably mostly the latter.

Did it turn you on?

Not at all. I was a late developer in that sense. I must
have been sixteen the first time I looked at porn and had
a successful wank.

So the first time you wanked was watching porn?

I'd tried a bit before that without pictures, and it didn't

work. Then I tried with *Sky* – which was one of the lad mags along with *Loaded*, I think it was the tamest of the lot – and just thought, I can't do it. Then I remember very clearly being sixteen and going on this same website that continued to exist, The Hun, and it happening. From then on, as is quite common, it was very much all the time.

Always watching porn?

No, not at all.

So it wasn't as if wanking with no porn was no good and wanking with porn was good – it just so happened that your first successful wank was with porn, and that was great, and it just unleashed the dragon?

Yeah, completely. I think this is fairly common, but the number of times it was happening was just obscene. It was just in toilets, wherever, random places, all the time. Just obscene amounts for a while.

Is wanking watching porn and wanking not watching porn quite a different thing?

Over time it's got harder to do it without. I need some kind of stimulus. As time has gone on, I'm less physically sensitive than I was before, so it's harder to get to that stage. Sometimes that extra impetus is needed.

Does that feel like an age thing?

I said it was age, but to be honest it's mostly a question of habit. The porn aspect of it creates a moment that's

336

separate, and that feels especially important when you have lots of people around, and a kid.

It helps almost to demarcate it, in a way? To enter a place of fantasy, escapism.

Yes, and that influences the kind of porn I watch, which is generally very soft. People kissing is the biggest turn-on, in a way. I wouldn't put on a long porn film and watch the whole thing, but I get almost nothing out of just watching two people having sex, it doesn't really give me anything.

You need a narrative, or a story?

Yeah that is really important, in terms of fantasy. That's always been the biggest thing.

How has it been when you have veered into more hardcore territory?

My experience of hardcore stuff is aggressive and close up and fast and all the things I don't find in any way attractive. None of those things turn me on at all, so I've never stuck it out for long. Even in terms of role-play or different situations, I've got no interest at all in S and M type stuff, or servants or subservience of any kind. It doesn't do anything for me.

So the woman being treated aggressively is not a turn-on?

No, completely the opposite. To the point where if I'd been watching something and it got to that stage, even if the woman's hair is held, it cuts me off completely.

Because you think about the women being in pain?

I would never want to be in that situation, where I'm doing that to somebody. That's the entirely selfish part of it. The second thing I feel is that it doesn't look okay. It doesn't look consensual. Whatever the ethics or the reality of that is, it doesn't look consensual. But it's not just that. It's the other thing as well, because you're in the mode of putting yourself in that situation, and they happen simultaneously. I would never put myself in that situation, so it doesn't turn me on, and on top of that I feel uncomfortable witnessing it.

My sense is that a lot of people – at least those who give it some thought – feel the same on a rational level, but they're turned on by this power dynamic that they wouldn't want to recreate or be part of in real life, and so they experience this disconnect. Whereas for you, it feels as if that's quite aligned? Even within the fantasy realm of porn you are turned on by the sort of sex you want to have in real life?

Yes. The only thing that's outside of that is the specific circumstance or the specific people that are in it, in terms of age and gender. I watch stuff with older women and men. The MILF thing is a thing for me, for sure. I watch some gay porn too. I find myself in a strange position with that, because it does turn me on but I'm not really imagining myself in that position.

I know you're in a monogamous relationship and you aren't planning on having sex with anyone outside of that. Does the idea of doing stuff with men now feel like a more remote possibility?

338

It feels as unlikely as anything else, I would say.

When you're watching gay porn, does that feel less worrying to you? People talk about being worried about porn performers, but my sense is that usually they're worried about the women. When I hear my gay male friends objectifying men, I find it a lot less objectionable than when I hear straight men objectifying women. I suppose I'm curious how porn fits in with that.

Yeah, I think you're right about people worrying more about the women. It's difficult to say, to some degree, because I'm not interested in watching violent porn. Maybe that's an irrelevant thing to say, because I suppose the ethics could still be dodgy no matter what kind of porn it is. When you're watching somebody being double penetrated and seemingly in great pain, the ethical issues are more obvious. Since the stuff I've watched is extremely soft, and it's more just about the scenario, I've never thought about it. But neither have I ever watched gay porn and asked myself about the ethics. I'm certain that the same issues apply, without question.

I also prefer soft stuff, because it feels more real. That's also why I find scenes from films much more of a turn-on, paradoxically.

Believability is extremely important for me too. I remember watching this gay sex scene in *Queer as Folk* – it's quite explicit, it's the scene when two characters first get together – when I was whatever age and being really turned on by it, because they were good actors and it felt like a proper scene, you know? That plays a massive part. When sex is well done in films, the emphasis can't be too much on the groin area, so there's more of the rest of the body. By its nature it can appear more tender, there's more kissing, there's more top half stuff. I'm not really that interested in seeing a dick going into a vagina, it just doesn't do it for me at all. Or a dick going into anything.

Any orifice?

Yeah, no. That's the thing that pisses me off about porn – and again, I know this is a standard argument – you see almost nothing of the man. At the very beginning of it, you might get the odd shot of his back. It's not that I need to see a man because it makes it more arousing, but it does create a more realistic picture.

I read recently that only one third of women can experience orgasm through penetrative sex. I never realized that, because I've never had a problem with it, but it totally blew my mind. I'm tempted to say that the obsession with penetration and close-ups and the general phallocentrism of porn might have increased the pressure on women for that to be the thing that they enjoy, but it's clearly not that simple or one directional, right? With the younger generations, porn will increasingly be their first taste of what sex should look like. There will probably be fewer formative moments with sex scenes in films, let alone actual sex, and more will be with porn. I know it sounds grandma-esque but I worry about what young, malleable brains will make of that slamming, getting your pussy pounded, coming on people's faces kind of stuff when they've no real-life encounters to contextualize it with. Or else, real-life encounters with people who also learned all they know from porn.

340

There's nothing redeeming about that whatsoever. I'm sure there are people who like to have cum on their face, both men and women, but there's no way of portraying that in a porn film without it looking like exploitation.

I remember a friend told me that she was having sex with the guy that she was going out with at school and he'd tried to come on her face, and she'd violently pushed him to the floor. She said this strange, superhuman strength swelled up in her. I think she really shocked him. When she told me, I was genuinely bewildered by this idea of come on someone's face. That's a sign of how naïve I was at the time, I had no idea it was a thing. Nineteen-year-old me felt a pure sense of, Why would you want to do that, that's such a weird thing to do. It seemed like there was nothing sexual about it at all, like it was done purely to humiliate someone. Now I'm older and more worldly, I realize that there's most likely tons of people actively turned on by that.

There must be. I was listening to a podcast by Jon Ronson, *The Butterfly Effect*, about the creation of Pornhub. He goes into the algorithms involved in choosing what turns people on. Going by that, there must be people who are turned on by cumshots. When you go into the subcategories of that stuff it's mind-boggling, the level of detail is unbelievable.

Can you give me an example?

If you're ever searching for something, let's say you start writing 'next-door neighbour', you type in the word 'next' and a great list immediately flashes up: 'next-door neighbour', 'next to my ass', 'next in line for a fuck', 'next put a razorblade up my ass'. There are a ludicrous number of categories. But then the question is, did the desire to do all of those things come out of having seen them? To return to the original question: do people think, I really would like somebody to come on my face! Or I'd really like to come on somebody's face! Or did they see it and think, Oh, that looks interesting!

Can we talk a bit about the relationship aspect? Have you and your wife always been open about porn, and does it feel important to be open about it?

We've talked about it but it's not a conversation that we have a lot. We're open about it, but not massively so. Part of the context is that it's difficult sometimes to find the time and the space to have as active a sex life as you might want, especially with a kid and during a national lockdown. With different working hours, you end up not getting to that point as often. And then it becomes a physiological need. I don't have to watch porn, but I do have to masturbate because the need literally builds up. My wife's the same, so we both do it. Having said that, it's not in an entirely cold way – I don't think of wanking like I do, say, going to the toilet. But I do feel it's a necessity. More than I probably would have thought previously.

What do you mean by that?

I haven't always felt like I must make sure that I have a wank – I've never seen it in that way. I have done it because it's a fun thing to do, a satisfying thing to do. Now it is that, but it's also a massive tension relief. And it's clearly more regular when there's not the opportunity to have sex as much as you might want.

When you've been in relationships in the past, have you also masturbated, or has the sex been frequent enough that you've not needed to? It seems that for you masturbation is not exactly a compensation for sex, but when there is less sex, the need becomes more profound. Let's say you're in a place where you're having the sex life of your dreams, do you imagine that you would still masturbate?

In the past I've always done it, almost regardless of what's happening in my sex life. The need is less pressing, I suppose, when my sex life is good – although, again, it feels strange to talk about a physiological 'need', because that sounds quite cold and doesn't reflect how I think of it. It doesn't feel like a substitution for sex, and nor is it preferable, obviously. You know how people often say that they're using porn because they don't feel like they're getting enough out of their sex life? That's not how I class it, and I'm not just saying that because this is being recorded, either. It doesn't feel like it's a substitute. It feels like something that just needs to pass through the system. When you're not in a relationship and you're not having sex at all, then it's just part of life, just something to do.

Would you feel weird if you didn't or couldn't talk to your partner about porn and wanking? It seems important that you've had that conversation and it's out there. If you didn't have that, would you feel guilty?

Maybe. I feel more comfortable that we've talked about it, but I don't feel like it's such a big deal either. And I haven't told her exactly what I watch... Occasionally the topic of attraction will come up and she'll ask me, Do you still see men that you find attractive? And I say,

343

Yeah, of course. But I don't tell her every time that I'm watching gay porn, and nor do I tell her what other kinds of porn I'm watching. Although actually we have talked about that. She finds the whole MILF situation hilarious. I think I'd feel strange if we hadn't had a conversation about it at all, but having said that, I probably did it before we had a conversation about it. And then we talked about it and I felt better – that's probably how it went.

I'm fascinated by the question of how private our sexuality is, and should be. How important it is to have privacy around it, and what happens to that once you enter into a monogamous relationship. I wonder, with people who really get into porn – and maybe this is just hopeless romanticism or backseat psychologizing – whether it's because they want something for themselves? Maybe they struggle to find the intimacy they want from real connections, and so porn functions as a portal to some other place of intimacy, even though on the surface, it's anything but.

There's also a sense of intimacy with yourself, which is quite powerful, and also entirely private. Those two things really add something to the experience. I haven't really thought about it before, but what you just said makes me think that having that kind of privacy, having things that only you are party to, is important. In a relationship with someone, regardless of whether or not you've got kids, you're with that person a lot of the time. If you've got kids, there's no privacy whatsoever. So it becomes more of a thing, I suppose. Also, this is jumping, but the thing that makes me feel weird sometimes is having a daughter and watching porn. Sometimes that makes me think: What am I doing? This feels completely not okay.

Can you unpack that?

Would I want my daughter to be doing that?

To be doing what?

To be a porn actress.

Why not?

Because I'd feel really weird about it.

Why would you feel weird?

Because she's my daughter.

You know, I listened to a podcast this week about Andrew Cuomo resigning[13], and one of the things they quoted him saying, in this very sober voice, was, 'I do on occasion say "Ciao bella"'. For some reason that really tickled me. Anyway, he essentially refused to take responsibility for anything he'd done, and instead said that he'd realized that, unbeknownst to him, his views about women were out of date, but that as the father of two daughters, he wanted to say that he'd never treated women in a way that was different to how he would want them to be treated, and that's the God honest truth. That was just intriguing, because aside from totally missing the point that the behaviours he calls 'out of date' are causing people discomfort and harm, it feels like an admission that he wants his daughters to be objectified and perved on by people

13 Andrew Cuomo served as the 56th governor of New York from
    2011 to 2021, resigning amid a spate of sexual misconduct
    allegations.

like him all the time. The fact that he can't see it as a problematic statement is fascinating in and of itself – it's a real lack of awareness about what being an old-school man means. Anyway. The sense of not wanting your daughter to become a porn actress: does that come out of the social stigma attached to it, or something more fundamental?

I don't know, I haven't unpacked it at all. I think it's a reflex, but then by implication that's saying, Okay, well these women here have chosen to do porn that you are watching – that's not a worthy or worthwhile thing. Which is a bit hypocritical.

This is why Jon Ronson is so great, because he really gets to the heart of that society-wide hypocrisy. I wonder if there's something quite primal and caste-like about the psychology of it, in the same way that in various societies around the world throughout history, butchers or people who carried night soil have been ostracized and looked down on. There's this tendency to shun anyone who is associated professionally with the parts of us that we regard as most shameful. Today those people are porn actors and sex workers, even more than butchers or abattoir workers or sewage workers or rubbish collectors.

That's true. For me, though, it's possibly not about the stigma of it. I think you'd be hard pressed to find a parent who would be comfortable with their child becoming a porn actor. I don't think you're going to find many parents who are comfortable with their child's sexual life, full stop, and that's no different if it involves a profession. Although in parenting terms, it's entirely contextual. If my daughter came to me when she was twenty or twenty-one and said, Look, I really want to do this, it's a good way of making money, I feel completely in control, it's an ethical company, it's run by women or whatever, then I'm not going to say, I disown you as my daughter, but I'm clearly not going to watch. It's such a funny thing. Anyway, that's occasionally what I feel guilt about. I don't often feel guilt watching porn, apart from when I feel I've touched upon something that feels completely exploitative or when that thought passes through my head.

You seem relatively unashamed about your sexuality.

Unashamed about being bi?

No, I don't mean being bi, specifically. A lot of people are 'unashamed' about their sexuality in a public-facing way, but they achieve that by conforming exactly to what society tells them their sexuality should be. I feel like you are genuinely curious and in touch with what actually turns you on and unashamed about that.

Yeah, I'd agree. That's how I've felt since I've been sexually active, give or take a few years at the beginning.

Where do you think that comes from? Is shame not a particularly strong thing for you?

I don't feel ashamed a lot. I can't say that I feel shame about things I've done. It's not as if my family is super open or anything. I never talked about sex with my parents ever, it never came up. But I do come from a family that's very no nonsense about things in general, they just get on with stuff. It feels like quite a practical lack of shame.

347

A household that doesn't talk about that stuff seems like it would be the ideal place for shame to blossom. But if it's just that there's no importance attached to it, and either way is fine, then you're not going grow up feeling, I'm a bad person if I do this.

That's exactly what it was. I've just remembered – I did feel shame once because of porn. We were having a party – was it a Halloween party? – in our house, and I was playing music on my computer. Somebody went on my computer and did a search for hidden files and found some porn, and then proceeded to play it on the computer, in the presence of everybody in the room. Which was really very shit.

Gay porn?

It was gay porn, yeah.

Have you ever watched porn with someone else?

Yes, twice. Once with a previous girlfriend, we decided we thought it'd be fun to try it, and then it wasn't at all. It was really weird. Or not weird: just unsatisfactory for everybody.

How did that work? You put it on and then started kissing while you were watching and then started having sex with it still on?

Essentially that, yes, but the problem was it was a different turn-on for both of us at different points. So it started off as a mutual activity that we were both doing, but became something we were doing separately. The

348

second time was with my wife. There's a porn actress slash company owner called Erika Lust, it's all porn made by women. We got a DVD and watched some of that together. And that was good, it was really nice, but it was just an additional bit of foreplay – because of the quality of the porn, it was pretty nice and well directed, so it just added to the mood. It was effective, but only in the context of wanting to add an extra layer of something else. We've talked about doing it again.

ZERO AGAIN

As I was drawing close to the end of this project, a friend sent me Audre Lorde's 'Uses of the Erotic: The Erotic as Power'. She was incredulous that I'd not yet read it – as was I, once I had. As its title suggests, the essay examines what it would mean and what it would take to harness the power of the erotic throughout our lives – importantly, not just within what we think of in a compartmentalized way as our 'sex lives', but across the board. The erotic, for Lorde, is a 'deeply female and spiritual' force 'rooted in the power of our unexpressed or unrecognized feeling', which resists the hyper-productivity drive and objectification that capitalism requires of us. The pornographic appears in the essay as the polar opposite of eroticism: in emphasizing sensation stripped of any emotive dimension, it 'is a direct denial of the power of the erotic, for it represents the suppression of true feeling'.

Lorde's essay is glorious, and it made me feel quite strange – not because I disagreed with what she was saying, but if anything, the opposite. Reading it brought me a sense of comfort and conviction that rippled out from deep down, and this reaction made me think about my own porn-related publication. Perhaps I was wrong to have done this book as a compilation of messy, ugly conversations brimming with contradiction and ambiguity. Perhaps I should have stayed within the safety and the poeticism of critical theory, where nobody specific needed to be spoken about. Above anything, shouldn't I have at least attempted to create something beautiful, lasting, like Lorde had? I ought to have tried to set out an alternative vision that would give solace, as opposed to inviting people to simply chew whatever cultural fat appeared on the plate in front of them at that particular moment.

And then, as I was reading, Lorde seemed to reach out a reassuring hand. Responding to the way that our society deems a life which truly embraces the erotic as abnormal and dysfunctional, she writes: 'Giving into the fear of feeling and working to capacity is a luxury only the unintentional can afford, and the unintentional are those who do not wish to guide their own destinies.'

By this point, it's obvious to me that there isn't a single or overarching motivation for writing this book. Rather, it's the convergence of a lot of different impulses – which makes the attempt to provide any kind of conclusion or summation, as I am now doing, somehow overwhelming. Yet reading Lorde on acting intentionally, I heard myself saying to myself, not for the first time: *Yes, that's exactly what this book is trying to do.*

What I've come to realize about porn over the course of these conversations is that what scares me the most about it – what I now believe has always scared me the most about it – is the way that the shame and the silence and the guilt and the awkwardness surrounding it, in combination with its compulsive and private nature, work to produce a sense of passivity, a lack of agency and responsibility, that come through on the rare occasions we do speak of it in any earnest way. Of course, it is hardly surprising that things are this way; porn is not just a standalone phenomenon, but is part of a capitalist socioeconomic context that Pamela Paul has dubbed 'the pornification of the world'. In our present-day society, the productive apparatus endeavours not only to sell us products but to create needs, and ultimately, induce addictive behaviour in us. This applies not just to pornographic content, but anything that seduces us to behave as consumers in certain ways; as Giorgio Tricarico writes, 'Porn can surely be considered an uncanny object on the shelves, but it's the whole, invisible supermarket itself, the trademark of our capitalistic and technological world, wrapping us up with its apparently innocuous coils' that is arguably the most unsettling thing of all.

Speaking of intentionality in this context does, I fully admit, throw up a whole host of problems. When we have fully accepted the implications of living in an invisible supermarket, we may well end up accepting the inevitability of the trajectory that we're on as a society – we may, after thinking about it and talking about it, conclude that there is no way out of the automatic doors. I still believe, though, that this isn't incompatible with maintaining a sense of agency and responsibility over our own practices, or at least, a more conscious understanding of what it is that we are doing. I still believe that this consciousness is preferable to burying our heads in the sand – or the shelves.

I would also say that, as dismal and hopeless as it is to think about the pornification of society, it is in contemplating this aspect of our reality and how different it is, already, than the one Lorde was writing from, that I can feel content in the fact that I haven't attempted to write a work of critical theory that looks anything like hers. I can even entertain the thought that in a way, the time for such treatises has passed. This is not to say that what Lorde writes is outdated; on the contrary, I believe that most of the people I was speaking to would agree with the essence of what she writes about the superior value of the erotic over the pornographic. I certainly do. Yet here we are, in this society where porn makes up a considerable portion of the traffic across the entire internet, where it is instantly accessible on the devices that most of us carry around and have some kind of addictive relationship to, and where porn surrounds us. Here we are in an age where it is perfectly conceivable that someone not dissimilar from me might, over a glass of wine at a dinner party, speak with friends about the importance of the erotic as opposed to the pornographic, and then, later on that same evening, watch a video entitled 'Parents Keep Leaving Me Alone With My Cum-Hungry Stepsister' or 'Small tits hungarian BABE has romantic sex of a lifetime'. We can say that porn is not truly stimulating, but it is also true that many of the people who would say that go to porn when they are looking for sexual stimulation.

Of course I cannot speculate whether or not, were Lorde alive today, she would embrace CrashPad, or Pornhub, or Beautiful Agony, or Literotica, just as I cannot say these things about any of my contemporaries without speaking to them. What seems less controvertible is that a Lorde born in the early nineties would have an awareness of and familiarity with both pornography and our societal steeping in it in a way that made her eschewal of it an even more politicized act, therefore in need of an alternative form of justification. Writing today, I believe, Lorde would likely have felt compelled to further engage with pornography before dismissing it – to illustrate, more, that she was coming to the topic from a place of understanding, of street-smartness. That she wasn't closing her eyes to what is a daily reality for swathes of the population – something which is, in a sense, all of our realities. It seems to me that if we are to talk about what is truly erotic, what people really want, we have to find a way of doing so that engages with porn also. Whether or not we deem that a potentially viable expression for it, or a proxy adopted in lieu of something that is missing, it still needs to be part of the conversation. And the conversation, I increasingly feel, have come to feel over the course of this book, needs to be exactly that: a real conversation.

354

I want to end with a final thought from Lorde, who writes as a cautionary note: '[The] internal requirement toward excellence which we learn from the erotic must not be misconstrued as demanding the impossible from ourselves nor from others.'

I cite this here for I believe that while not demanding the impossible is fundamental with respect to many things, it is particularly so with porn. Certainly, when I look back on how I was before having these talks, the arguments I had with exes, I feel like it's a perfect summation of what I used to do: I demanded the impossible, and not getting it, was stuck spinning round in feelings of outrage, and the fear of being hurt and disregarded. My over-reactions, I believe, came out of an unwillingness to face the reality – or perhaps, to accept that there are multiple realities that we move through. Certainly, I have for a long time been unwilling to confront the idea that much of the economic structure of contemporary first-world society is geared up to keeping us passive, and hooked, and often acting against our more conscious or rational instincts. I have been unwilling to acknowledge both myself and the people around me as at the behest of greater forces of which we are not wholly in control, because that has felt too terrifying. A certain amount of peace has come from arriving at the sense that we are not totally in control, but not totally out of it either – that there is room for personal choice, even if the greater picture remains highly worrying.

In this vein, I would submit that a first step towards intentionality around porn, instead of demanding big, immediate and likely impossible changes of yourself or of others, should be to talk about it. However horrendous the prospect seems initially, I would suggest that it is most likely less impossible than it might feel. I would also say that, hearing about what has happened in the lives of some of the people I spoke with after our conversations, I do have the sense that the talking can, sometimes, be the hardest stage of the process; that sometimes the changing and becoming more intentional in one's behaviour comes naturally, at least in small ways.

I mentioned that when I sent my initial email call-out to friends asking them to participate in my project, several people responded by saying they weren't sure whether they'd really have anything to say as their thoughts around the topic hadn't crystallized yet. My favourite comment in this vein was from a friend who wrote, 'I feel like I need to read the book you're going to write about it first, to prepare.' Seeing this, I smiled beatifically. Then a few seconds later, the jolt of fear came: would I ever be able to write the kind of book that would inform and prepare someone to talk to other people about porn?

Now, as I'm coming to the end of the project, I ask myself, in a moment of cold sobriety, whether or not I think I've assembled that book. Hardly, is one possible answer. Far from putting forward a wildly original thesis, I haven't even proposed any of my own thoughts on porn, and I emerge from this project feeling less sure what my position is than when I went in.

Another possible answer, though, is yes. Yes, I have written that book. I can say that because I now believe quite fervently that the only way to prepare for conversations about porn is to have conversations about porn, with the people around you, as you would do with anything else. I've written the book that I hope comes as close as possible to encouraging people to do that – if only in an 'I can do a better job of it than this' way. Because, in all likelihood, you can.

Works referenced and recommended

Katherine Angel, *Tomorrow Sex Will Be Good Again: Women and Desire in the Age of Consent* (Verso, 2021).

Katherine Angel, *Unmastered: A Book on Desire, Most Difficult to Tell* (Penguin, 2012).

Jean Baudrillard, 'Stereo-Porno' in *Seduction*, translated by Brian Singer (New World Perspectives, 1990).

James Baldwin, *Another Country* (Penguin Classics, 1962).

Judith Butler, *Gender Trouble* (Routledge, 1990).

Nell Dunn, *Talking to Women* (Silver Press, 2018).

Andrea Dworkin, *Pornography: Men Possessing Women* (Putnam, 1981).

Shiori Itō, *Black Box,* translated by Allison Markin Powell (Tilted Axis Press, 2021).

David Farrier and Dylan Reeve, *Tickled* (Magnolia Pictures, 2016).

Mark Fisher, *Capitalist Realism: Is There No Alternative?* (Zero Books, 2009).

Ariel Levy, *Female Chauvinist Pigs: Women and the Rise of Raunch Culture* (Simon & Schuster, 2005).

Andrea Long Chu, *Females* (Verso, 2019).

Audre Lorde, 'Uses for the Erotic: The Erotic as Power' in *Sister Outsider: Essays and Speeches* (Crossing Press, 1984)

Joseph Lee, Lisa Marchiano, and Deborah Stewart, hosts, 'SHADOWLAND: Prostitution - The Story of Kay', This Jungian Life (podcast), 2 September 2021.

Joseph Lee, Lisa Marchiano, and Deborah Stewart, hosts, 'PORN: Technology, Consumerism & Soul', This Jungian Life (podcast), 20 January 2022.

Emily Nagoski, *Come as You Are* (Scribe, 2015).

Maggie Nelson, *Bluets* (Wave, 2009).

Maggie Nelson, *The Argonauts* (Graywolf Press, 2015).

Maureen O'Connor, 'Pornhub is the Kinsey Report of Our Time' in *New York* Magazine, 12 June 2017 (https://www.thecut.com/2017/06/pornhub-and-the-american-sexual-imagination.html).

Reuters, 'Billie Eilish says watching porn as a child "destroyed my brain"', *Guardian*, https://www.theguardian.com/music/2021/dec/15/billie-eilish-says-watching-porn-gave-her-nightmares-and-destroyed-my-brain

Jon Ronson, *The Butterfly Effect*, podcast series (2017).

Jon Ronson, *The Last Days of August*, podcast series (2019).

Amia Srinivasan, *The Right to Sex* (Bloomsbury, 2021).

Giorgio Tricarico, *Lost Goddesses: A Kaleidoscope on Porn* (Routledge, 2017).

Saskia Vogel, 'Men of a Certain Age: On Sex, Privacy, and Pornography', *Lithub*, 23 February 2018 (https://lithub.com/men-of-a-certain-age-on-sex-privacy-and-pornography/).

Adrian Nathan West, *The Aesthetics of Degradation* (Repeater Books, 2016).

Acknowledgements

This book owes almost everything to the people who agreed to speak to me in parks, hotels and Zoom rooms, whom I wish I could name and thank here, but who will instead have to make do with an unindividuated but boundless cloud of gratitude. You are all brilliant.

The rest it owes to Jacques Testard, the best editor I could wish for, Angelique Tran Van Sang, agent extraordinaire, and Adrian Bridget, beloved friend whose support and insight has seen me across many a lake of doubt.

Thank you to the Fitzcarraldo dream team: Clare Bogen, Tamara Sampey-Jawad, Joely Day, Rosie Brown, Charlotte Jackson and Ray O'Meara.

Finally, thanks to my friends and my family. This book, and these couple of years, have made me realize just how lucky I am to have you all.

Fitzcarraldo Editions
8-12 Creekside
London, SE8 3DX
United Kingdom

ISBN 978-1-80427-040-0

Design by Ray O'Meara
Typeset in Fitzcarraldo
Printed and bound by TJ Books

fitzcarraldoeditions.com

Fitzcarraldo Editions